FRANCES HODGKINS

PAINTINGS AND DRAWINGS

IAIN BUCHANAN

MICHAEL DUNN

ELIZABETH EASTMOND

THAMES AND HUDSON

First published in Great Britain in 1995
by Thames and Hudson Ltd, London

British Library Cataloguing-in-Publication Data

A catalogue record for this book is available from the British Library

ISBN 0-500-09247-8

Printed and bound in Hong Kong

FRANCES HODGKINS

PAINTINGS AND DRAWINGS

Seated Woman, c.1926
Tate Gallery, London

CONTENTS

ACKNOWLEDGEMENTS

As a result of Frances Hodgkins's special position as a New Zealand expatriate artist, her works, and the documentary material related to them and to her life, are now divided between New Zealand, Australia and Great Britain. In the course of researching this book, we have come into contact with many private owners of her works, the staff of commercial and public art galleries, in addition to archives and libraries in all those countries. In particular, we would like to thank the following people and institutions for their help.

In New Zealand:

Dorothy Alice Field, who as copyright-holder extended permission to reproduce the works by Frances Hodgkins in this book; Linda Gill, editor of Frances Hodgkins's letters, for her expert advice and support; E. H. McCormick, to whom as biographer of Frances Hodgkins we owe a great deal and who generously lent photographs to be used in the book; Ron Brownson, research librarian at the Auckland City Art Gallery, for allowing us to consult the typescript by E. H. McCormick of Frances Hodgkins's letters and for providing material related to Hodgkins in the Art Gallery collection. We are indebted to Roger Collins who made available his research on Hodgkins in France prior to its publication, and to Avenal McKinnon, and Gretchen Albrecht and James Ross for information on the location of works by Hodgkins. Among commercial gallery owners, John Gow (John Leech Gallery), Peter Jarvis (Ferner Fine Art), Jonathan Gooderam (Jonathan Grant Gallery), Dunbar Sloane (Dunbar Sloane Ltd) and Marcia Shaw (Tinakori Gallery) put us into contact with owners of Hodgkins's works and provided photographs of her works for use in the book. Peter Shaw, curator of the Fletcher Challenge Collection, allowed us to view the works by Hodgkins in the collection. We are grateful to Jetta and Bruce Cornish, Adrian Burr, Maurice and Beverley Allen, Sir Ron and Lady Trotter, Lyn and Frank Corner, Elizabeth Steiner, the Honourable Philip Burdon and Ros Burdon, and other unnamed owners who gave us access to Hodgkins works in their collections and agreed to their reproduction. Amanda Gibbs of the Auckland City Art Gallery, Auckland University Art Collection, Jill Trevelyan of the Museum of New

ACKNOWLEDGEMENTS

Zealand Te Papa Tongarewa, Victoria University Art Collection, Anna Crighton and Neil Roberts of the Robert McDougall Art Gallery, Oliver Stead of the Dunedin Public Art Gallery, Tim Garrity and Rosemary Entwisle at the Hocken Library kindly allowed us to see works in storage, supplied photographs and arranged permission for works to be reproduced. We also thank the Ministry of Foreign Affairs and Trade for permission to reproduce works in their collection and the staff of the Alexander Turnbull Library, the National Library of New Zealand, Auckland University Library and Fine Arts Library for making available material on Hodgkins.

In Australia:
Patricia McDonald at the Art Gallery of New South Wales, who arranged access to works in storage; the conservator Stuart Laidler, who made a series of paint cross-sections of *The White House*, and the Gallery for permission to reproduce Hodgkins paintings; and the Art Gallery of South Australia for photographs and agreeing to the reproduction of two Hodgkins works.

In Great Britain:
The staff of the Tate Gallery Archive who made available documentary material on Hodgkins and related British artists, and the Tate Library, especially Meg Duff and Krzysztof Cieszkowski, as well as the Gallery for permission to reproduce works; Anna Miles of the Tate Conservation Department, who provided invaluable information on the condition and painting techniques of works by Hodgkins in the Tate; the staff of the National Art Library, the Witt Library and the Conway Library for their assistance in the documentation of Hodgkins's works and exhibitions; Liz Reintjes, Alexis Hunter, Hugh Stevenson, Antony and Deyman Eastmond for their invaluable support in providing photographs of Hodgkins's works or arranging for them to be made; Francis Eastmond and Martin Robertson for help in locating works; Myfanwy Piper, Mary Spencer-Watson and especially Kitty West and Nancy Moore, who gave access to their collections, agreed to the reproduction of works and generously shared their memories of the artist and her work; the collectors who wished to remain anonymous, for their generosity in agreeing to the inclusion of works from their collections in the book; Alistair Smith and the staff of the Whitworth Art Gallery for showing us works in storage and granting permission for their reproduction. In addition we thank the British Council, Government Art Collection, Department of National Heritage, New Zealand High Commission, Manchester City Art Gallery, Birmingham Museums and Art Gallery, Salford Art Gallery, Bristol City Art Gallery, Sheffield City Art Galleries, Cecil Higgins Art Gallery, Leeds City Art Gallery, the Towner Art Gallery and Museum, the Ferens Art Gallery, Wakefield Art Gallery, Victoria and Albert Museum, Glasgow Art Gallery and the Scottish National Gallery of Modern Art for showing us Hodgkins works and agreeing to their reproduction.

We would also like to thank the following institutions for their permission to reproduce works in their collections: the National Gallery of Canada, Ottawa; the Carnegie Museum of Art, Pittsburgh; the Albright-Knox Art Gallery, Buffalo; the Musée Departemental de Rochechouart, Limoges; and the Musée Picasso, Paris.

Elizabeth Eastmond is grateful to her father, Gregory Eastmond, for entertaining her son Fenner while she was 'on the Frances Hodgkins trail' at various locations in Somerset and Dorset and also Frances Eastmond, Janet Wensley and Linda Ruthe for their assistance with child-care.

We are especially appreciative of the encouragement and expertise of Elizabeth Caffin and the staff of Auckland University Press. We are also grateful to Colleen Sherman who typed much of the text.

Finally we would like to thank the University of Auckland for various grants towards the costs of research in New Zealand and Great Britain for this book, and the New Zealand Arts Council for financial support towards the costs of its production.

INTRODUCTION

'She has kept the artist well in front of the human being', wrote Frances Hodgkins approvingly in 1943 of Myfanwy Evans's draft for the first monograph (in the Penguin Modern Painters series) on her work.[1] *Frances Hodgkins: Paintings and Drawings* aims to retrieve and develop that close attention to the art. Fifty years on, our project is, we feel, more than timely, given Hodgkins's considerable significance as an artist, particularly over the last two decades of her life when she was among the artists at the forefront of British modernism. For while much has been written on Frances Hodgkins's life, notably the invaluable biographical studies of E. H. McCormick,[2] and while much unpublished material, including letters, survives, surprisingly little analysis of her art in relation to its shifting contexts and in terms of close readings of individual works has been achieved.[3]

A crop of smallish exhibitions both in New Zealand and in Britain clearly bear testimony to a recent resurgence of interest in Hodgkins in both countries.[4] In Britain this has developed both as a result of a general reassessment of artists of the years 1920–1950 — Cedric Morris and Cecil Collins, for instance — and of the reevaluation of neglected women artists such as Winifred Nicholson.[5] In New Zealand Hodgkins is regarded as the major historical expatriate artist and as something of a cultural icon, being seen as an exemplar of the complex issues surrounding expatriatism, of crucial concern until relatively recently to a country like New Zealand.[6] Useful perspectives on Hodgkins's situation as a woman artist have emerged[7] and the 1993 publication — in New Zealand's women's suffrage centenary year — of *Letters of Frances Hodgkins* has provided a wonderfully rich and engaging resource for further Hodgkins art-historical study.[8] Our intention then has been to shift the focus back to the work. Frances Hodgkins's own expression, 'artist well in front of the human being', does not necessarily imply a separation, but a prioritising of the work in relation to the life and this emphasis has been enormously enriched by the material now available both on the artist's life and on the lives of other artists of the period. Our project has something in common with two other recent studies of women artists: Frida Kahlo and Berthe Morisot. Both, like Hodgkins, have been the subject of full biographies which were subsequently followed by detailed art-historical studies of their work.[9] Did their status as 'exceptions' to the roles more acceptable for their gender result in this initial focus on the conditions of their lives and their exceptional personalities, so delaying serious evaluations of their work? This is not to suggest that the attention to the work in the later studies, as in our own, necessarily becomes 'free' of the 'life', of course, but rather that the emphasis has radically shifted, with a judicious use of biographical material which, in conjunction with the other tools of critical contextual analysis, can usefully enrich the discussion of art practice.

The period of almost fifty years since Frances Hodgkins's death also enables us to look at her achievements alongside recent reassessments of other artists of the important late period of her career. One of these is John Piper, some of whose concerns in the 1940s were shared and inspired by Frances Hodgkins, whom he much admired, as his letters to her reveal.[10]

In New Zealand Frances Hodgkins's position is somewhat ambiguous: well known as the country's major historical artist, frequently exhibited, yet little studied in a critical sense and posing a problem for nationalist historians in that the main body of her art practice relates to European art and has little relevance to local movements such as the dominance of regional landscape in New Zealand art of the 1930s and 1940s. This has led to the construction of separate chapters dealing with issues of expatriatism in order to include her work within the parameters of local art histories.[11] The evaluation of expatriate artists like Frances Hodgkins must thus be qualified in different ways according to their two major contexts. In Britain exhibitions like the Minories Gallery's 1990 *Frances Hodgkins — The Late Work* may signal some resurgence of interest, as does her inclusion in Frances Spalding's recent *British Art since 1900*. But why has Hodgkins still not been accorded similar serious attention in Britain — the context for her late work — as artists like Piper, Nash, Winifred Nicholson or Ben Nicholson, with whom she exhibited so frequently in the 1930s and 1940s and with whose achievements hers are on a par? Why was she not included in recent major reassessments of aspects of twentieth-century art like the Royal Academy's 1987 *British Art in the 20th Century* or in productively revisionist exhibitions like the Barbican's 1987 *A Paradise Lost, The Neo-Romantic Imagination in Britain 1935–55*? In the late thirties and forties her work was consistently shown both in groupings with Sutherland, Nash, Moore and Piper and also with the younger Neo-Romantics: John Minton, for instance, and the 'two Roberts', Colquhoun and McBryde. She was one of the five artists in *Recent Paintings by Francis Bacon, Frances Hodgkins, Henry Moore, Matthew Smith, Graham Sutherland* at the Lefevre Gallery in 1945. She was included, with Nash and Sutherland, among the most recent exponents of romanticism in Piper's 1947 *British Romantic Artists* and earlier, in 1940, had been one of a small group of artists chosen to represent Britain in the *Biennale di Venezia*. These questions may seem more pressing to New Zealand-based historians addressing the evaluation of this country's major historical artist, but the study of Frances Hodgkins's posthumous artistic reputation is important as her achievement was substantial. In the case of Mary Cassatt, an American artist whose contribution to Impressionism was significant and has only relatively recently been reassessed, it has been suggested that she suffered a 'double disability': that as a woman artist her importance has been underestimated and that as an American she represented 'an anomaly to art historians working within strict national categories'.[12] It is pertinent to consider whether either or both of these factors of gender and nationality have played a part in the lack of a serious focus on the contribution of Frances Hodgkins to modernism in Britain in the 1930s and 1940s.

Hodgkins's omission from all the major general books on women artists which have emerged over the last two decades is also surprising and disappointing, although in terms of national histories, Britain, unlike the United States, Australia and New Zealand, has yet to produce a general history of British women artists in which she would surely appear . . . or, as born in New Zealand, would she? Interestingly, in Britain in the 1930s, nationality could provide an obstacle to fame, it seems: reviewers of Hodgkins's pivotal 1930 exhibition at the St George's Gallery declared that had the artist been of *French* birth, she would be 'enjoying European renown'.[13] On top of that, even in the 1930s, lack of clear adherence to a particular 'school' could prove problematic and marginalise some artists: Eric Newton felt impelled to defend what he called 'The Centre Party' in British painting when Surrealism and abstraction seemed to be drawing artists into opposing camps.[14] Frances Hodgkins was one of his four representatives of a kind of independent mid-way position.

Frances Hodgkins's death, and the end of her long career as an artist, occurred at a time of major transition in British art and life: the war was just over, new beginnings were in the air and two major art movements were in transition. Neo-Romanticism, with which she was so closely associated in the 1940s, was losing its impetus and the impact of abstract expressionism was beginning to be felt. One context then was becoming unfashionable — and to remain so for a considerable time — the other, in its increasing impatience with the 'object', with any signs of allegiance to representation, had the effect of marginalising artists like Hodgkins who worked the boundaries between representation and abstraction and who also painted on a more modest scale. Although her work did appear in some group exhibitions over the 1950s and 1960s in Britain, these factors may also have affected her subsequent evaluation. In a sense this notion of 'lack' in her late work (because not fully abstract) coloured the assessment of Hodgkins in New Zealand's major attempt at a reevaluation of her achievement in the 1969 Centenary Exhibition, for here the curators concluded that 'the oppressive dictates of the subject and her incomplete realization of pictorial space place severe limits on her achievement'.[15] Greenbergian modernist notions, prevalent in the 1960s, were clearly the subtext here.

Now, in the 1990s we can benefit from a different cultural context, one in which notions associated with postmodernism have arguably freed us from the limiting effects of binary constructs such as the abstraction versus Surrealism or the abstraction versus representation dualisms cited above. We are also, perhaps, freer of unproductive notions of nationality and of gender difference. Also of relevance to a clearer appraisal of Frances Hodgkins's art are views associated with recent critical perspectives on modernism, like those of Frances

Spalding, for whom British art no longer needs to be 'judged by the yardstick set by Continental or American art', so enabling a celebration of British art's 'imaginative fertility as well as its literalness'.[16]

The trajectory of Frances Hodgkins's long career of almost sixty years presents a kind of paradigm of the gradual transition of an artist from parochial beginnings, through years of experimentation to emergence as a significant modernist voice. Her contribution, particularly in her later years, was to produce work which, while inspired by external stimuli, explored a range of marvellously exuberant and idiosyncratic painterly effects frequently free of any literal relation to the subject, with an approach to colour which in its subtlety, sheer beauty and powerfully suggestive qualities is a major strength of her art. The more literary reviewers of the period put this gift of Hodgkins rather elegantly, although they were also alert to the problems of capturing these qualities in language, frequently making comparisons with other arts: for Eric Newton, Hodgkins 'can build up in paint the exact equivalent of the deliciously complex sounds that are at the disposal of a master of orchestration'. But he adds, 'To call her colour "delicious" is merely to praise it without giving an inkling as to its quality' and continues, 'Frances Hodgkins needs a finer adjustment. Hers is twilight colour. It is queer and surprising. Moreover it continues to be surprising. Looking at her best gouaches, the eye, long after first impact, goes on receiving little subsidiary shocks of delight.'[17] For Myfanwy Evans Hodgkins's colour 'has the same quality as some fine poetry . . . . She has no formula, but the colour of each picture is as indicative of a mood as a blushing and sensitive skin.'[18] The terms 'delicious' and 'delight' and the evocative physicality of Evans's analogy with skin provide a key to the unique effect of Hodgkins's art, and its qualities of buoyancy, vitality, sensuous *jouissance* have frequently been remarked. One of New Zealand's major artists of the post-war period, Colin McCahon (a painter of a very different kind, but one who deeply admired Hodgkins), concluded his introduction to the Auckland City Art Gallery's 1959 Hodgkins exhibition with observations which both celebrate the unique painterly *joie de vivre* of Hodgkins's art and situate it in relation to other contexts:

> Frances Hodgkins's paintings from 1930 to the time of her death in 1947 became frequently joyous and free from convention, particularly in the last years of her life. Then her lack of dependence on specific subject matter — with the ever present overtones of human suffering, which realist painters can seldom if ever avoid — disappeared and her world became increasingly a place of intuitive freedom and spontaneous happiness rarely found in the work of a New Zealand painter and seldom in contemporary art.[19]

The influence of Frances Hodgkins has not yet been fully explored in relation either to New Zealand artists like Gabrielle Hope or May Smith or as an often quoted role model for contemporary New Zealand women artists, or to British artists like John Piper and some of the younger Neo-Romantics such as John Minton. We hope our text will stimulate studies such as these.

But what factors lay behind the remarkable leap for Frances Hodgkins (aged sixty in 1929) from a position of relative neglect to one, from the early 1930s, within the British avant-garde? A comparable artist, the Scot Jeka Kemp, travelling in Europe and North Africa in the early 1900s, based like Hodgkins in Paris and exhibiting there, studying with her in Brittany in 1908 and painting then in a similar vein of muted Impressionism, gave up painting in the late 1920s precisely at the time Hodgkins's career was gaining momentum.[20] A letter of 1928 gives a strong sense that she is on course at last: 'I have *changed* & *evolved* & *experimented* — but am none the worse for that. My present work is consistent — I shall sink or swim by it — I think swim . . .'.[21] In Britain the economic situation was hardly encouraging, but it was perhaps that combination of Hodgkins's talent and her extraordinary tenacity together with various other crucial factors in the late 1920s which provided the possibilities for her remarkable 'late phase'. Her connections with Arthur Howell of the St George's Gallery have been well-documented and there is no doubt that this and her 1930 exhibition there were crucial.[22] But other factors should not be overlooked, particularly the important exhibiting context of the Seven and Five Society from 1929, and the supportive and professional friendship of Cedric Morris and Lett Haines. There was also the interest and support of such key art-world figures as Duncan Grant and Matthew Smith and the wealthy collector and gallery-owner Lucy Wertheim (whom Hodgkins advised against calling her new gallery Young Masters: 'How can I pass as a young master?'[23]). The decisions to discontinue teaching and to base her practice in Britain, rather than returning to New Zealand or France, were also significant, the latter to the developing of an exhibiting and critical context for her art. It has recently been suggested that the death of her mother in 1926, although causing her much grief, perhaps also had the effect of absolving the expatriate 'spinster' daughter from a long-standing sense of guilt, so releasing that energy and focus characteristic of her late work.[24]

But perhaps one other small factor has been overlooked. In a letter of 1928 from the south of France Frances Hodgkins makes amusing reference to a biscuit, a biscuit with magical properties which one could perhaps playfully add to that list of factors contributing to her transition to what she called 'the moderns'. She eats, she writes, 'every day for lunch a biscuit with *Vouloir c'est Pouvoir* printed on it — which enables me to do just anything I want — it acts like magic.'[25] The letter was written at the same time and place as her prescient declaration that her current work was 'consistent' and that she would 'swim' as a result of it. The message itself, aptly enough in French and suggestive of the inspirational qualities of French art for Frances Hodgkins, evidently cast a most propitious spell on her future.

ELIZABETH EASTMOND

1. FH to Katharine West, 4 April 1943. Myfanwy Evans's *Frances Hodgkins*, Penguin Modern Painters, Harmondsworth, was finally published in 1948.

2. E. H. McCormick's *The Expatriate*, Wellington, 1954 and his *Portrait of Frances Hodgkins*, Auckland, 1981. See also Lindsey Bridget Shaw, 'Still Life: Self Portrait, The Late Development of Frances Hodgkins', in *Frances Hodgkins — The Late Work*, exhibition catalogue, Minories Art Gallery, Colchester, 1991, pp.31-38.

3. Anthony S. G. Green's 'Reflections on the Hodgkins Exhibition', *Ascent*, Frances Hodgkins commemorative issue, December, 1969, pp.29-43 and Charles Brasch's 'Frances Hodgkins at One Hundred', *Landfall*, 92, Sept. 1969, pp.265-7, are exceptions. See Bibliography for recent articles by Iain Buchanan, R. D. J. Collins, Anne-Marie Davison, and Pamela Gerrish Nunn. Also see Avenal McKinnon's introductory essay in *Frances Hodgkins 1869–1947*, exhibition catalogue, Whitford & Hughes, London, 1990, the introduction by Liz Reintjes and essay by Rosemary Pawsey in *Frances Hodgkins — The Late Work* and the introduction by Jill Trevelyan in *Frances Hodgkins*, exhibition catalogue, Women's Suffrage Exhibition, Museum of New Zealand Te Papa Tongarewa, Wellington, 1993.

4. See Exhibitions, p.172.

5. Cedric Morris, Cecil Collins and Winifred Nicholson exhibitions, Tate Gallery, London, 1984, 1990 and 1987 respectively.

6. E. H. McCormick, *The Expatriate* and, more recently, Lindsey Bridget Shaw's 'Still Life: Self Portrait'.

7. Jill Trevelyan, introduction, *Frances Hodgkins*.

8. Linda Gill, ed., *Letters of Frances Hodgkins*, Auckland, 1993.

9. Hayden Herrera, *Frida Kahlo: The Paintings*, New York, 1992 and Anne Higonnet, *Berthe Morisot's Images of Women*, Cambridge, Mass., 1992.

10. John Piper to FH, c.Sept. 1941.

11. Both Anne Kirker's *New Zealand Women Artists*, Sydney, revised ed., 1993, and Michael Dunn's *A Concise History of New Zealand Painting*, Sydney, 1991, have valuable chapters dealing with the issue of expatriate artists.

12. Griselda Pollock, *Mary Cassatt*, London, 1980, p.5.

13. Despite Roger Fry's emphasis on the French school and the continuing influence of his writings at this time. The reviews: *Spectator*, 18 Oct. 1930 and *Daily Express*, 13 Oct. 1930.

14. Eric Newton, 'The Centre Party in Contemporary Painting', *Listener*, 23 May 1934, pp.862-3.

15. David Armitage & Ian Roberts in *Frances Hodgkins 1869–1947, A Centenary Exhibition*, exhibition catalogue, Auckland City Art Gallery, 1969.

16. Frances Spalding, *100 Years of Art in Britain*, exhibition catalogue, Leeds City Art Galleries, 1988, p.6.

17. Eric Newton, 'Frances Hodgkins', *Listener*, 2 Oct. 1941, p.473.

18. Myfanwy Evans, 'Round the Art Exhibitions', *Listener*, 18 April 1940, p.778.

19. Colin McCahon, introduction, *Frances Hodgkins, Paintings and Drawings*, exhibition catalogue, Auckland City Art Gallery, 1959, p.6.

20. Irving Grose, introduction, *Jeka Kemp 1876–1967*, exhibition catalogue, Belgrave Gallery, 1977.

21. FH to Lucy Wertheim, 13 Feb. 1928.

22. Arthur R. Howell, *Frances Hodgkins, Four Vital Years*, London, 1951.

23. FH to Lucy Wertheim, c.4 Aug. 1930.

24. Lindsey Bridget Shaw, 'Still Life; Self Portrait', p.38. Also Linda Gill, ed., *Letters of Frances Hodgkins*, pp.5-6.

25. FH to Jane Saunders, Jan./Feb. 1928.

1869–1913

MICHAEL DUNN

I feel that if I had known what was before me, I should never have had the courage to begin.

FRANCES HODGKINS, MAY 1913[1]

THE EARLY YEARS

Short though it was, Frances Hodgkins's last visit to New Zealand in 1912–13 was a significant one. On her return from Europe, she exhibited recent works with some success in her home town of Dunedin and also in Wellington where her mother and sister then lived. Not only did she sell some watercolours which entered local collections but there were reviews of her exhibitions at Australian and New Zealand venues as well as accounts in newspapers based on interviews with the artist. Her quoted comments provide some telling clues as to how she saw herself at that time. This visit ended her direct contact with New Zealand and concludes the early phase of her painting career.

From her remarks it is clear that she valued her overseas success in Paris, limited though it was, as her greatest achievement. 'A Dunedin Girl who Conquered Paris' read the head-line in the *Otago Daily Times*.[2] This was despite the fact that she had originally gone to England and it was there, not in France, that her artistic reputation would be made. She observed that the artist 'craves naturally for Paris'.[3] It was in Paris that she found the excitement and openness to modern painting missing in London. 'The French are so eager for new ideas; they give them such a welcome; and the progress must come with new ideas, mustn't it? We can't go on with modern minds painting like the old masters.'[4]

Yet the Dunedin article acknowledged that her recognition had been limited. 'In her own art, in her own circle, among Parisian painters in watercolour, Miss Hodgkins has suc-ceeded, has "arrived". A small success, yet a definite arrival.'[5] One sign of this success was her appointment as a teacher at the Académie Colarossi. She was, apparently, the first woman to hold such a post. Colarossi's was a rival to the more famous Académie Julian which had studios in both Right and Left Bank locations. Its fees were much lower than Julian's and its courses flexible enough to allow terms of one week's instruction.[6]

Frances Hodgkins must have known that watercolour was not the preferred medium of major French painters. Yet she used only watercolour up to that time. French artists used watercolour for sketches rather than paintings intended to make an impression at the Salon. Among French nineteenth-century artists who used watercolour for significant works are Eugène Delacroix (1798–1863), Paul Huet (1803–69) and Constantin Guys (1802–92). Of Hodgkins's immediate contemporaries, the American painter John Singer Sargent (1856–1925), also an expatriate, made brilliant use of watercolour in his *plein air* sketches of Venice and elsewhere in a style that has connections with her approach. Although Sargent exhibited extensively in Paris, he made his public reputation in Paris and London with his portraits in oil. The painter who did most to give watercolour serious recognition in France and the United States as a medium for creating important works was Paul Cézanne (1839–1906) but it was not until after his death, in 1907, that a sizeable selection of his watercolours was shown at the Bernheim-Jeune Gallery and at the *Salon d'Automne*. By 1911 his watercolours were influencing modern American painters.[7] Cézanne used watercolour in a structural way to establish spatial and formal relations and his approach was quite unlike Hodgkins's, which remained tied to the older impressionistic concerns of evoking light, colour and atmosphere.

Frances Hodgkins had first learned the use of watercolour in Dunedin from her father, William Mathew Hodgkins (1833–98).[8] Hodgkins was a gifted amateur painter of landscapes who, in addition to his activity as an artist, was also President of the Otago Art Society. In 1880 he delivered an address to the Otago Institute entitled 'A History of Landscape Art and its Study in New Zealand'.[9] William Mathew Hodgkins, like many amateur artists in the British colonies, preferred watercolour as a medium because of its portability, its small scale and speed of drying. In his address he mentioned the impression made on him in London by seeing the sketches of J. M. W. Turner. He recommended the study of good examples of painting but also the observation of nature and atmospheric effects.[10] His own paintings deal exclusively with landscape, often seen in extensive semi-panoramic views. His bold approach suggested the play of light and dark and changing weather conditions by merging land and sky, or sky and water. To her surprise Frances Hodgkins found his painting in 1913 better than she expected. 'I was glad to feel, on returning to New Zealand, that his work had a breadth and value which, coming with educated eyes, I was scarcely prepared to find.'[11]

Her father's example was clearly influential, probably not only for his lessons and encouragement but also because of the importance he placed on art. In his later years painting meant more to him than his regular job as a solicitor.[12] Frances and her sister Isabel, also an amateur painter, benefited from his enthusiasm and what went with it. This included the company of artists, a collection of their paintings in the house, and books and magazines devoted to the arts.[13] From these she would have gained her initial understanding of modern painting. Her sister Isabel (1867–1950), also taught watercolour by her father, was immediately successful in selling her watercolours at Art Society exhibitions.[14] Her rather pretty colouration and landscape subjects of a kind similar to her father's made few demands on her audience. She was usually regarded as more talented than Frances Hodgkins, who was to an extent forced to work in her shadow.

When Isabel married a Wellington solicitor, William Field, in 1893, she left Dunedin. But she continued to paint, exhibit and sell works up to 1901, the year of Frances Hodgkins's first trip to Europe. The example of an elder sister who took painting seriously enough to exhibit, even after her marriage, must have provided Frances with stimulus and a sense of competitiveness.

In Frances Hodgkins's earliest works, though, it is noticeable that she largely avoided landscape. She thus removed herself from direct competition with her father and sister.[15] This indicates her independence of outlook, as well as a lack of sympathy for wilderness landscapes with mountains and lakes. From the start she favoured the familiar and intimate over the grand and remote wonders of nature. It was the family maid Phemie putting out the washing, or children she knew at play, who attracted her attention. She liked, too, domestic settings, houses, backyards and the still-life objects they provide, like wheelbarrows and water-tanks, as well as hens, ducks, and the family dog. Such things never lost their importance for her, and their equivalents may be found in her last paintings of the 1940s.[16]

Her desire to paint people asserted itself early in her studies of children and portraits of her sister Isabel and of Ethel McLaren. She showed little interest in painting male sitters, who appear infrequently in her works. She presented few of these early subjects formally but rather depicted them in a more casual manner.

There is a modesty of ambition and scale in these watercolours as well as obvious shortcomings in drawing the human figure. The origins of her style and subjects lie in British Victorian painting. Her paintings are of contemporary subjects, they deal with the everyday not with the myths and allegories favoured by the influential Pre-Raphaelite movement. Her use of posed models in outdoor settings recalls the ideas of the British, Dutch and French realist painters, but her subjects lack the scale, the seriousness of political message and the confrontational dimension of large oils like Millet's *The Gleaners* or Ford Madox Brown's *Work*. A closer resemblance is found in the watercolours of a prominent woman painter of the time, Helen Allingham R.W.S.[17] Allingham, whose paintings of English domestic subjects featuring women and children were greatly sought after in the 1880s and 1890s, did a number of works similar to early Hodgkins. These include *The Clothes-Line*, which has a young mother pegging out clothes on a make-shift line similar to that in Hodgkins's *Washing Day at Cranmore*, 1890.[18] In both cases, the standing figure of a young woman, set in a domesticated suburban landscape is the central focus. Allingham even includes a flock of geese in the meadow recalling that in Hodgkins's *A Goose Girl* of 1893. The baby seated playing with clothes pegs on the ground, too, is like the children found in Hodgkins's art. Allingham's work, often compared with that of Birket Foster, is full of such innocent activities as a girl feeding rabbits or children at play. Hodgkins's *Girl Feeding Poultry*, 1890,[19] is this type of subject, though painted without Allingham's surer grasp of descriptive figure drawing.

Hodgkins could see some original British works at Dunedin and Christchurch, in exhibitions, or the art galleries.[20] Also, she had access to reproductions in publications like *Royal*

FIGURE 1
Helen Allingham, *English Countryside*
Watercolour, 255 x 380mm
Dunedin Public Art Gallery

Academy Pictures Illustrated. Many works were available reproduced by steel engravings in illustrated magazines before the 1890s and after that in photographic reproduction. By these means she was able to widen out her range of visual material.

In 1893 Frances Hodgkins began to take lessons from a visiting Italian painter, Girolamo Pieri Nerli. The first mention of this is in a letter to her sister Isabel dated June that year.[21] She notes that she wants 'to make the most of Nerli's lessons and that Nerli has been most awfully good to me and gives me an extra lesson on Saturdays at his studio'.[22] Nerli (1860–1926) had studied art in Florence in the studio of Tiberio Ciseri before travelling to the South Pacific in 1885.[23] He spent some years in Sydney and Melbourne prior to visiting Dunedin in 1889 on the occasion of the New Zealand and South Seas Exhibition.[24]

Nerli worked in a variety of media, mainly oil, but also pastel and watercolour. Although he painted some landscapes, he was mostly occupied with figure painting, especially informal portraits and intimate studies of girlhood, old age and modern life. In 1889 one of his watercolours, *A Portrait of a Lady*, attracted the eye of the reviewer for the *Otago Witness*, 'a watercolour portrait of a lady in modern, walking costume is a pretty and at the same time a most truthful piece of work'.[25] This watercolour is quite possibly the study, now in the

Auckland City Art Gallery, which Nerli exhibited in Sydney that same year with the title, *The First at the Rendez-Vous* (Fig. 2).[26] Even more to the point, it was owned by William Mathew Hodgkins during the 1890s and he probably bought it from the New Zealand and South Seas Exhibition. William Mathew Hodgkins was an admirer of Nerli's painting of which he owned more than one example. He also sat for his portrait to Nerli probably in 1893.[27]

It is highly likely that Frances Hodgkins first met Nerli in 1889–90 and had been familiar with his figure studies since that time. The opportunity to learn from him when he came back to Dunedin in 1893 was clearly not to be missed. Although she does not specify it, Frances would certainly have been taught figure painting and portraiture by Nerli. His knowledge in these areas was unmatched in the colonial city and his concept of figure painting, as well as his technique and style, were more modern, spontaneous and painterly than anything being done there at that time. The impact of Nerli on Hodgkins appears immediately in 1893 and influenced all her subsequent New Zealand work. Despite this, she was unwilling in later life to give him much credit. The opinion given by Myfanwy Evans in 1948 that Nerli was 'a comic character' and that 'from him she did not learn much' hardly squares with the reality of the 1890s.[28]

In 1893 Hodgkins painted *The Girl with the Flaxen Hair* (Pl. 1), a work that, despite some weaknesses in drawing, marks a development in conception and execution. Proportionately the girl's head is larger and she confronts the viewer more directly than in the earlier portraits. Hodgkins has vignetted the head and shoulders of the girl against the untouched areas of paper — a device Nerli used in some of his watercolour studies.[29] This contributes to an informal, unfinished quality, matched by the execution of the girl's smock which has runs of paint. Hodgkins has allowed paint to merge wet on wet on the paper and stop at irregular intervals. In the hair she has used a sponge to lift areas of paint and create an effect of shine and movement, at the expense of detail. This kind of watercolour technique reflects Nerli's awareness of modern French and Italian approaches to sketching, where the process of painting is allowed to take on an element of the improvised and the accidental.[30] His acquaintance with the Australian Heidelberg painters, especially Tom Roberts and Charles Conder, would have complemented his European experience.

McCormick points out that this 'study' was not exhibited by Hodgkins perhaps because it fell outside the usual definition of a portrait.[31] It is a study of girlhood and innocence as much as a portrait, and it relates to Nerli's several paintings of girlhood painted in Dunedin in 1893–94.[32] Nerli's focus on the colour of the young women's hair — he favoured an auburn colouration — is reflected in Hodgkins's watercolour, in which the warm colour of the girl's flaxen hair is complemented by the blue colouration of her smock. This 'conscious' emphasis on the aesthetic values of colour combinations at the expense of description mirrors again Nerli's relatively sophisticated understanding of trends in modern European art. A later, more accomplished work of this type is *George*, where the modelling of the face is more developed and assured. This is particularly obvious in the placing of the nose in relation to the lips and eyes which in *The Girl with the Flaxen Hair* are out of alignment.[33] Also in

FIGURE 2
Girolamo Pieri Nerli, *The First at the Rendez-Vous*, 1889
Watercolour, 387 x 270mm
Auckland City Art Gallery

FIGURE 3
Head of an Old Woman, 1895
Watercolour, 498 x 373mm
Theomin Gallery, Olveston, Dunedin

George Hodgkins carried the broad style of painting into the facial areas, whereas in *The Girl with the Flaxen Hair* the face is tentatively painted compared with the hair and smock. Already Frances Hodgkins showed a preference for a painterly manner of working from the model rather than a tight, more precise method of drawing. This made her more comfortable with Nerli's approach than with some of the alternative conventions.

Not that she confined herself to one direction all the time. In 1895 she took classes at the Dunedin School of Art and Design, where Nerli had been appointed an instructor.[34] Her competition portrait, *Head of An Old Woman* (Fig. 3), which won a prize at the New Zealand Academy of Fine Arts, indicates another approach to painting a head from life. In this case, the drawing is more literal in its rendering of the features and the head is modelled more systematically in the round by the use of deep chiaroscuro.[35] It is a characterisation of age, somewhat reminiscent of van der Velden's portraits, where the dark shadows can be seen to symbolise encroaching death. Petrus van der Velden (1837–1913) was a Dutch painter, then based in Christchurch, who had been a member of the Hague School of realists.[36] Van der Velden had shown a fine characterisation of age, *Old Jack* (Fig. 4), at the Otago Art Society in 1893.[37] He preferred a dark palette and pronounced tonal contrast of the type Hodgkins used in her *Head of an Old Woman*. But this manner, while successful with the public, was an aberration and was soon discarded. McCormick records the telling comment she is reported to have made in 1913, on seeing the painting again, that it should be burned.[38]

From 1895 onwards, after success at the South Kensington art examinations, she was qualified to practise as a teacher.[39] Her art classes were to provide her from then on with a small, irregular income. Teaching was to stand her in good stead, too, in her later years in Europe. She exhibited regularly at the local art society exhibitions, in Dunedin, Christchurch and Wellington and on two occasions even sent works to Auckland.[40] Increasingly she was able to sell her watercolours and could think in terms of a professional career as a painter. Her decision to become a professional artist was undoubtedly a gradual one, arrived at over a period of years. A factor was the interest of her father and probably the example of Nerli and van der Velden. The itinerant Nerli doubtless suggested the bohemian appeal of being a painter. His studio in The Octagon was a focus for painters from its establishment in 1894.[41] Nerli also encouraged a number of women painters, one of them probably being Grace Joel (1865–1924), a Dunedin woman a few years older than Hodgkins.[42] Joel studied in Melbourne and later made a career as a painter in London. She kept in touch with Nerli in England and in her will left a portrait of Nerli and a work of his to the Art Gallery of New South Wales.[43] Hodgkins knew Grace Joel but they do not appear to have been friends. Another woman painter friend was Dorothy Kate Richmond (1861–1935), a Wellington artist who made a career as a teacher and painter of still life and landscape.[44] In her account of New Zealand women artists, Anne Kirker credits Nerli with stimulating Grace Joel and Frances Hodgkins to extend their study of art overseas.[45] She points out that by doing so they were able 'to realise their ambitions in a way not open to a woman in colonial society'.[46] This is certainly true, but the sense of freedom and independence colonial life allowed may well have contributed to the decision Frances Hodgkins made to become a painter. Dunedin was a centre of learning and numbered several prominent women, like Anna Paterson Stout (1858–1931), a member of the Franchise League, in its intellectual community. Stout was foremost among those who helped achieve the right to vote for women in 1893. The late nineteenth century in Britain, France, Canada and the United States witnessed a dramatic rise in the number of professional women artists.[47] Among these are a few, like the American painter Mary Cassatt (1844–1926), who gained success in Paris, and rather more like the Canadian Emily Carr (1871–1945), who achieved fame in their own country.[48]

Nerli's *Portrait of a Young Woman Artist*, c.1889, provides an image of this trend towards professionalism for women painters, and bears witness to his encouragement and support of women pupils in his classes. Looking back in 1913, though, Hodgkins did not wish to encourage others to follow her example. 'I would hesitate to recommend a New Zealand girl to follow the road I travelled. It is too hard for a woman . . . . The obstacles far exceed a woman's small advantages. Often I felt like giving up.'[49]

These thoughts and misgivings were yet to come as she continued to work and exhibit in the period leading up to her first departure for Europe in 1901. Of her paintings of the years 1896–1900 a group of images of the Maori occupy prominent positions. The New Zealand Maori had long fascinated European artists, some of whom, like the Bohemian painter Gottfried Lindauer (1839–1926), devoted a large part of their output to portraits of the old-time Maori and to figure compositions based on Maori myth or customs.[50] In his works there is a pronounced ethnographical content which is largely absent from Hodgkins's watercolours. She would undoubtedly have known of Nerli's paintings of Pacific subjects, some made in Samoa in 1892, others in Fiji.[51] Nerli had also painted some subjects based on the Australian Aboriginal. These paintings are small, sometimes in watercolour and have a less serious programme than Lindauer's in terms of documenting exotic lifestyle, customs and manner of dress.[52] Nerli's studies appear to have been painted directly *en plein air*, like Hodgkins's, and are free of the hermetic quality so pronounced in Lindauer, whose works can appear dry and artificial.

Hodgkins's paintings of the Maori are almost entirely concentrated on studies of women and children. Quite a few are heads, vignetted against the paper in the manner she first learned from Nerli. She has painted the heads quickly with extensive use of the wet-on-wet technique he favoured. There is minimal suggestion of costume — mainly an indication of a shawl or scarf loosely tied round the shoulders or hair.[53] Like Nerli she appears to have been attracted to the subjects because of their exotic quality and the opportunity to convey a childlike innocence of expression. Her Maoris have smiling or pouting faces dramatised by large eyes and lips.[54] The subjects solicit the viewer in an obvious way, as if begging for attention and emotional response. For example, *Maori Girl*, 1896 (Fig. 5), has the sentimental appeal of a kind favoured in late Victorian paintings of children or animals by artists like Sir John Everett Millais (1829–96) or Sir Edwin Landseer (1802–73).[55]

By detaching the heads from any background, Hodgkins divorces the images from a

FIGURE 4
Petrus van der Velden, *Old Jack*, 1893
Oil on canvas, 932 x 600mm
Dunedin Public Art Gallery

FIGURE 5
Maori Girl, 1896
Watercolour, 348 x 244mm
Dunedin Public Art Gallery

specific context. She thus makes it easier to excise any disturbing problems of poverty or social inequality from the situation. The Maoris are the 'other' in a transaction where there is an assumed hierarchy between viewer and viewed. There is nothing to indicate that Hodgkins felt very deeply about the actual circumstances of the South Island Maoris — a people largely dispossessed of their land and culture by the European settlers. Statements she made in a letter to her sister Isabel in 1899 indicate a distinct lack of concern: 'they (The Maoris) are mostly a rather degenerate lot I think, but still hugely interesting from an artistic point of view'.[56]

Apart from her studies of heads, Hodgkins also made more ambitious watercolours showing full-length figures going about simple tasks such as gathering mussels, digging potatoes and making a bag. While Hodgkins did not present an idealised Polynesian lifestyle, her Maoris seem to epitomise a simple, timeless way of life, close to nature, to the sea and the land.[57] Her female figures may be engaged in manual labour, yet there is no suggestion of oppression or social injustice. As McCormick has pointed out, they can be compared with the figures of European peasants found in British, French, Dutch and Italian painting of the late nineteenth century.[58]

Undoubtedly Hodgkins knew the images of Dutch fishermen and their families brought to New Zealand by Petrus van der Velden.[59] In these paintings van der Velden reflected the Hague School's interest in the lives of the working poor. But it was French painting of the 1840s onwards in which the labour of the peasantry was given its most memorable form.[60] Major artists such as J. François Millet, Jules Breton and Jules Bastien-Lepage specialised in painting large oils devoted to the harsh lives and labour of peasants in France. While these images did range in attitude from sentimentality to graphic political statements about conditions in rural areas, there was a pronounced interest in scenes of honest toil. In some of these paintings, notably the famous *The Gleaners* of Millet painted in 1857, women are the main actors and are shown as monumental, even noble, figures. Their ethnic costumes give a grace and picturesque aspect, as for example, in Jules Breton's *Return of the Gleaners*, 1859.[61] In Breton, and Bastien-Lepage, the viewer is kept at a reassuring distance from the disturbing aspects of rural labour. These paintings suggest a contentment, an innocence and singularity of life that are as comforting as they are unbelievable.[62]

Frances Hodgkins's paintings of the Maori can be related to this well-established tradition. While her works are less ambitious in scale and complexity, they present attractive dignified images of Maori women dressed in European-style costume. *The Bag Maker*, 1898 (Fig. 6), for example, sits calmly at her task; the voluminous folds of her costume echo the simple, large forms found in Millet and endow the figure with presence. She is anonymous, yet stands for a type. She is non-threatening, even reassuring, in her apparent contentment with her lot in life. While there is no sign of luxury, equally there is no squalor. The girl's features have a wistful expression which helps to involve the viewer on an emotional level.

The Mussel Gatherers, Puketeraki, 1900 (Fig. 7), represents one of the last of these works, executed before she left for Europe. It is also one of the more effective in its contrast of the standing woman in the foreground with a male figure beside a beached boat, further back in space. The contrast in scale between the male and female figures, as well as the contrast in definition, is effective and gives compositional variety to the watercolour. Hodgkins's mussel-gatherer stands still — as if posed for the artist — holding her flax basket in one hand. This posed stillness recalls especially Bastien-Lepage.

Bastien-Lepage (1848–84) was one of the most popular and influential French painters whose work featured models posed *en plein air*. He often used a single large figure of a peasant standing in the foreground looking directly at the viewer. His paintings were certainly known in New Zealand and in Australia.[63] The wistful expression of Hodgkins's mussel-gatherer evokes the mood of Bastien-Lepage's peasants. His children, in particular, gaze appealingly at the spectator, eliciting the sentimental response Hodgkins often seeks in her Maori imagery.

It could be argued that Hodgkins manipulates her Maori subjects to find equivalents to known types of imagery from European art. One work, called *A Maori Picnic*, 1900, shows a group of Maoris around a fire cooking food. Without being told the title, it would be easy to identify the group as gypsies from a work by a British painter like George Clausen. In fact, Hodgkins herself painted a similar kind of scene, soon after, in Rapallo, called *Gypsy Cara-van*.[64] Certainly, in these early Maori studies, Hodgkins is content to work within a limited range of ideas showing no real desire to develop a deeper understanding of her subjects or their lifestyle. Already she shows a reluctance to engage herself with political or social issues to any great extent.

It seems that the Maori subjects gave her a popular and identifiable kind of work on which to build her reputation. Probably, too, there was the hope that she could make some sales of these watercolours and help towards funding her first trip to Europe. It is remarkable that although there are landscape backgrounds in a number of Hodgkins's studies of the Maori, she rarely did landscapes by themselves. But once in Europe she devoted much of her time to subjects that are of an essentially landscape nature.

However, there is one landscape from these years, *Mountain Scene*, 1897 (Pl. 2), which shows her ability in this area. While the subject is similar to the snow-capped mountain paintings favoured by her father, the treatment is different. She has painted the watercolour in the direct wet-on-wet technique learnt from Nerli. This is apparent in her painting of the alps in the background and in the suggestive, almost calligraphic treatment of the foreground. As with Nerli, she has allowed the unmarked areas of paper in the lower margin to suggest incompleteness and speed of execution. This adds to the impression of immediacy generated by the handling of the paint.[65] Hodgkins presented the subject as fragmentary and discontinuous. There is no focus on a well-known or named scenic feature.[66] She has painted the imagery so that the surface of the paper is always apparent and the sense of illusionistic space and recession is diminished. For example, there is little sky, and the river appears to tilt up towards the viewer rather than recede in one point perspective. Her positioning of the key mountain motifs to one side and the absence of framing devices in the

FIGURE 6
The Bag Maker, 1898
Watercolour, 300 x 185mm
Private collection

FIGURE 7
The Mussel Gatherers, Puketeraki, 1900
Watercolour, 432 x 248mm
Private collection

foreground further contribute to the unconventional feeling of the work. This modernity of conception almost certainly reflects Nerli's influence, which included ideas drawn from European painting and Japanese prints.[67] Japanese prints and the camera helped to undermine older conventions of order and composition.

On at least one occasion Frances Hodgkins painted a modern industrial subject, *The Harbour*, c.1898, with factory buildings and smoking chimneys.[68] It was only a slight study but one that again reveals her receptivity to new ideas in the years before her departure in 1901. That openness and ability to respond to what was vital in art would enable her, in Europe, to progress from a limited provincial background to a place in the mainstream of British painting of the 1930s and 1940s.

FIRST YEARS IN EUROPE: 1901–1912

Early in February 1901 Frances Hodgkins sailed for Europe.[69] Although this voyage did not sever her contact with New Zealand, it does mark the start of her long, productive years in Europe and Britain. Gradually she was able to evolve from being a minor provincial water-colourist to achieving the status of a leading British artist at the time of her death in 1947.

Initially her plans were quite modest. She intended to visit the major art centres, paint and take classes to improve her work. Like many colonial artists she then would return to a life of painting and teaching in New Zealand. But her first taste of Europe spoiled her for life in Wellington. After a short return to New Zealand in 1903–5,[70] she sailed again for Europe, this time staying much longer, until late 1912. On coming back to New Zealand and Australia she was to stay only a matter of months and this visit seems more like an interlude in her European career than an attempt to base herself in the Antipodes. Perhaps significantly she was hailed in Australasia as an 'ultra-Impressionist', more of the French school than the New Zealand.

Hodgkins left for Europe at a time of great change and vitality in French art. The first years of the twentieth century were to witness the widespread acceptance of Post-Impressionist styles and the overthrow of academic traditions in teaching and practice.[71] Hodgkins's method of working from nature *en plein air*, recording effects of light and weather, indeed attempting to be truthful to appearances with structured space and unity of time and place, came under serious question. During her first decade in Europe she remained an Impressionist long after it ceased to be avant-garde. She did not respond to the Cubist painters Georges Braque and Pablo Picasso until the 1920s, even though she must have seen or heard of their paintings in Paris long before then. She certainly knew of the Italian Futurists and attended the first Futurist Conference at the Bernheim Gallery in January 1912.[72] She heard Filippo Marinetti (1876–1944) expound his theory that all the old art of museums and academies should be destroyed. She remembered him saying 'represent the psychic cause and effect of things — the mental abstract, not the physical concrete'.[73]

These too were the years of the widespread influence of Paul Cézanne and the Fauves. Paris remained the magnet for artists interested in what was new and exciting. Yet, like most British colonial painters, Hodgkins first went to London in hopes of learning more about contemporary painting. She recalled in 1913: 'On leaving New Zealand I went first to England — seeking schooling, but I did not find what I wanted. I was looking for colour and light, and I didn't find it.'[74] There were exceptions in painters such as Arthur Melville or Frank Brangwyn, but she turned increasingly to France for stimulus. Her style of painting *en plein air* from the motif derived from French Impressionism. And she certainly admired painters like Renoir, Monet and Sisley. Her interest in spontaneity, in freshness, in light and colour accords most easily with the Impressionists and their host of followers. In these years the gifted American painter John Singer Sargent (1856–1925) made some of his finest water-colours in a style derived, like hers, from French Impressionism.[75] He too painted similar subjects, boats in harbour, townscapes with figures and landscape on a human scale. Her awareness of French art, and the considerable amount of time she spent in France, contrib-uted greatly to her identity as a painter. Understandably her painting did not evolve sys-tematically in one way. She naturally responded to a wide range of stimuli while testing various styles and techniques. She remained in these first European years a watercolourist. She kept within the conventions of realist and Impressionist painting and executed much of her painting rapidly from the model or the motif. Her subject matter continued to include studies of women and children but she interpreted these increasingly with greater assur-ance and different stylistic emphasis.

In Europe she delighted in painting landscapes and scenes set in the old towns of France, Britain, Italy and Holland. At first these can appear somewhat touristy, the imagery of a colonial attracted by a heritage which was known secondhand rather than from personal experience. They have even been called 'vulgar'.[76] Only gradually did her discrimination improve and the obvious give way to more subtle presentation.

By exhibiting in group shows such as the Royal Academy, London, and the Paris Salon, she tried to place her works in a truly European context. In 1907 she was able to hold her first solo exhibition in London.[77] Between 1908 and 1912 she made a determined bid to posi-tion her art in Paris and to gain a reputation there. She exhibited at both the Old and the New Salons as well as at other venues.[78] While her watercolours did receive mentions in some reviews, they did not bring her much fame. But she did make strides towards the independence of a professional artist who could support herself from her painting and teaching.

Of the paintings she did on her first trip, those made in North Africa deserve special consideration. In these works there is a vitality and breadth of conception which looks for-ward to her achievements of the period 1906–12.

It was in late 1902 that Hodgkins decided to travel to North Africa to paint in Morocco.[79] She was accompanied by a Mrs Ashington, who proved a congenial companion during her exploration of Tangier and a subsequent caravan journey to Tetuan. While her journey can be seen as symptomatic of her search for exotic subject matter, she was attracted also by her love of sunlight, colour and warmth. Tangier, located strategically on the Strait of Gibraltar, consisted of an old walled Moorish town and more modern suburbs reflecting the successive dominion of European powers like the Portuguese, Spaniards and the English. To Hodgkins, still painting *en plein air* and sensitive to the play of sunlight on her subjects, Tangier provided a heightened sensation of colour. Late in life she saw her time in Morocco 'as the real beginning of her painting career'.[80]

She was attracted by the Moorish aspects of the old city, by its people with their flowing robes and dark skins, by the crowded markets and the arched openings of elegant buildings. She painted a number of market scenes in Tangier dating from this trip and several which appear to have been made later from sketches.[81] In such works she used displays of fruit or pottery to provide the occasion for a heightened, decorative use of colour. Hodgkins also made sketches of individual sitters like her study of a Soudanese, and of a Jewess (both in 1903). In choosing to travel to North Africa, Hodgkins was hardly doing anything novel, though her caravan trip to Tetuan was adventurous for a woman at that period.[82] Since the time of Delacroix in the 1830s French and British artists had been attracted to North Africa, at first drawn by a romantic longing for the remote and exotic, later by the attraction of cheap, congenial conditions for painting.[83] Many of these images exude a sensuality and eroticism in the rendering of women in fanciful or compromising situations — an aspect totally absent from Hodgkins's view.

The closest affiliations with her approach are found in the watercolours of Arthur Melville (1855–1904).[84] Evans recorded that Hodgkins was unimpressed by most English watercolours when she arrived in London. They appeared 'dim and pretty, tasteless and colourless'.[85] She adds, 'the only ones that attracted her at all were those of Arthur Melville, with their brilliant blobs of colour in a toneless but sensitive waste'.[86]

Melville, though little remembered today, was at the peak of his reputation when Hodgkins first visited Europe. He was a friend of Frank Brangwyn and was often considered to have helped him achieve the stronger colouration that distinguishes his mature work. Like Hodgkins, Melville was not noted as a draughtsman; rather he was admired for the breadth of his conceptions and 'full blobs' of colour laid on over a softer ground of lighter washes.[87] Significantly Melville often painted in locations such as Spain and Egypt, where he made a number of watercolours of market scenes not unlike those of Hodgkins in Tangier. An example is the *Orange Market, Saragossa*, 1892.[88] In watercolours such as this, open stalls of fruit allowed him to use strong, saturated colour freely, unrestrained by tight drawing or tonal modelling.

Hodgkins's *Orange Sellers, Tangier*, 1903 (Pl. 3), is a good example of her work done in Morocco. This watercolour was a commission for a wealthy Dunedin businessman, Mr D. E. Theomin.[89] It is a market scene painted in full sun so that the glare of light corrodes the forms of buildings rendering them visible by the shadows they cast. She has indicated the

FIGURE 8
Arthur Melville, *A Moorish Procession*, 1903
Watercolour, 593 x 798mm
National Gallery of Scotland, Edinburgh

fully robed figures by blobs of blue and mauve shadows so that they provide a foil for the warm colours of the oranges and onions strewn on the ground in the front of the picture.

By choosing a low viewpoint, Hodgkins tilted the fruit and vegetables towards the picture plane so that the impact of the orange and red colours is maximised. Because there is a minimal amount of descriptive drawing the artist could merge the individual fruit into a larger mass of orange and red which functions as colour first, fruit second. Hodgkins eliminated the sky in this and related images, as did Melville in many of his comparable scenes. Melville was noted for his technique of interspersing dabs and patches of colour with empty spaces.[90] In her Moroccan watercolours Hodgkins appears to have been indebted to this method.

In 1913 Hodgkins saw her trip to Morocco as a search for 'colour and light' and 'freedom' of treatment.[91] These remarks reflect her desire to break away from what she felt was the conservatism and drabness of British art. But her path from 1903 onwards was neither consistent nor in one direction. Frances Hodgkins returned to Wellington just before Christmas in 1903. At first she planned to settle there, open a studio and take pupils. She also prepared for an exhibition to be held jointly with her friend and European sketching companion, D. K. Richmond.[92] Although Hodgkins received good reviews for her watercolours, and some sold, she found it hard to adjust to Wellington. The decline in her output as a painter in itself suggests a problem with her new environment.

The capital was not an art centre in the way Dunedin had been in the late nineteenth century. Its most prominent painter, James Nairn (1859–1904), was to die soon after she arrived in Wellington, an event which had little advantage for Hodgkins in providing an opportunity to take his place.[93] Instead it was Miss Richmond who ultimately filled Nairn's position as a teacher and regular contributor to exhibitions at the New Zealand Academy of Fine Arts.

Among Hodgkins's dated watercolours of 1904–5, figure compositions are important and these compositions sometimes have a specific European or exotic connotation, as if the artist were nostalgic for the world she had left behind and found there a fresher source of inspiration than in her Wellington environment. Why else would she have felt the need to dress up her sister's laundress as a Dutch housewife unless it was a ploy to gain sales from the local audience?[94]

One of her most ambitious paintings of 1904 is *Ayesha* (Pl. 4).[95] The name Ayesha, that of Mohammed's favourite wife, itself has a distinctively Eastern overtone. Hodgkins carries this exotic mood through the costume, the headscarf and the musical instrument the girl appears to be tuning. *Ayesha* is very rich and warm in colour not only in the costume but also in the background. Hodgkins has filled the surface with colour leaving no apparent areas of untouched paper. Ayesha's head, observed from a posed model, is drawn skilfully in a three-quarter view and cast in a cool, bluish shadow. In technique Hodgkins has varied her paint application from broad, irregular washes on the costume to tighter, wedgelike application in the background. She manages to evoke here something of the warmth and mystery of North Africa — still a fresh and inspirational memory. *Ayesha* has been criticised for being contrived, when in fact it belongs to a type — well known in French art — and found, for example, in the works of the Orientalists, or the posed models of Corot.[96] Its acceptance in New Zealand at that time is proved by its ready purchase for the Dunedin Public Art Gallery the year it was painted. Perhaps Hodgkins saw this as a demonstration piece — a work that combined a degree of imagination with a display of technical mastery. Although she turns towards us, the girl's self-absorption distances her from us.

Another important work of this Wellington period is *Babette*, 1905.[97] *Babette* appears to have been posed from the same model as *Ayesha*, yet is treated in a very different manner. No longer posing as an exotic beauty, Babette is shown as a modern European girl, her name now evocative of France, not the East. Whereas *Ayesha* is strongly coloured, *Babette* is reduced to an off-white range — only the girl's auburn hair provides an accent of warm colour. Clearly Hodgkins is concerned with using the model to convey a range of ideas and formal concerns. In no sense is *Babette* a portrait, rather it is a study of mood and feeling. Hodgkins has put special emphasis on the girl's hand fingering her hair. The hand is larger in size than is justified by natural scale, yet provides a foil for the reflective, near melancholic features of the sitter.

FIGURE 9
The Idlers, 1905
Watercolour, 230 x 210mm
Private collection

Apart from these watercolours, Hodgkins painted a few images of the Maori. In 1905 she visited Rotorua, probably to find models for these paintings. One of the dated works of that year is *The Idlers* (Fig. 9), a loosely handled study of the two women and a child in front of a house.[98] While the composition is more elaborate than in her earlier Maori paintings, her focus is still on women and children seen from an outsider's viewpoint and with no deep insight into their life and customs. Indeed the title itself suggests a disapproving or at least condescending tone. Her plans to paint the Maori as a means of stimulating her art in New Zealand seem to have quickly fallen through.

It is hardly surprising to find her deciding to return to Europe for she had friends and supporters there and by this stage it must have been obvious that only in Europe could she realise her ambitions as a painter.

Frances Hodgkins returned to Britain early in 1906. After renewing old acquaintances, she went to Venice in April and took rooms in the Casa Frollo on the Giudecca canal. In a letter to her mother she drew a comparison between the scale and spaciousness of her new quarters and her Bowen Street studio in Wellington.[99] There is a sense of excitement in her mention of the lapping of the canal water and the glimpse of the great church of Santa Maria della Salute through her window. She would have known that Venice was a city that had inspired some of Sargent's most vivid and colourful watercolours. However, it was not in Venice that she was to paint her most memorable Italian works but in the nearby fishing village of Chioggia.[100]

At Chioggia she painted several works based on the subject of fishing boats in the harbour. It was the colour of the boats' sails that attracted her more than the vessels themselves.[101] She was well aware of the potential of this kind of subject through her contact with the Newlyn School of artists and her friendship with the painter Norman Garstin (1847–1926) in particular.[102] Hodgkins went to Newlyn first in 1902 but had already been in contact with Garstin at Caudebec in Normandy the previous year.[103] Newlyn itself is a small fishing village in Cornwall which was chosen by painters like Stanhope Forbes R.A. (1857–1947) as an English equivalent to Brittany towns such as Concarneau in France where there were established artist colonies.[104] The founders of Newlyn were in the main artists who had studied in France and admired the works of Bastien-Lepage. Like him they chose to depict scenes of village life based on observation from nature. Newlyn artists like Garstin, who took sketching classes in Europe, introduced Hodgkins to the subject matter found in her Chioggia watercolours and the many related themes in her paintings at Concarneau and elsewhere in provincial France and Holland. She felt more comfortable with the simpler subjects such villages provided than with the spectacular imagery of Venice.

An interesting example of her work at Chioggia is the large watercolour *Red Sails*, 1906 (Pl. 5).[105] In this instance, the composition has a greater breadth and structure than in her earlier works. This is achieved by the trapezoidal mass of the sails which juts up into the picture plane and is boldly lopped off by the frame. In the lower region, the deep blue reflection of the hull provides a tonal and colour contrast. It is blue, the sail orange and red. The

FIGURE 10
Stanhope Forbes, *Preparations for Market, Quimperlé, Brittany*, 1883
Oil on canvas, 1690 x 1340mm
Dunedin Public Art Gallery

91 SAINT-VALÉRY-SUR-SOMME. — Sur le sable. — LL.

Postcard of St Valery-sur-Somme

sail seems old, tattered, and saturated with the warm colours of the sun as if with time they have stained its fabric in their own glowing image.

In its almost decorative grandeur *Red Sails* recalls the paintings of Sir Frank Brangwyn (1867–1956). Brangwyn was noted in his watercolours for his 'sweeping touch', his colourism and his decorative power.[106] Often, as Hodgkins does here, he positions the viewer down low so that the masses of clouds, buildings, boats or figures rise dramatically above us to give enhanced grandeur to the scene. Also, as Hodgkins does, he makes the most of pattern and surface shapes at the expense of detail.

It is characteristic of Brangwyn and of Hodgkins in watercolours such as this to relate areas of colour, like the sails, to the picture plane and to acknowledge its flatness. Also, the sketchy, untouched areas of the quay to the right allow us to see the paper and follow its presence into the image. Hodgkins continued to paint a series of watercolours of fishing vessels in Europe over the next few years. A good example is the work entitled *Fishing Boats*, probably painted in Concarneau, 1911.[107] In this work an evening effect is achieved but with the shapes of the fishing boats' masts and hulls creating structures and patterns on the paper surface.

Interestingly, images of boats in harbour were common in French painting of the time. The expatriate New Zealand painter Sydney Lough Thompson based himself in Concarneau and often painted its sardine fleet.[108] He was influenced by many of the same artists as Hodgkins, including Lucien Simon, whose broad vigorous handling and sense of design appealed to both painters.[109] The Fauve painters, who included in their number Raoul Dufy and Henri Matisse, often found in fishing boats and their sails the ideal motif for studies in bright, primary colours.[110] Dufy, Manguin, Derain and Matisse exhibited such works widely in France, especially Paris, from 1904 onwards. Comparatively Hodgkins's *Red Sails* is restrained but there is the beginning of formalist interests that would align her more closely with these artists' works in the 1920s.

Increasingly after 1907 Hodgkins began to spend less time in Britain and more time in Europe. She lived for a period in Holland where her continued interest in picturesque European villagers and townscape is evident. Among the artists Hodgkins specifically mentioned as influential at the time were the Dutch painters Anton Mauve (1838–88) and the Maris brothers Willem and Jacob.[111] All were members of the Hague School to which Petrus van der Velden had belonged before emigrating to New Zealand. The continuities with the Newlyn School approach and that of French artists like Simon can be found in her Dutch imagery.

In one example, the subject is a small bridge over a Dutch canal (Pl. 7).[112] In addition to the bridge and buildings there is a group of children dressed in national costume which gives the scene a somewhat exotic look, as happens with Simon's Breton peasant subjects. Hodgkins painted the scene broadly with largish washes and blobs of subdued colour which coalesce into an overall atmospheric unity. She has indicated houses faintly in the background; the children and ducks help give a feeling of domesticity and calm so typical of the Dutch painting she admired.

A powerful work of the same period is *Dordrecht*, c.1908 (Pl. 8).[113] Here the composition is held to the picture plane by a wall of architectural forms, culminating in a domed structure. Her use of architecture in this and related works, while important thematically, is in no sense topographical.[114] Seen in a dull but resonant light with heavy cloud and rain, the buildings on the river mass together giving a feeling of structure and solidity which is unmatched in her art up to that time. The figures of children in the foreground add a measure of scale to the view without unduly contributing a narrative dimension. The girl at the left is one of Hodgkins's more felicitous inventions and her gaze extends the space laterally beyond the frame. While the watercolour is low in tone, it has colouristic richness in its combination of deep blue and amber.

Works such as this from her second European period appear as a decided advance over her more illustrative scenes of towns in Italy and France of 1901–3. From late 1908 until 1912 Hodgkins was based in France. She lived a life of poverty supplementing sales of her watercolours by taking classes for sketching in places like Concarneau and St Valery-sur-Somme.[115] In 1909 she was asked to teach watercolour at the Académie Colarossi in Paris. Like Julian's, Colarossi's also depended on a large number of women artists for its clientele.[116] While Hodgkins later recalled this 'invitation' with pride, she taught there only for a few months in the winter of 1909–10. In 1911 she opened her own painting school in Paris, where she conducted classes, some attended by New Zealanders like Cora Wilding (1888–1982).[117]

It seems reasonable to expect that it was during these years that her understanding of French art grew and put its stamp on her style of painting. She was certainly in a position to see works by major modernist masters such as Picasso and Matisse. However, her vision remained an Impressionist one, concerned with light in all its variety of effects from muted indoor studies to luminous outdoor subjects such as *Summer*, c.1912 (Pl. 9).[118] In this example her technique changes to allow long, almost calligraphic strokes or lines to detach themselves from literal meaning and animate the surface with an ephemeral, shimmering effect.

She used this approach also in her views of the Seine of about 1912. A number of prominent American watercolourists who studied in Paris at the same time as Hodgkins evolved their technique in a similar way. An example is John Marin (1870–1953).[119] In his case he wanted to reveal the pulse and vitality of all things, to convey a sense of life. We know that Hodgkins had listened with interest in 1911 to the Futurist Marinetti, who encouraged greater freedom from appearances and more emphasis on sensation.[120] This appears to have appealed to Hodgkins. The watercolours of 1911–12 seem to reflect an urge for change and greater expression in handling. It is possible to sense the need to move away from the restrictions of later Impressionism towards something fresh.

In the period from 1906 to 1912 Hodgkins continued to paint, alongside her other subjects, an important series of images of women and children. These paintings continue the-

Postcard of Paris showing the Académie Colarossi down the street at left

matic interests which can be traced back to her beginnings as a painter in Dunedin. The pleasures of domestic life, of motherhood and children, even of security, emerge in these works with a poignancy perhaps enhanced by her own exclusion from them. Almost unconsciously she created in paint a world she sacrificed to pursue her lonely path as an artist. She evokes, too, some of the freedoms of modern women at the start of the new century and contrasts them with the conventional restraints of traditional peasant society in France and Holland.[121] In her paintings women and their relationship with friends and family assume a special significance.

Among Hodgkins's watercolours depicting young modern women in a contemporary setting *The Window Seat*, 1907 (Pl. 6), is one of the more appealing.[122] It is also one of the best documented because she won a prize for it in the Franco-British Exhibition in 1908, in the Australian section for women's art.[123] *The Window Seat* evokes the colours and atmosphere of an interior at night lit by a standard lamp which is reflected in the window panes of the room. Subdued in pose and soft in focus her figures are romantic in mood. Both women are in evening dresses whose subtle green and pink colours give a touch of glamour to the scene. The moment she shows here is one of intimacy and reflection. The women's proximity to one another and their poses suggest friendship and mutual concerns. It is part of the appeal of such a work, as is the case with French *Intimiste* imagery, that we are allowed access to personal and everyday moments normally confined to the privacy of one's home.[124]

Hodgkins must have seen some of the small paintings of domestic scenes by Edouard Vuillard (1868–1940) and Pierre Bonnard (1867–1947), where interior spaces become the setting for the confidences of friends, family and mothers with children.[125] In this watercolour Hodgkins seems comfortable with the subject as if familiar with the sitters. This was indeed the case, for the women she depicts are Maud and Una Nickalls.[126] Hodgkins had met Maud as early as 1901 at Norman Garstin's class at Caudebec, Normandy. She became friends with her and stayed with the family at their home, Wispers, near Stedham, Sussex, in November and December 1907. That provided the occasion for painting *The Window Seat*.[127]

Hodgkins also painted women together outdoors suggesting freedom from constraint, well-being and wholesomeness — a degree of vigour. An example is *The Hill Top*, c.1908 (Fig. 11).[128] A similar quality emerges from the paintings of American artists in Paris at the turn of the century, like Robert Reid (1862–1929), whose women suggest the emancipation so much associated with the United States, and to some extent with Australia and New Zealand.[129]

A comparable spirit in literature can be found in the heroines of Henry James's novels set in Europe. Hodgkins herself belonged to the growing number of women who came to Paris to learn and to take part in the vital art scene to which they were to make an important contribution, even if one often downplayed and dismissed by some critics as feminine in character.[130] Undoubtedly Hodgkins had the ambition to succeed as a painter, not as a woman painter, but in so doing she had no need to suppress or deny her perspective on life and art shaped by her experiences as a woman.

FIGURE 11
The Hill Top, c.1908
Watercolour, 750 x 570mm
Museum of New Zealand, Te Papa
Tongarewa

Perhaps at no other period did Hodgkins's painting have such buoyancy of feeling. Her imagery is remarkably unconcerned with the melancholic and tragic aspects of life, though she was to experience more than her share of them. As she was to write much later to her friend Jane Saunders: 'I try to focus on my work — my cherished escape — but life is all very difficult.'[131] Even images like *The Convalescent* exude the virtues of a loving home into which illness may enter but never cast a shadow for too long.[132] In this case the pose of the woman seated on the bed suggests concern, patience, and moral support. The energetic brush-strokes and the presence of light act to dispel any suggestion of gloom.

Of her paintings of women and children from this period, two of the finest examples are in the Dunedin Public Art Gallery. They are *Woman and Child* (Fig. 12) and *Summer* (Pl. 9), both undated but around 1912.[133] In *Woman and Child* the tender kiss of the young woman who embraces the baby gains in feeling by the way Hodgkins has woven the two figures together by long, ripply strokes of paint. The pool of shadow fuses the heads, adding intimacy by manifesting the affectionate bond in her formal construction of the work. Similar thematic concerns are found in the imagery of Impressionist artists such as Mary Cassatt.[134]

In *Summer* Hodgkins makes a baby the centre of attention. Although in this case the painting includes three figures, it is the baby who is at the focal point of the composition and who is the object of the women's thoughts. Hodgkins has painted the women's faces indistinctly, even blurred them, as if they are out of focus. By this technique she could suggest their preoccupation and loss of self in the child whose head she drew clearly. Taken in combination with the sunshine and outdoor setting, Hodgkins achieved in this watercolour an image which celebrates the maternal and domestic side of life and identifies such values with health, well-being and the future of society. This gives her watercolours of women and children the optimism and infectious vitality which she shares with much French Impressionist art. It was the French qualities of her painting that attracted most attention when she returned to Australasia late in 1912.

Frances Hodgkins sailed for New Zealand for the last time in October 1912.[135] She called first at Melbourne, where she held a successful exhibition of her works, then went on to Wellington arriving in time for Christmas. On this occasion it was immediately apparent that she would not be staying long. She returned to Australia to exhibit in Sydney and Adelaide before going to Dunedin. Her reception at Dunedin and the response to her show there, while good, were surpassed by the turnout of politicians and members of Wellington high society when she held her final show in the capital. In October 1913 she left Wellington en route via Sydney to Naples.[136] She appears to have painted very little on this busy tour oriented as it was to exhibitions and sales — clearly she now saw her future as lying in Europe and her connections with the Antipodes being on a sentimental and family level, not an artistic one.

In the reviews and responses to her work in Australia and New Zealand Hodgkins was identified with modern French painting. One writer observed: 'the Impressionist wave that has swept over the Latin quarter of Paris has certainly caught this clever little lady in its

FIGURE 12
Woman and Child, c.1912
Watercolour, 475 x 459mm
Dunedin Public Art Gallery

back-wash, though she keeps aloof from the passing insanity of the Futurists!'.[137]

Some writers, such as A. G. Stephens, saw a development in the paintings. He wrote, 'Almost the newest work in her collection is by far the best. The subject is a spring day in Paris; with a white and blue and purple sky, thrilling with wind, blown over a white building shut between the green passages of a tree, a bridge, and a river boat on the Seine.'[138] A reviewer for the *Sydney Morning Herald* noted that her efforts form an up-to-date statement of modern watercolour art in France.[139] Looking back in 1948 Myfanwy Evans observed: 'Frances Hodgkins knew all about what was being painted in Paris in the first twelve years of the twentieth century.'[140] Yet Evans sees the main influences as lying with Impressionism, with Renoir, Monet and Sisley.[141]

To even the most casual observer it was apparent that Hodgkins had evolved into an exciting, well-informed cosmopolitan painter. She was now ready to build on the foundations she had laid in those twelve, tumultuous years and push her art further forwards.

---

1. A. G. Stephens, 'Frances Hodgkins', Supplement to *The Bookfellow*, Sydney, 1 May 1913, pp.ix-x.

2. *Otago Daily Times*, 8 May 1913.

3. Ibid.

4. Ibid.

5. Ibid.

6. See Barbara H. Weinberg, *The Lure of Paris: 19th Century American Painters and Their French Teachers*, New York, 1991, p.279.

7. See M. Kushner, ed., *The Modernist Tradition in American Watercolours, 1911–1939*, Evanston, 1991, pp.10-11.

8. Stephens, p.ix: 'Her father had taught her to paint.' For W. M. Hodgkins, see P. Entwisle, *William Mathew Hodgkins and His Circle*, Dunedin Public Art Gallery, 1984.

9. See Entwisle, pp.156-62, for a transcript of this address.

10. Entwisle, p.162.

11. Stephens, p.ix.

12. Entwisle, p.25: 'eventually, it [painting] seems to have been his predominant concern'.

13. For a discussion of the general social context, see E. H. McCormick, *The Expatriate: A Study of Frances Hodgkins & New Zealand*, Wellington, 1954, pp.18-49.

14. See Entwisle, pp.127-32.

15. For example, early works exhibited in Dunedin at the Otago Art Society include *A Game of Marbles*, 1891, *Little Models*, 1891, *The Young Anglers*, 1892, and *A Goose Girl*, 1893. See E. H. McCormick, *Works of Frances Hodgkins in New Zealand*, Auckland, 1954, pp.224-5.

16. See A. McKinnon, *Frances Hodgkins, 1869-1947*, London, 1990, Pls 25-32. Items include farmyard implements, outhouses, disused steam-engines, brick walls etc.

17. For Allingham, see M. B. Huish, *Happy England as Painted by Helen Allingham, R.W.S.*, London, 1903. Allingham, born in 1848, was the first woman painter made a full member of the Royal Watercolour Society, in 1890. She died in 1926.

18. See Huish, Pl. 11, and pp.59-61. He notes, 'The figure of the woman still smacks somewhat too much of the studio' and that 'the figure detaches itself too much from the rest of the picture', p.60. These observations could also apply to Hodgkins's work.

19. Robert McDougall Art Gallery.

20. An important instance was the New Zealand & South Seas Exhibition held in Dunedin in 1889–90, which had representative displays of British painting by artists such as Lord Leighton. We know that Hodgkins copied a work by Marie Seymour Lucas, called *The Tyrant*, in 1891. See E. H. McCormick, *Portrait of Frances Hodgkins*, Auckland, 1981, pp.16-17.

21. FH to Isabel Field, 9 June 1893, quoted McCormick, *Works*.

22. Ibid.

23. For Nerli, see P. Entwisle, M. Dunn, & R. Collins, *Nerli: An Exhibition of Paintings and Drawings*, Dunedin Public Art Gallery, 1988; also M. Dunn, 'Girolamo Nerli: An Italian Painter in New Zealand', *Art New Zealand*, 49, 1988, pp.60-65; also A. Davison, 'G. P. Nerli and Frances Hodgkins', *Art New Zealand*, 58, 1991, pp.78-82.

24. See Entwisle, Dunn & Collins, p.47.

25. *Otago Witness*, 28 Nov. 1889, p.21.

26. See Entwisle, Dunn & Collins, pp.119-20.

27. This famous work is now in the Hocken Library Collection, Dunedin.

28. M. Evans, *Frances Hodgkins* (Penguin Modern Painters), Harmondsworth, 1948, pp.5-6. See also McCormick, *Works*, pp.34-35, for a useful discussion of the issues.

29. For example, his portrait of Arthur Hadfield Fisher, 1894, for the Carisbrook Cricket Club.

30. For Italian painting in Florence in the period 1860–80, see Norma Broude, *The Macchiaioli: Italian Painters of the Nineteenth Century*, New Haven, 1987. Broude deals extensively with the sketch, but mainly with regard to oil painting.

31. McCormick, *Works*, pp.37-38.

32. See Entwisle, Dunn & Collins, Cat. nos. 112, 113, 117, for examples; also Davison, pp.80-81.

33. Auckland City Art Gallery. *George* is dated c.1896 by McCormick, *Works*, p.142.

34. See *Evening Star*, Dunedin, 20 July 1895, p.3. He had been appointed in February.

35. Nerli did paint a few early works of this type. See Entwisle, Dunn & Collins, pp.96-97.

36. For van der Velden, see T. L. R. Wilson, *Petrus van der Velden*, Wellington, 1976.

37. See Wilson, p.155. The painting is now in the Dunedin Public Art Gallery.

38. McCormick, *Works*, p.134.

39. McCormick, *Expatriate*, pp.33-34. He gives a good account of her routine of classes and visits to Wellington to see Isabel and her family.

40. In 1897 she exhibited three paintings at the Auckland Society of Arts, and in 1898 at the Industrial and Mining Exhibition.

41. See Entwisle, Dunn & Collins, p.57. The studio was shared with L. W. Wilson and J. D. Perrett.

42. For Joel, see Frank Dickinson, *Grace Joel: Paintings & Drawings*, Dunedin Public Art Gallery, 1980; also R. D. J. Collins, 'Grace Joel and Australia', *Bulletin of New Zealand Art History*, 14, 1993, pp.29-40.

43. See Entwisle, pp.122-3.

44. See Louis Johnston, 'Dorothy Kate Richmond 1861–1935', MA thesis, Univ. of Auckland, 1991.

45. Anne Kirker, *New Zealand Woman Artists*, Wellington, 1986, p.19.

46. Ibid.

47. For the latest general account, see W. Chadwick, *Women, Art and Society*, London, 1991, pp.210-34.

48. Hodgkins, in fact, taught Emily Carr, in France in 1911. See McCormick, *Portrait*, p.69.

49. Stephens, p.ix.

50. For a general introduction to the topic, see L. Bell, *The Maori in European Art*, Wellington, 1980.

51. See Entwistle, Dunn & Collins, pp.18–19.

52. There is a thoughtful discussion of Hodgkins's Maori paintings in McCormick, *Works*, pp.54-57.

53. The earliest of the Maori studies are dated 1896. See McCormick, *Works*, pp.140-3, for a list of these.

54. Nerli sometimes painted extremes of expression in his images of Aboriginal or Polynesian subjects, ranging from laughter to a sullen moodiness.

55. The origins of this kind of presentation can be traced back in English art to Thomas Gainsborough's so-called 'Fancy' pictures of rustic children. An earlier source lies in the painting of peasant children by the Spanish artist Murillo (1617–82).

56. FH to Isabel Field, 28 April 1899. Quoted McCormick, *Works*, p.54.

57. This identity, of course, has a great deal of truth. See M. Orbell, *The Natural World of the Maori*, Auckland, 1985.

58. See McCormick, *Expatriate*, p.41.

59. See Wilson, pp.47-58.

60. See Nochlin, *Realism*, Harmondsworth, 1971; also R. Rosenblum & H. W. Janson, *Art of the 19th Century*, London, 1984, for a general survey.

61. Reproduced Nochlin, p.117. The painting is in the Musée, Arras.

62. See Rosenblum & Janson, pp.221-2. See also A. Boime, 'The Macchiaioli and the Risorgimento', in *The Macchiaioli Painters of Italian Life 1850–1900*, Los Angeles, 1986, pp.33-71, for a discussion of the propaganda role of paintings of Italian peasants in the late nineteenth century.

63. A major work by Lepage, *The Potato Gatherers*, 1878, was bought for the National Gallery of Victoria. See Virginia Spate, *Tom Roberts*, Melbourne, 1972. Lepage was influential on the Glasgow School of Painting, of which James Nairn, who emigrated to New Zealand in 1890, was a member. See R. Billcliffe, *The Glasgow Boys*, London, 1985.

64. *Maori Picnic* is in a private collection. It shows the same standing male figure used in *The Mussel Gatherers, Puketeraki*, suggesting the practice of introducing or combining figures from different studies. *Gypsy Caravan*, 1901, is reproduced in McCormick's *Portrait*, p.42.

65. Nerli usually sketched landscapes in oil *en plein air*. On the whole he avoided grand mountain subjects, and preferred the low key and intimate, as did the French Impressionists.

66. The subject has been identified by Charles Brasch as the Dart River, near Lake Wakatipu. See McCormick, *Portrait*, pp.30-31. McCormick's uncertainty about the subject is evident from his earlier reference, *Works*, p.144, to its having been painted in South Canterbury.

67. Oriental items can be found in several of Nerli's works, for example, *The Sitting*, 1889. See Entwisle, Dunn & Collins, p.18.

68. Private collection.

69. She left on 6 February and had reached Marseilles by the end of March.

70. She made no mention of her first trip back to Myfanwy Evans, who omits it from her book. See Evans, *Hodgkins*, pp.6-7. She also makes no mention of it in the interviews she gave to the press in 1913.

71 For a general introduction, see George Heard Hamilton, *Painting and Sculpture in Europe: 1880–1940*, Harmondsworth, 1967, pp.7-184.

72. See Stephens, p.ix. 'I had the pleasure of being present at the first Futurist conference held in Paris — a remarkable meeting.'

73. Ibid, p.x.

74. Ibid, p.ix.

75. See Donelson F. Hoopes, *Sargent Watercolours*, New York, 1976. Sargent, unlike Hodgkins at this stage, also worked in oils. His watercolours were done almost for relaxation.

76. See John Rothenstein, *Modern English Painters*, vol. 1, London, 1962. 'I also detect a distinct strain of vulgarity!', p.129.

77. In March at Paterson's Gallery.

78. For example, she exhibited at the New Salon — *Salon de la Société des Beaux Arts* — in 1911 and 1912 — and at the *Société Internationale des Aquarellistes* in 1911. For a detailed discussion, see Roger Collins, 'A Long Attachment: Frances Hodgkins in France' in *Writing a New Country*, J. Ross, L. Gill, & S. McRae, eds, Auckland, 1993, pp.84-95.

79. Letters date her arrival to December 1902. She left in April 1903. See McCormick, *Expatriate*, pp.80-83.

80 See Evans, *Hodgkins*, p.7.

81. One of the latter is *Orange Sellers, Tangier*, 1905, Museum of New Zealand. It was presumably painted in New Zealand.

82. See Evans, *Hodgkins*, p.7: 'Tetuan, where few white women had ever been'. Evans's account is based on interviews with the artist and no doubt reflects her assessment of the situation.

83. See G. M. Ackerman, *Les Orientalistes de L'Ecole Britannique*, Paris, 1991. Her friend Norman Garstin had worked in Tangier. See his article 'Tangier as a sketching ground', *Studio*, vol. 11, August 1897, pp.177-82. The attraction continued in the early twentieth century. Matisse spent time in Algeria in 1906 and in Morocco in 1912. See *Matisse in Morocco: Paintings and Drawings: 1912–1913*, National Gallery of Art, Washington, 1990.

84. For Melville, see Agnes McKay, *Arthur Melville, Scottish Impressionist*, Leigh-on-Sea, 1951; also R. Fedden, 'Arthur Melville', *Annual of the Old Watercolour Society*, no. 1, 1923–4, pp.39-59.

85. Evans, *Hodgkins*, p.7.

86. Ibid.

87. See Fedden, pp.41-42.

88. Reproduced McKay, Pl. 38. Another good example is *A Moorish Procession*, 1903, National Gallery of Scotland, Edinburgh, reproduced Ackerman, p.215.

89. Mr Theomin gave her the commission in December 1902. See McCormick, *Works*, p.176.

90. This is commented on by W. Shaw Sparrow in *Frank Brangwyn and His Work*, London, 1910, p.177.

91. Stephens, p.ix.

92. This exhibition was held at McGregor Wright & Co.'s Art Gallery in February 1904.

93. Nairn died in poverty on 22 February 1904, aged 45, and a committee was set up to raise funds for his family. See Robin Kay & Tony Eden, *Portrait of a Century: The History of the New Zealand Academy of Fine Arts 1882–1982*, Wellington, 1983, pp.42-43.

94. See McCormick, *Expatriate*, p.97.

95. *Ayesha* was purchased from the artist at the Otago Art Society's Annual Exhibition in 1904 for £21.

96. See McCormick, *Works*, p.72. It is also called 'an unconvincing fiction' by Peter Entwisle in his accession notes, Dunedin Public Art Gallery, 1987. See also, Peter Entwisle, 'Frances Hodgkins at the Dunedin Public Art Gallery: A History of the Collection and a Checklist', *Bulletin of New Zealand Art History*, vol. 14, 1993, p.41.

97. Dowse Art Gallery, Lower Hutt.

98. Private collection. This work was exhibited at the New Zealand Academy of Arts in 1905, at Wellington.

99. Letter dated 18 April 1906.

100. Chioggia is a seaport on the Adriatic, twenty kilometres from Venice. It had been a port since ancient times and was noted for its fishing fleet and fish market. It had long been popular with British and American painters.

101. She wrote, 'The red and yellow sails are the feature of Chioggia, otherwise it would be quite uninteresting.' Quoted McCormick, *Portrait*, p.61.

102. For Newlyn, see Caroline Fox, *Painting in Newlyn 1900–30*, Penzance, 1985; also *Painting in Newlyn 1880–1930*, Barbican Gallery, London, 1985. See also Michael Jacobs, *The Good and Simple Life, Artist Colonies in Europe and America*, Oxford, 1985, ch. 8, pp.143-66 especially.

103. See McCormick, *Expatriate*, p.57.

104. Forbes wrote to his mother in 1884, 'Newlyn is a sort of English Concarneau and the haunt of a great many painters.' See Fox, *Painting in Newlyn 1900–30*, p.9.

105. Once owned by the artist's brother Percy Hodgkins, it was donated by him to the Dunedin Public Art Gallery in 1956. It is sometimes also known as *The Orange Sail*.

106. See W. Shaw Sparrow, pp.177-8.

107. The painting was bought by public subscription from an exhibition of works in 1913. See accession notes by Peter Entwisle, 1987, Dunedin Public Art Gallery. A related work, *Dusk in the Port, Concarneau*, is in the Auckland City Art Gallery Collection.

108. See Julie King, *Sydney Lough Thompson at Home and Abroad*, Robert McDougall Art Gallery, Christchurch, 1990. Hodgkins knew Thompson in France.

109. For Simon, see exhibition catalogue, *Lucien Simon*, Musée des Beaux-Arts de Quimper; also G. Mourey, 'The Art of Lucien Simon', *Studio*, vol. 25 (109), 1902, pp.157-70.

110. See Judi Freeman, ed., *The Fauve Landscape*, Los Angeles County Museum of Art, 1990, pp.59-121 especially.

111. They are referred to by Evans, *Hodgkins*, p.7; also McCormick, *Portrait*, p.64.

112. McCormick, *Works*, p.187, notes that the work is dated indistinctly and that the probable reading is 1907.

113. Purchased from the artist's Dunedin exhibition in 1913. Hodgkins was in Dordrecht from May 1907 until mid 1908. The weather was exceptionally wet which may account for the mood of the painting.

114. A comparison can be made with works of an artist like Jacob Maris such as his *Harbour Scene*, c.1885, Rijksmuseum, Amsterdam. See Fritz Novotny, *Painting and Sculpture in Europe 1780–1880*, Pelican History of Art, Harmondsworth, 1960, Pl. 135b.

115. See McCormick, *Expatriate*, pp.132-43.

116. It was located in the rue de la Grand Chaumière, Montparnasse, See Marie Adelaide Belloc, 'Lady Artists in Montparnasse', *Murray's Magazine*, (8) Sept. 1890, pp.371-84.

117. See McCormick, *Expatriate*, pp.140-1, for an interesting account of Hodgkins's teaching methods as described by

Wilding. Wilding was a founder of the Sunlight League which helped run children's health camps.

118. This work is undated but was purchased for the Dunedin Public Art Gallery in 1913. The date 1912 is accepted by McCormick, *Works*, p.192.

119. See S. Reich, *John Marin: A Stylistic Analysis and Catalogue Raisonné*, 2 vols, Tucson, 1970.

120. Stephens, p.ix; also, Evans, *Hodgkins*, p.9.

121. Subjects of women and children are common in late nineteenth- and early twentieth-century French art. See Chadwick, *Women, Art and Society*, ch. 8, for a discussion of the social context and problems for women artists at this period.

122. The watercolour was purchased in 1913 from Anthony Hordern's Gallery, Sydney.

123. She refers to winning the prize in a letter written from Rijsoord, Holland, on 6 July 1908. See typescript by E. H. McCormick, Art Gallery of New South Wales, Sydney.

124. Vuillard is the leading exponent of this kind of painting. See B. Thompson, *Vuillard*, Oxford, 1988. See also G. H. Hamilton, *Painting and Sculpture in Europe 1880–1940*, Pelican History of Art, Harmondsworth, 1967, pp.64-66.

125. Bonnard had one-man shows at the Bernheim-Jeune Gallery, Paris, in 1906, 1909, 1910, 1911 and 1913. We know Hodgkins visited this gallery when in Paris.

126. For the Nickalls, see McCormick, *Expatriate*, pp.84-85.

127. See typescript by E. H. McCormick, Art Gallery of New South Wales Library, Sydney.

128. Museum of New Zealand. This work was reproduced in Evans, *Hodgkins*, Pl. 1, to represent the early phase of her career. Hodgkins must have thought enough of the image to have kept a photograph after she had forgotten who owned the work, as the owner is listed as unknown.

129. See B. Weinberg, p.248.

130. For a discussion of this issue, see R. Parker & F. Pollock, *Old Mistresses: Women, Art and Ideology*, New York, 1981, pp.37-49.

131. Letter to Jane Saunders, 3 May 1942. Tate Gallery Archive, London.

132. Whitworth Gallery, Manchester.

133. *Woman and Child* was bequeathed to the gallery in 1956 by the artist's brother Percy Hodgkins. The date is McCormick's, *Works*, p.193. For *Summer*, see note 118 above.

134. For example, her colour print *Mother's Kiss*, 1890–91. See N. Mathews & B. S. Shapiro, *Mary Cassatt: The Colour Prints*, Washington, 1989.

135. An excellent account of her return journey and its social side is given in McCormick, *Expatriate*, ch. 7, pp.144-60.

136. She left on 17 October 1913. *Evening Post*, Wellington, 18 Oct. 1913.

137. Ann Cornstalk, 'Pages for Everywoman', *Lone Hand*, Sydney, 2 June 1913, p.xxxviii.

138. Stephens, p.ix.

139. *Sydney Morning Herald*, 15 May 1913.

140. Evans, *Hodgkins*, p.9.

141. Ibid.

1914–1930

IAIN BUCHANAN

Friends say my work is much stronger now than ever — I feel it is — perhaps the war has vitalised & fortified — who knows.

FRANCES HODGKINS, 10 JANUARY 1916

THE WAR YEARS 1914–20

It is quite significant that when Frances Hodgkins returned to Europe she chose France rather than England. France had always held a special importance for her — besides being the centre of the most advanced developments in painting, the French countryside was a constant source of subjects and inspiration. She had spent the last four years based in Paris and clearly intended to resume her life of teaching and exhibiting. The outbreak of war in August 1914 ended that dream. Her pupils, on whom she depended for financial support, returned to England and shortly afterwards she joined them. By the end of the year she was living at St Ives in Cornwall, where she was to remain apart from brief periods in London. For Hodgkins, after working in France since 1908, the return to England meant a renewed involvement with British painting and all the restrictions it imposed. The wartime artistic situation was succinctly defined by the painter Wyndham Lewis, who wrote in 1915: 'The English have never been so insular and "English" as at the present moment.'[1] Frances Hodgkins was equally susceptible to this influence and by the end of the war her earlier French manner had been replaced by one based on an English approach to subject and treatment.

Hodgkins knew Cornwall well and had already spent part of the summer of 1902 in Penzance, working in close contact with her former teacher Norman Garstin. Cornwall, and in particular Newlyn, had been established as an artistic centre in the 1880s under the influence of French art and in conscious imitation of Brittany, where many Newlyn painters such as Stanhope Forbes and Norman Garstin continued to hold classes during the summer months.[2] Like Brittany, the Cornish countryside offered picturesque local subjects drawn from the customs of the villagers and fishermen, as well as attractive settings for *plein air* landscape painting. Garstin himself had praised the variety of scenery, ranging from rocky coves to moorland farms, in a 1909 article on 'West Cornwall as a Sketching Ground'.[3]

At first Frances Hodgkins renewed her friendships and was associated with Norman

Garstin, Moffat Lindner and Stanhope Forbes, older members of the Cornish School, who continued to exhibit at the Royal Academy and to paint in a tonal and subdued form of Impressionism, influenced by Whistler and the French artist Bastien-Lepage. The conservative nature of art in St Ives was particularly striking to her after the experimentation of Paris, a feeling she expressed to her mother in February 1915 — 'I find I am too modern for people down here and I am conscious of the cold eye of distrust and disapproval by the older members of St Ives.'[4]

The interviews Hodgkins gave in Australia between 1912 and 1913 reveal an admiration for Monet, Pissaro, Degas and Sisley.[5] Her own art remained basically Impressionist in style and approach, grounded in an immediate response to nature. Light and movement were her chief interests but she detected a shift in art away from pure aestheticism towards a more vigorous and robust style. Certainly she knew the works of the Post-Impressionist painters Gauguin, Van Gogh and Cézanne, which had been recently introduced to Britain by Roger Fry's *Manet and the Post-Impressionists* exhibition of 1910. While some British artists such as Vanessa Bell, Duncan Grant and Spencer Gore had already absorbed these influences and were working with non-objective colour and a flattened treatment of form, for Hodgkins such experimentation was a more cautious process and Post-Impressionist practice only gradually enters her painting.[6]

During the war she avoided the usual St Ives landscape motifs, concentrating instead on figure painting. There is a move towards a greater emphasis on form and structure in the treatment of her Impressionist subjects. Over these years she painted many portraits, some of them commissions from her pupils and friends, and this became a valuable source of income. Landscapes are much less prominent and the Impressionist combination of figure and landscape, common to her earlier work, is largely abandoned. Only in part can this change be explained by a wartime demand for portraits and the restrictions on outdoor sketching imposed in July 1915. It is more symptomatic of an artistic revaluation in which she gives up her exclusive dependency on watercolour, introducing both oil and tempera paint as well as an increased scale to her paintings. Watercolour was now too restricted a medium for the kind of work she wanted to produce. Among the earliest of these new oil and tempera paintings are *Loveday and Anne* (Pl. 11) and *Mr and Mrs Moffat Lindner and Hope* (Pl. 12), both of which she exhibited at the fashionable National Portrait Society in February 1916.[7]

It is debatable to what extent *Loveday and Anne* can be defined as a portrait. Certainly it is quite different in subject and treatment from the more conventional society portraits exhibited at the National Portrait Society by artists such as Ambrose McEvoy and Sir William Orpen. This may account for the reaction of John Salis in *New Witness* who wrote: 'This is the exhibit of a pyrotechnic artist in paint, it is not portraiture, or if it is, I never want to meet Loveday and Anne.'[8] In fact, the sitters were local models — two fishermen's daughters. A similar interest in painting ordinary working-class sitters is also found in Walter Sickert's pictures such as *The Blue Hat* (1914) and in Harold Gilman. *Loveday and Anne* has an informal quality: it is an exercise in painting in which the central bowl of intense blue flowers serves to link the rather disconnected figures.

Moffat Lindner, who bought *Loveday and Anne,* also commissioned a large portrait group of his family from Hodgkins at the beginning of 1916. *Mr and Mrs Moffat Lindner and Hope* is executed in tempera, unlike *Loveday and Anne,* but has a similar appearance though it is much bigger, remaining the largest of Hodgkins's surviving works. This is in keeping with recent French art where Bonnard and Vuillard had introduced a more structured treatment and greater scale to the Impressionist portrait. Hodgkins places the Lindners outside, posed against a large studio window which serves to define the groupings. She retains the Impressionist interest in light, which is reflected in the window and falls directly onto the sitters, but the figures and their relations are given greater emphasis and importance. The greenish flesh tones, commented on negatively by a number of contemporary critics, are quite common in the works of Vuillard and Toulouse-Lautrec. Vuillard himself did a number of portraits of artists and close friends such as *The Painter K— X— Roussel and his Daughter Annette,* 1903 (Fig. 13), where the figures are placed in unposed groupings and the setting imparts a definite mood to the scene.[9] Hodgkins, like Vuillard, had a sympathetic understanding of children, and Hope, clad in a violet dress, is the centre of the composition, the only figure to look directly out of the scene. Tempera for Hodgkins was an extension of her usual water-colour method in terms of scale and permanence but, as yet, she had not developed an oil-painting technique. This was to come later in works such as *The Edwardians* (Fig. 14), painted around 1919, where the colours are richer, the paint applied in quite thick impasto, and the tonal range much more developed.[10] Otherwise, in terms of mood, structure and lighting the painting is quite similar to *Mr and Mrs Moffat Lindner and Hope.*

A more sombre quality is apparent in the paintings Hodgkins did of Belgian refugees, where she tends to suppress her bright decorative colouration. The oil and tempera painting known as *Belgian Refugees* (Pl. 13) is probably identical with *Unshatterable,* exhibited at the International Society in Autumn 1916.[11] This patriotic subject had been taken up by a number of artists at the beginning of the war in response to the plight of Belgium. Among them were Frank Brangwyn, who treated the theme in a recruiting poster for the London Underground in 1914 (see Pl. 13), and William Lee Hankey in his etching of 1914, *The Flight from Belgium.* Both Brangwyn and Lee Hankey depicted family groups viewed from below, dramatically outlined against a stormy sky. Hodgkins adopted the then quite common formula for her own composition, painting the sky boldly in oils in a modulated grey-blue colour. The figures, reduced to a few summarily defined shapes, are almost sketch-like, although in places oil paint is used to reinforce the modelling of form. Like Brangwyn, she includes a nursing mother at the centre of the painting but no men are present, and her piled-up figure group is composed only of women and children. This is a distinctive feature of her refugee paintings, which always address the more intimate relations of mothers and children. *The Parrot,* a watercolour of three children, is closely related to *Belgian Refugees,* and was exhibited at the International Society in 1916. As no drawings are known from this period, Hodgkins

FIGURE 13
Edouard Vuillard, *The Painter K— X— Roussel and his Daughter Annette,* 1903
Oil, 582 x 531mm
Albright-Knox Art Gallery, Buffalo

probably used watercolours as preliminary studies for her more developed oil paintings. *Refugee Children* (Fig. 15), another tempera painting, is similar in subject to *Belgian Refugees* but much less monumental in treatment, being more of a personal response to three individual children.

At the end of 1918, Hodgkins came into contact with two much younger artists, Cedric Morris and Arthur Lett Haines, who were then just at the beginning of their careers.[12] Lett Haines, who acquired *Belgian Refugees*, had sublet her studio at Eldon Road, Kensington and later she stayed with them at Newlyn. Cedric Morris later recalled visiting her St Ives studio, where the walls were lined with paintings of children, 'compositions in which textural effects were juxtaposed with an emphasis on pattern'.[13] Many of these pictures must have come from the group of twenty-two watercolours of young children Hodgkins exhibited at the International Society in October 1918. They were done over a two-month period in a concentrated burst of activity. Only a few seem to have survived, but from the exhibition titles it is clear that two infants named Peter and Lilian were recorded asleep in no less than eleven separate studies. The group of watercolours was hung along one wall of the Private Gallery in a special display next to work of Alfred Munnings. The subject of mothers and children is often found in French Impressionist painting and was treated by Mary Cassatt and Lucien Simon among others, but studies of sleeping children are much less common and they indicate again Hodgkins's unusual approach to portraiture.

Cedric Morris and Lett Haines were in Newlyn for a short period from 1919 to 1920 and through them Hodgkins probably came to know a younger and more progressive group of artists, painters such as Ernest and Dod Proctor and Harold and Laura Knight, and the sculptor Frank Dobson. The most important of these artists was Laura Knight, who had been established at Newlyn from 1907, painting coastal scenes and large-scale figure subjects which she exhibited regularly at the Royal Academy.[14] Perhaps the most successful woman painter in Britain, Laura Knight was a friend of Norman Garstin, who had written an article on the Knights in the *Studio* of 1913.[15] He praised their paintings as avoiding 'all suspicion of abnormality. Sanity of outlook and lucidity of statement are the dominating factors of their work.' At that time Laura Knight's painting was Impressionist in handling and treatment, concerned with recording the effects of light in strong bright colours. She excelled at figure painting and produced a series of large compositions in open-air settings which she had worked up from drawings of models. A typical example is the nude study *Daughters of the Sun*, exhibited at the Royal Academy in 1911.[16]

Frances Hodgkins certainly knew Knight's work and was somewhat influenced by her subjects and large-scale format. In a letter of August 1915 she records a visit of Laura Knight to St Ives when she painted one of her favourite subjects — a group of thirteen nude boys bathing.[17] The following summer at Chipping Campden Hodgkins painted a large watercolour of boys bathing in a pool. This work, entitled *Lady Juliana's Gateway*, was exhibited in October 1916 at the International Society but does not appear to have survived.

In general, Laura Knight is more naturalistic and less experimental in style than Frances

FIGURE 14
The Edwardians, c.1919
Oil, 1016 x 1016mm
Auckland City Art Gallery

FIGURE 15
Refugee Children, c.1916
Tempera, 600 x 720mm
Private collection on loan to Manchester City Art Gallery

FIGURE 16
Laura Knight, *The Green Feather*, 1911
Oil, 2147 x 1533mm
National Gallery of Canada, Ottawa

FIGURE 17
My Landlady, c.1920
Watercolour, 406 x 419mm
Auckland City Art Gallery

Hodgkins. She was an accomplished artist in both oil and watercolour, who remained content to paint within the accepted academic style and whose work never shows the sketchy and informal qualities of *Loveday and Anne* or *Refugee Children*. Around 1918 Hodgkins did, however, paint some rather more conventional and highly finished portraits. The *Portrait of Beatrice Wood* is representative; it was commissioned in early 1918 and exhibited at the International Society that summer. The concern of the artist is less with a defined characterisation than with suggesting the elegance of the fashionable young woman, complete with fluffy dog. She is placed against a low horizon and painted in a free and brilliant manner not dissimilar to that of Laura Knight's *The Green Feather* of 1911 (Fig. 16).

Many English painters reacted unfavourably to the second Post-Impressionist exhibition organised by Roger Fry and held in the winter of 1912–13, while Hodgkins was in Australia. The exhibition included large selections of works by Picasso and Matisse and also paintings by Derain, Vlaminck and Herbin, giving a greater emphasis to recent art than the 1910 showing.[18] Among the critical British artists was Walter Sickert, who found Matisse to be nonsense and rejected the bright colours of Post-Impressionism.[19] He continued to work in his own version of Impressionism: sombre paintings of everyday life, music halls, pubs and shabby interiors, which, though naturalistic, also have a poetic dimension.

Around 1919 Hodgkins painted a number of these subjects, clearly under the influence of Sickert rather than Roger Fry and his followers. Two examples are *My Landlady* (Fig. 17) and *Seaside Lodgings*, which were exhibited together at the International Society in 1919. Like Sickert's *Ennui* of around 1914 (Fig. 18),[20] these paintings have an anecdotal quality: an event is suggested but left undefined. The spare monochromatic treatment of *My Landlady* contrasts with the flamboyance and bright decorative pattern found in Hodgkins's earlier watercolours, a change indebted to Sickert. The landlady, removed and self-absorbed, is placed within a carefully delineated Edwardian interior of rather faded gentility. Hodgkins's concern is less with formal values than with the play of light on objects and surfaces. *My Landlady* has a somewhat ironic quality, another feature found in Sickert, whose picture titles often give his sitters a mock grandeur. The theme was also treated by Harold Gilman and Nina Hamnet, who painted *Portrait of a Landlady* in 1913.[21]

Landscape is not so significant in Frances Hodgkins's work at this time, partly because of the wartime prohibition on sketching within sight of the coast imposed in 1915. Most of her landscapes were done during her summer classes held inland at Chipping Campden (1916), Burford (1917), Porlock (1918), Ludlow and Great Barrington (1919). A great many of these watercolour landscapes are threshing scenes, a subject which appears as early as 1917, when *Threshing in the Cotswolds* was shown at the International Society. Another group was done in 1919 at Great Barrington. A number of these watercolours are dominated by the farm machinery, a fascination which was to return during the Second World War. The large watercolour, *Threshing Scene* (Pl. 14), is representative of a move away from the animated colour and interest in light of her Impressionist landscapes towards a more structured composition and restricted colour effect. The paint is thinly washed over an initial drawing in a range of closely related hues. A series of sweeping movements defines the composition, in which the figures are dwarfed by the steam-powered threshing machine.

In a letter of around August 1917 to Hannah Ritchie, a prospective pupil who had sent her some watercolours for criticism, Frances Hodgkins gave a rare indication of her approach to landscape watercolour, adding her own versions of Ritchie's subjects as diagrams with detailed notes.[22] Several points emerge from the letter, which is very revealing of her own painting methods. Hodgkins emphasises the importance of structure: prominence must be given to the chief object of the sketch, and the rest of the composition subordinated to it. Charcoal should be used to give definition to the drawing. She suggests a large scale: 'Make it look immense and impressive.' In colour, pure paint only should be employed, mixed with black for deeper tones. She names her favourite colours as transparent viridian, lemon yellow and aurelian. Hodgkins stresses the importance of keeping the colour fresh: 'the older I grow in Water Colour I realise the great charm is freshness and lovely colour'. She adds that the watercolour painter should strive to 'get the character and essential spirit of the place in the simplest manner'.

During the summer of 1919, Hodgkins was at Ludlow, which had been the setting for the sketches Richie had sent two years before. Her watercolour *Ludlow* (Fig. 19) is a large square-format view of the bridge Ritchie had treated earlier and illustrates many of the points expressed in her letter. The composition is reduced to a few elements: the sweeping bridge which dominates the scene and leads into depth, the simplified flat shapes of the houses beyond and the distant castle outlined against the sky. The paint is thin and freely handled, the quite transparent colours restricted to a few carefully chosen hues. The watercolour has more emphasis on structure than lighting, and is more tonal than Impressionist in appearance.

By the end of the war, Hodgkins was reworking her art and beginning to experiment in response to contemporary artistic movements. She knew the work of the Vorticists, then the most advanced artistic group in England, which included among its members the painters Wyndham Lewis, Edward Wadsworth, David Bomberg and C. R. Nevinson, as well as the sculptors Gaudier-Brzeska and Jacob Epstein.[23] The Vorticists employed a severe abstract and geometrical style influenced by Cubism but closer to Italian Futurism in their fascination with modern subjects and dynamic movement. As early as 1917, in a letter to G. F. Mann, Director of the Art Gallery of New South Wales, Hodgkins had praised the work of Nevinson and Epstein, writing that 'the War has produced nothing very remarkable or exclamatory in Art. Nevinson and Epstein perhaps are the most significant and personal.'[24]

Morris and Lett Haines were friendly with a number of the Vorticists and both Wyndham Lewis and Wadsworth were visitors to Newlyn.[25] Hodgkins herself, in a number of letters, rather inaccurately referred to Morris and Lett Haines as Futurists. Something of their influence is apparent in her *Portrait of Lett Haines* (Fig. 21), an oil sketch of around 1920, made in response to a number of portrait drawings that Morris and Lett Haines had done of her. In a Post-Impressionist manner, the colours are bright and harsh, the unmodulated paint crudely

FIGURE 18
Walter Sickert, *Ennui*, c.1913–14
Oil, 1524 x 1124mm
Tate Gallery, London

FIGURE 19
Ludlow, c.1919
Watercolour, 565 x 565mm
Auckland City Art Gallery

FIGURE 20
Bridge with Distant Landscape, c.1919
Pencil & watercolour, 263 x 209mm
Auckland City Art Gallery

applied to make a series of rhythmic patterns. The schematic and angular treatment of the head is strongly expressive and rather more abstractly treated than Morris's own *Self Portrait* of 1919, to which it is closely related.[26] The *Portrait of Lett Haines* was an experiment, a painting intended for a close friend and not public exhibition, but it is significant as the first indication of the path towards abstraction her art was to follow during the 1920s.

THE YEARS IN FRANCE AND ENGLAND 1921–24

Early in December 1920 Frances Hodgkins arrived in the south of France. Having made the decision to leave St Ives for good, she gave up her studio and banked around £200, on which she hoped to exist for a year, supplemented by her earnings from pupils. The next four years, from 1921 to the end of 1924, she divided between France and England: almost all of 1921 she spent in France, from January 1922 until the end of 1923 her base was Burford near Oxford, and she returned again to France for most of 1924.

Hodgkins had already formed the intention of working in France by June 1920, when she wrote to her mother, 'I badly want to get back to France, and rub off some of the rust of ages.'[27] It was partly an escape from gloomy England to the warmth and cheapness of the south, but perhaps more important was the opportunity to renew her art through a fresh involvement with France and French painting. These were her years of experimentation, when, under the impact of French modernism, she attempted to give her art a more advanced look. Unfortunately much of this important period still remains obscure — she seldom dated her works and, probably because of the experimental nature of her painting, held few exhibitions.

In France she remained an outsider, a foreigner working in France rather than a participant in the art scene. She was not based in the artistic centre of Paris and never made the contacts which were vital to further her career. In England she fell out of the art exhibition circuit and had only a small exhibition of black and white drawings in November 1923 at the Little Art Rooms, Adelphi. The most significant exhibition of her works in 1924 was the two paintings, three watercolours and two drawings which she showed at the November *Salon d'Automne* in Paris. Apart from these exhibitions, her work is known only through descriptions in her letters and the few surviving oil paintings, watercolours and drawings.

After a brief period at St Tropez, Hodgkins made her base at Cassis near Marseilles. Initially she was attracted to the Provençal landscape and began a series of black chalk landscapes of the region. She now concentrated on drawing in an attempt to develop the formal basis of her art. At least five drawings have survived of what was intended to be a distinct group.[28] These landscapes were not meant as studies for future paintings, but as self-sufficient works. A letter she wrote early in February 1921 makes this apparent: 'I am sending off my Cassis set of drawings to Mr Frank Rutter to see if he can arrange to show them in London and possibly have them reproduced in a portfolio.'[29]

FIGURE 21
Portrait of Arthur Lett Haines, c.1920
Oil, 433 x 381mm
Whereabouts unknown, photograph
Auckland City Art Gallery

The Cassis drawings are notable for their boldness and strength of design in what was for her a new medium of black chalk. She had used it previously but only to outline forms which she subsequently defined in watercolour. *Mediterranean Landscape* (Fig. 22) conveys strongly the bare and rocky quality of the Provençal mountain landscape behind Cassis. Hodgkins emphasises the mass and structure of the mountains as a series of planes, defined by the tonal treatment of the black chalk. The lighter, more flattened foreground contrasts with the densely modelled mountains. Her strong distinction between the black and white areas of the paper further serves to convey the effect of harsh southern sunlight. The drawing has a rhythmic quality, a sense of her rapidly defining the mountains and foliage in a series of bold strokes.

Her cuboid forms are comparable to Cézanne's painted landscapes in terms of structure and the way in which he built up his subjects in carefully modulated strokes of the brush. Cézanne, of course, was closely associated with Provence, having lived and worked in the region for much of his life. Hodgkins was probably aware of his well-known aim to make a more permanent art out of the sensory qualities of Impressionism. Certainly her concentration on form mirrored a general artistic shift away from the Impressionist emphasis on recording fleeting effects of light towards a more structured and timeless art. These ideas were

FIGURE 22
Mediterranean Landscape, c.1921
Black chalk
Private collection

FIGURE 23
Olives, St Tropez, c.1921
Black chalk, 252 x 318mm
Hocken Library, Dunedin

FIGURE 24
Les Martigues, c.1921
Pencil, 375 x 419mm
Tate Gallery Archive, London

promoted in England through Roger Fry's doctrine of 'significant form', a term which emerged in his writings during the war years.[30] Fry himself had done a number of paintings at Cassis in 1915, strongly under the influence of Cézanne.[31] These were the years of the 'Cézanne cult' in English painting, initiated by the Cézanne retrospective exhibitions of 1907 in Paris. By 1918–19, the English painter Charles Ginner, in an article entitled 'The Cézanne Stunt', was able to note the predominant influence of Cézanne and the 'extraordinary affinity between the landscape of Provence and the art of Cézanne'.[32] He went on to argue that it was a mistake for English painters to apply Cézanne's formula to the quite different landscape of England. Hodgkins was not alone in her black chalk drawings of Cassis; Muirhead Bone also did a number of similar drawings around Marseilles, which were exhibited in 1922 at the Grosvenor Galleries.[33] They are rather more literal renderings of landscape but share with Hodgkins's drawings a pronounced tonal emphasis.

The other painter closely associated with Provence was Van Gogh and his influence is evident on Hodgkins's *Olives, St Tropez* (Fig. 23). After the drama of the Cassis landscapes, *Olives, St Tropez* has a more intimate and enclosed feeling. The choice of subject recalls Van Gogh, who painted many scenes of olive groves in Provence between 1889 and 1890. The spreading, twisted forms of the olive trees, and the pattern of light and shade on the ground, convey a rhythmic intensity common to Van Gogh's paintings and also found in his drawings of tilled fields. The tree in the foreground climbs around the edge of the sheet, defining and enclosing the tunnel-like space. The luxuriant organic life of southern France is much more pronounced in this drawing, and the trees writhe with an expressive force.

Hodgkins left Cassis towards the end of January and moved west to Martigues, a fishing port on the other side of Marseilles. There she concentrated on figure drawing, as she explained in a letter of 28 February 1921, 'We draw in the cafes in the evening — Such types — largely Spanish in certain quarters. Such beauty & bearing.'[34] A number of small drawings have survived from this group of cafe scenes, executed in black chalk and stylistically quite unified (see Fig. 24). Though some have been dated to around 1928, their stylistic similarity and use of the black chalk technique suggests an earlier period.

Certain of the drawings show card players, a theme closely associated with Cézanne, who did a number of versions of the subject. One of the most elaborate is *Chez M. le Chef* (Fig. 25), where the structure of the composition and the characterisation of the figures around the table recalls Cézanne's *Card Players* in the Barnes Foundation. The treatment of objects on the mantelpiece links the drawing to the earlier watercolour *My Landlady* (Fig. 17), but now the figures and objects are defined in a volumetric sense, influenced by Cubism. Parts of the drawing, such as the head of the young woman to the left, are worked out carefully in tonal planes; elsewhere only the chalk outline serves to indicate the form. Overall, like the Cassis landscapes, there is an emphasis on form and structure reinforced by the tonal treatment of the heads and bodies.

Hodgkins's rapid mastery of this tonal approach to the figure is confirmed by an elaborate charcoal drawing entitled *The Cinema* (Fig. 26), which was reproduced as the frontis-

FIGURE 25
Chez M. le Chef, c.1921
Black chalk, 275 x 425mm
Auckland City Art Gallery

piece to the June 1922 issue of the magazine *Colour*.[35] Rather more confident in its concentration on the heads of the children, the drawing was probably done on her return to England in 1922, as Myfanwy Evans mentions that Hodgkins drew children by candlelight in the cinema around this date.[36]

Closely related to these charcoal drawings and in a sense equivalent to them, are some watercolour and gouache paintings of Breton women and children, which Hodgkins carried out in Brittany probably towards the end of 1921. One example, the watercolour *Mother and Child* (Fig. 27), is again quite tonal in approach; the oval structure of the mother's head is defined largely in terms of volume and colour effects are kept to a minimum. As in her drawings, Hodgkins is concerned with formal simplification and a careful placement of the figures on the sheet; this interest supplants her earlier interest in picturesque Breton costume.

It took some time before these artistic developments entered her paintings. The few paintings that can be dated to around 1924 show a Cubist treatment of form and a more simplified approach to composition, but are less resolved than her contemporary work in drawing and watercolour. Many of these oil paintings were owned by her Manchester friends, Jane Saunders and Hannah Ritchie, who were in close contact with Hodgkins over these years and probably bought them directly from her.

Still Life with Gloxinia and *Three Children* (Pl. 15) were both owned by Jane Saunders and are closely related in their technique and approach to the subject. Hodgkins painted the quite bright colours onto a white ground in a series of thinly applied hues. In *Still Life with*

FIGURE 26
The Cinema, c.1922
Charcoal
Tinakori Gallery, Wellington

FIGURE 27
Mother and Child, c.1921
Watercolour, 406 x 361mm
Auckland City Art Gallery

FIGURE 28
Fabric design, c.1925
Gouache, 141 x 305mm
Tate Gallery Archive, London

Gloxinia a Cubist treatment is given to the objects on the table, which are viewed as a series of intersecting facets; but the rendition of table and space remains traditionally perspectival. The use of a white base and transparent layering of the surfaces can be compared to Gris' *Bottle of Wine and Water Jar*, painted some years before.[37] As yet however, her approach to form remains closer to earlier analytical Cubism than to the synthetic manner then being employed by Picasso, Braque and Gris.[38] She also seems unaware that in true Cubist painting no distinction was made between space and object in terms of treatment. This is apparent from *Three Children,* where the figures are treated in a simplified Cubist manner, but not the picture space, which is largely left undefined. Indeed, much of the painting is still experimental; the pose of the central child is unresolved, as is the relationship between the head and body of the figure on the right.

The Red Cockerel (Pl. 16) of 1924 is the most successful of Hodgkins's Cubist-inspired compositions and certainly her most abstract painting up to that date. The hanging birds of Hodgkins's painting remain quite naturalistic but are rendered as a series of interlocking planes which blend into one another, forming a fluid pattern across the picture. The painting is still constructed in terms of colour planes but they are now carefully related to one another through the restricted choice of colours and smooth brushwork. The predominant greens and blues are richer and more subdued than in *Three Children*, giving a sombre effect related to early Cubism and reminiscent of Marcoussis.

THE MANCHESTER PERIOD 1925–27

Frances Hodgkins spent the years from 1925 to 1927 in Manchester, not from choice but rather through a series of external circumstances. She had returned to England early in 1925, disillusioned and disheartened after her year in France, with the intention of emigrating to Australia. By now her funds were so depleted that a friend had to advance her the fare. Her passage was booked for June, but while she was staying with her friends Hannah Ritchie and Jane Saunders in Manchester, her work came to the attention of Forrest Hewit, the Chairman of the Calico Printers' Association, a large textile company. He asked Hodgkins to submit some designs to the Association, which resulted in her being taken on as a designer in June 1925.[39] While Manchester was not an important artistic centre like London, Hodgkins showed work in the local galleries, found friends and pupils and, most importantly, created a series of paintings inspired by the local women and children.

About her work for the Calico Printers' Association very little is known; her contract was not renewed and she remained for only six months. Hodgkins found textile design repetitive and demanding work, but it meant security at a time of financial difficulty. There are only a few surviving designs from around this period (Fig. 28), and it is not certain whether any were ever put into production. Myfanwy Evans mentions as her most successful designs some 'model' scarves,[40] but the one surviving handkerchief in the Dunedin Public Art

Gallery (Fig. 29), decorated with a stylised farmyard scene, is not a typical design of the period and must have been made at a later date.

Frances Hodgkins had an opportunity to view the latest in fabric design when in August 1925 she was sent by the Calico Printers' Association to the Paris *Exposition Internationale des Arts Decoratifs et Industriels Modernes*.[41] This huge exhibition, held in the centre of Paris on the Pont Alexandre III and adjoining banks of the Seine, was ostensibly dedicated to international modern decorative art, but was largely a showpiece for French luxury goods and interior design. Four of the pavilions were allocated to Paris department stores and decorated as fashionable apartments with furniture, carpets, tapestries and sculptures. Artist-designers such as Sonia Delaunay and Raoul Dufy were well represented and indicated quite different contemporary approaches to fabric design.[42] Dufy's fabrics for Bianchini-Férier, influenced by Cubist painting, still remained organic and naturalistic in their forms. By contrast, Sonia Delaunay's 'simultaneous' fabrics, exhibited on her stand with Jacques Heim, were based on geometrical patterns whose sharply contrasting colours formed very dynamic designs. Dufy was also responsible for a series of fourteen large figurative wall hangings, which decorated one of the three barges the couturier Paul Poirot employed to display his collection. As two of the hangings show Poirot's models at the races and in his salon, they give a rich compendium of his current designs.[43] In a long letter to her sister, Frances Hodgkins described her impressions of the exhibition and in particular of the *Pavilion d'Elégance*, where the collections of Laurin, Worth, Carlier and Callot were on display: '200 above life-size gold and silver mannequins, clothed in ravishing frocks in exquisite colour schemes'.[44] This experience, combined with the discipline of designing fabrics, must have reinforced an already pronounced decorative tendency in her painting. Colour and pattern now become increasingly important in paintings such as the *Double Portrait* (of Hannah Ritchie and Jane Saunders) (Pl. 17), where the influence of Matisse appears for the first time.

The *Double Portrait* is dated usually around 1922, but it was not completed in fact until 1925, and was reworked considerably over the intervening period. An earlier watercolour study of Hannah Ritchie and Jane Saunders has a quite different composition (see Pl. 17). The sitters' clothes and poses were changed for the oil and only the checked sofa is retained from the earlier painting. The influence of Matisse is most apparent in the almost abstract stylisation of the faces, reduced to simplified shapes and flattened forms. The attention to the rich decorative patterning of the sofa and the sitters' clothing clearly reflects her current work as a fabric designer. The intense red of Hannah Ritchie's coat recalls Matisse's use of similar expressive colour effects in paintings such as *La Robe Verte*, and is complemented by the more subdued violet-blue of Saunders's dress.

The large and highly finished drawing *Seated Woman* (Fig. 30), executed in pencil and black chalk, is closely related to the *Double Portrait* in its format and attention to the decorative pattern of the clothing, now conceived as a series of interlocking shapes repeated in the background. According to Hodgkins's own recollection it was included in an exhibition at

FIGURE 29
Handkerchief designed by Frances Hodgkins, c.1940?
242 x 257mm
Dunedin Public Art Gallery

FIGURE 30
Seated Woman, c.1926
Pencil & black chalk, 940 x 600mm
Tate Gallery, London

the Mansard Gallery — either May 1929 or in 1930 — but may have been executed some-what earlier.[45] Matisse did a number of similar works, both in lithograph and in his draw-ings for the series *The Plumed Hat* of around 1919. Rather more posed and monumental than the figures in Matisse, Hodgkins's sitter shares his approach of a naturalistically observed head, combined with a more abstract, decorative treatment of the clothing. The rhythmic and simplified quality of Matisse's line drawings was an important influence on Hodgkins's *Adoration* (Fig. 31), part of a group of studies of women and children she made around 1925. The subject exists in two versions, one in Auckland, the other at the Whitworth Art Gallery (Manchester), and appeared initially in her one-woman exhibition of November 1926 at All Saints, Manchester. In the Auckland version the line serves to define the form but also acts as a flat rhythmic pattern on the surface of the paper. The Whitworth drawing is modelled more fully in watercolour, the figures' forms and movements exactly defined.[46] The inti-macy of the groupings, the way the women focus on the twisting child and the title itself recall similar themes in Italian Renaissance painting such as the Virgin and Child with St Anne or the Holy Family.

Another group of watercolour studies depicting Lancashire mill girls is closely connected in theme and treatment with the 'Mother and Child' series. The two surviving watercolours called *Lancashire Mill Girls* have a similar piled-up figure composition to *Adoration*.[47] The women's shawls, a typical local costume, define the models' heads and convey a sense of rhythmic descending movement to the watercolour. A letter of January 1923 to Hannah Ritchie shows that Hodgkins's interest in painting these local subjects preceded even her brief visit to Manchester early in 1923. Hodgkins wrote, 'I want to make pictures of these hungry sad eyed women and children in Manchester photographed in the D. News. I won-der if it would be possible to get the use of a room in one of the missions and get the women to pose.'[48]

Hodgkins's interest in the subject may have arisen from social concern, and the surviv-ing studies have a remarkable intensity, but the result has little in common with social real-ism. Her approach remains formal; the sitters are viewed as models, and their local cos-tumes carry no more resonance than those in the studies she made in Brittany earlier in her career. This attitude is quite evident in *Lancashire Family* (Pl. 18), a major oil painting ex-ecuted towards the end of her time in Manchester. It was first shown in June 1927 at the London Group Exhibition and again the following year at the Claridge Gallery, when it was bought by Lett Haines.[49] The Claridge Gallery exhibition also included a thematically re-lated work, *Boy with a Boat* (see Pl. 18), now in Dunedin. *Lancashire Family* has a strong architectonic quality with its tightly structured figure group in which the bodies are treated like simplified cuboid shapes. Unusually square in format, the composition has a pronounced diagonal emphasis running from top right to bottom left of the picture. Apart from the in-tense blue stripe on the boy's toy boat, the colours are reduced to carefully modulated shades of green and brown. Hodgkins still retains the underlying religious theme of the *Adoration* drawings, the mother's shawl enclosing the children in the manner of an Italian Renaissance *Madonna della Misericordia*. In its emphasis on balance and order, the emotional restraint of the figures and coolness of colour, *Lancashire Family* has a distinctly classical feeling. At a time when the paintings of Picasso, Léger and Gris all indicate a return to the timeless forms and values of classicism, Hodgkins may have been influenced by this neo-classical direction in French art.[50]

Another oil from this period, *Lancashire Children* (Pl. 19), is associated in theme but executed in a richer manner, the now heavily applied paint taking on a more expressive aspect. The work is important as one of the first in a new painting style she was to employ into the early 1930s, in which the picture is built up in thick layers of paint and major changes are introduced to the composition, often during the process of painting. The theme of a view through a window with still-life objects in the foreground, frequent in her later work, appears here for the first time in an experimental form. The tightly packed figure group of *Lancashire Children* has an oppressively intense quality which prevents movement into the depth of the landscape beyond. In her later work this characteristic Manchester figure group was to be replaced by a more neutral combination of still life and landscape. *Lancashire Children* has the same monochromatic and sombre colouration as *Lancashire Family*, except in the sky, which is unusually blue and intense, almost Mediterranean in feeling.

While she was in Manchester Frances Hodgkins made a number of contacts which were to be important for her later career. The most significant was Lucy Wertheim, a wealthy Manchester art collector, who was later to open a gallery in London.[51] She met Hodgkins, probably early in 1926, at the home of the Dreys.[52] Raymond Drey, who was married to the Canadian painter Anne Estelle Rice, a friend of Katherine Mansfield's, was a well-known critic and wrote the introduction to the catalogue of Hodgkins's exhibition at All Saints, Manchester in November 1926. Both he and his wife collected Hodgkins's works.

Lucy Wertheim was to become one of the most important collectors of Hodgkins, although she confessed in her autobiography, *Adventure in Art*, that initially she did not fully understand her work. As most of Wertheim's Hodgkins collection was formed between 1926 and 1930, it gives an invaluable indication of the work Hodgkins was doing over this period.[53] Among the major oil paintings she acquired were *The Birdcage, Boy with a Boat, Still Life with Landscape, The Sisters* (Fig. 33), *The Farmer's Daughter, The Bridesmaids* (Pl. 20) and the *Portrait of Cedric Morris*. Some of these paintings were later offered for sale in her gallery and four Hodgkins works were included in the opening exhibition at her London gallery in October 1930.[54] Lucy Wertheim did not make a clear distinction between her own paintings and those that were for sale but although she continued to exhibit works by Hodgkins until the gallery closed in 1939, she acquired very little new work after 1930.

FIGURE 31
Adoration, c.1925
Pencil & watercolour, 529 x 378mm
Whitworth Art Gallery, University of Manchester

THE DECISIVE YEARS 1928–30

The period from 1928 to 1930 was perhaps the most significant in Frances Hodgkins's entire career, the time when she largely determined the course of her art and established her reputation. Over these years she abandoned the somewhat undirected experimentation of the early 1920s in order to concentrate on two main themes — portraiture and landscape. Her portrait sitters now are often placed in landscape settings and she adds a new variation, a combination of still life and landscape, which was to be of great importance in her future art. Along with this greater sense of purpose went an increased technical skill in oil painting. As her confidence grew, so did her artistic production — documented in a stream of letters to her friends — and from now onwards her work became far more visible to the public. In 1927 she began exhibiting with the London Group and the New English Art Club, and was admitted in 1929 to the Seven and Five Society, where she was to remain until 1934. Hodgkins had important one-woman exhibitions in April 1928 at the Claridge Gallery, in November 1929 at the Bloomsbury Gallery (with Vera Cuningham), and in October 1930 she was part of Lucy Wertheim's opening exhibition and had her own successful show at the St George's Gallery.

Arthur Howell, her dealer and owner of the St George's Gallery, described the period of his association with Hodgkins from 1927 to 1931 in his book *Four Vital Years*. He had first encountered her work in December 1927 at the New English Art Club Exhibition in the Burlington Galleries and, intrigued by her paintings, he became her sole agent for watercolours in March 1930.[55] He included her work in various group exhibitions and her one-woman show of October 1930 at his gallery really launched her career. Through his enthusiasm and activity on her behalf, Howell certainly played a major role in the establishment of Hodgkins as an important artist but whether he was solely responsible, as he suggests, is doubtful. In his book Howell minimised the assistance of Lucy Wertheim to Hodgkins and effectively suppressed Lett Haines and Cedric Morris from his account, although they had been among her most loyal supporters. Indeed, it was specifically Lett Haines and Morris whom Hodgkins singled out among her friends in a letter to Lucy Wertheim of early 1930: 'the fact that I am working here today — in a state of comparative liberty and independence I very largely owe to the friendship of Lett and Cedric'.[56]

Hodgkins had seen little of Morris and Lett Haines since 1920, when they had moved to Paris, but in 1927 she again came into contact with them at Tréboul in Brittany, where she spent most of the summer. From 1927 until 1931 is the time of her closest association with the paintings of Cedric Morris. His oil, *Corner in Tréboul*, of 1927, was painted in her presence and her own oil paintings of around this period, such as *A Country Window* (Fig. 37) and *Still-Life Landscape* (Pl. 23), share a similar thick application of paint and often quite laboured treatment.[57] At this period Morris was painting mainly landscapes and portraits in a direct and somewhat naive style (see Fig. 32). He employed a textured paint treatment,

FIGURE 32
Cedric Morris, *Herstmonceaux Church*, c.1928
Oil, 594 x 730mm
Towner Art Gallery, Eastbourne

usually quite intense in colouration, which was to influence both Hodgkins and the English painter Christopher Wood.

Over these years, once again, portraiture became an important part of Hodgkins's output, and she executed many portraits, mainly of her friends, both in oils and highly finished pencil drawings. Cedric Morris was himself a distinctive portrait painter, and between 1927 and 1930 Hodgkins made several portraits of him and of Lett Haines, coming gradually to adopt Morris's bright colouration and something of his direct approach to the sitter. Morris himself did a portrait of Frances Hodgkins in 1928. The *Portrait of Lett Haines* is the earliest of the group and was painted by Hodgkins in 1927 at Tréboul.[58] It has a similar treatment and colour range to *Lancashire Family*, executed in a series of subdued greens, browns and ochres. Lett Haines is rendered in an unconventional manner, caught asleep in an unguarded moment, which gives an informal and intimate atmosphere to the work.

Her subsequent portraits, such as *The Farmer's Daughter*, have a more direct quality under the influence of Cedric Morris. Two versions of this painting exist in quite different colour schemes; one, in subdued blues and greens, belonged to Lucy Wertheim and was shown at her inaugural exhibition in October 1930. The sitter, recently identified as Annie Coggan, is posed somewhat awkwardly in front of a landscape and close to the picture plane.[59] The paint, though quite thickly applied, is more fluid than in the *Portrait of Lett Haines*. Coggan's long hair, flowing down over her shoulder, introduces a sense of rhythmic movement to the painting, which continues into the background. A similar decorative treatment appears in Morris's *Portrait of Frances Hodgkins* of 1928, but Coggan's face, though simplified and almost naive, lacks his rather crudely caricatured effects. For Hodgkins the decorative aspects of colour, conveyed in a series of subtle variations, are more important than the characterisation of the sitter. At this period the landscape mainly serves to define the sitter in terms of structure, but in a number of pencil drawings such as *Mother and Child* (Salford), Hodgkins seems more concerned to place the figures within a landscape, which is now of equal importance.

Frances Hodgkins continued to experiment with the double portrait group first treated in tempera so many years before with *Loveday and Anne*, and more recently in the *Double Portrait* of Hannah Ritchie and Jane Saunders. *The Sisters* (Fig. 33), which was owned by Lucy Wertheim, is probably the work exhibited at the Claridge Gallery in 1928. There is also a double portrait drawing, perhaps of the same sitters, entitled *Two Sisters* (see Pl. 20), in Dunedin and another closely related painting in a blue-green colour range in a private collection.[60] By comparison with the drawing of *Two Sisters*, Hodgkins's approach in her paintings is to make the faces less detailed and observed. This is a simplified, almost child-like approach to portraiture, where the interest of the artist seems to be in relating the figures to each other and to the background by means of colour. Much of the awkwardness of the figures is a deliberate effect, consciously introduced by the artist, and can be parallelled in Marie Laurencin's female portraits of the late 1920s, which share the same naive approach to

FIGURE 33
The Sisters, 1927–28
Oil, 727 x 597mm
Auckland City Art Gallery

form and pastel colouration.[61] The most accomplished of these double portrait groups is *The Bridesmaids* (Pl. 20), which also belonged to Lucy Wertheim and was included in her gallery's opening exhibition of October 1930. Executed in an unusually intense green colour, *The Bridesmaids* shows an increased interest in defining the sitters. The bridesmaids are closely related to each other by their almost identical frontal poses, costumes, and their large hats, which merge subtly into each other in the centre of the composition. They are seated in a trellised arbour, the vines forming a decorative pattern behind their heads. Through a series of slight variations in head position and the treatment of their eyes and lips, Hodgkins is able to characterise each sitter quite differently in terms of expression.

Besides portraits Hodgkins concentrated on still life and landscapes, combining the two genres to create the distinctive still-life landscapes which were to be an integral part of her future artistic production. The subjects of still life and landscape were particularly associated with the Seven and Five Society, which included artists such as Christopher Wood, Winifred Nicholson and David Jones. Cedric Morris had joined the Society in 1926; and although he unsuccessfully proposed Hodgkins's election in 1928, she became a member the following year. From an initial submission in 1929 of two oils, *Boy in the Wood* and *The Garden*, and four watercolours, three of which were still lifes, she came to exhibit some of her most important new oil paintings at the Society's annual exhibitions. *Berries and Laurel* (Pl. 22) and *Pastorale* (1931), were followed by *Red Jug* and *Arum Lilies* (1932) (Pl. 26) and *Evening* (1933) (Pl. 28). Her last showing with the Society in 1934 was perhaps the most important and included *Flatford Mill*, *Wings over Water* (Pl. 25) and *Cut Melons* (Fig. 38). As Hodgkins often exhibited her paintings first with the Seven and Five Society, and only later in her one-woman exhibitions, the submissions she made can provide a valuable indication of the work she was doing at the time.

Founded in 1919, the Seven and Five Society was not simply an exhibiting society but a cohesive group of artists who shared some closely related attitudes to art.[62] By becoming a member, Hodgkins for the first time was associated with an advanced group of painters, many of whom held similar views on painting to her own. The members of the Society were all elected, one to four each year, and annual exhibitions were held, from 1929 onwards at the Leicester Galleries. The original rules of the Society, set down in 1926, specify a policy of unlimited membership and annual exhibitions but no clear artistic direction. All this was to be changed by Ben Nicholson, who became the secretary of the Society in 1926 and introduced a number of his friends, giving the group a unified approach to questions of artistic form and subject matter previously absent. Among the important artists to join over the ensuing years were Winifred Nicholson (1926), Christopher Wood (1927), David Jones and Len Lye (1928), Henry Moore and Barbara Hepworth (1932), and John Piper (1934).

H. S. Ede characterised some of the aims of the members in his foreword to the catalogue of the seventh exhibition of the Society in 1927 as follows:

The line of the Seven and Five is, I think, to break quite clearly from the representational in its photographic sense, though not like the Cubists to abandon known shapes. It is to use the everyday objects, but with such a swing and flow that they become living things, they fall into a rhythm in the same sort of way music does, but their vitality comes through colour and form instead of sound and time.

Ede emphasises the colour-based, lyrical treatment of form, the modified abstraction practised by many members of the group such as David Jones, Winifred Nicholson and Hodgkins herself. But there was another important aspect to their art not mentioned by Ede — an interest in child-like, or naive art, with its own unique aspects of expression and distinctive approach to form. Both Ben Nicholson and Christopher Wood had been strongly influenced by the Cornish 'primitive' painter Alfred Wallis, whom they had 'discovered' in 1928 at St Ives.[63] For Nicholson and Wood, the appeal of Wallis lay in his breaking of pictorial conventions and in the freshness of his effects. Wallis concentrated on paintings of the sea and old sailing ships, views of St Ives and its neighbourhood (Fig. 34). These he treated in an overall map-like manner with a restricted and unconventional use of colour. He painted on any material which came to hand, often pieces of cardboard in irregular shapes which determined the nature of his composition. Although seemingly quite unaware of the fact, Wallis thus echoed the contemporary interest in found objects and collage, the idea of the work of art as a self-sufficient object without outside reference.

Hodgkins was interested in naive art and certainly knew Wallis's paintings: Lucy Wertheim was an enthusiastic collector of Wallis, and much later in a letter to Dorothy Selby of 1945, Hodgkins recommended R. R. Tomlinson's book, *Children as Artists*.[64] While Hodgkins never went as far as Christopher Wood in the introduction of naive effects in her works, paintings such as *Wings on Water*, with its ships and harbour treated in a flattened and simplified manner, are partly indebted to Wallis's example (see Pl. 25). Nicholson and Wood often included Wallis-like sailing ships in their landscapes and a modified version of his pictorial structure.[65] Christopher Wood's *China Dogs in a St Ives Window* (1926) owes much to Wallis's rather thin and flat use of paint and prefigures many of Hodgkins's later motifs: the view through an open window to the landscape beyond, the simplified treatment of form and the decorative bric-à-brac of the china dogs. Like Hodgkins, Christopher Wood was strongly influenced by French art; they were both friends of Cedric Morris and up to Wood's early death in 1930 shared a similar approach to painting.[66]

The combination of still life and landscape, which was one of the major characteristics of the Seven and Five Society, was not, however, exclusive to the group and had already appeared in French painting in a variety of guises. It can be found in the synthetic Cubism of Picasso and Gris of the early 1920s, in the Fauvist paintings of Matisse and his followers and in the dream landscapes of Giorgio de Chirico. Usually in paintings such as Picasso's *St Raphael* series and Gris' *The Open Window* (1921), the still life is arranged on a table before a window which opens onto a landscape or city view.[67] For Picasso and Gris the emphasis is divided equally between the still life and the spatial ambiguities of the interior and exterior views. Christopher Wood and Winifred Nicholson in their still-life landscapes are rather

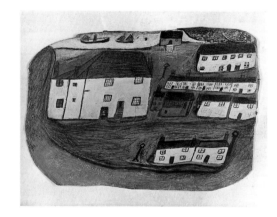

FIGURE 34
Alfred Wallis, *Houses at St Ives, Cornwall*, c.1935
Oil, 270 x 315mm
Tate Gallery, London

FIGURE 35
Still Life in a Landscape, c.1928
Oil, 813 x 721mm
Ministry of Foreign Affairs & Trade,
New Zealand

more naturalistic and conventional, usually maintaining a clear division between the still life in the room or on a window sill, and the landscape outside.[68] For them the landscape is the dominant element and their still lifes lack the abstract complexity and importance of the Cubists. More influenced by French painting in terms of form and colour, Hodgkins has a different approach to the still-life landscape, exploring its spatial ambiguities in a variety of arrangements and effects; and in the still-life landscape she found a theme rich enough to be a fundamental part of her artistic production until the end of her life.

The specific title *Still-Life Landscape* first emerges in the catalogue of her 1930 exhibition at the St George's Gallery, and was apparently suggested by Arthur Howell.[69] The theme, however, can be traced back to around 1928 and represents a logical extension of her still-life subjects into landscape. In fact Hodgkins did relatively few pure still-life paintings, but at this date and probably for the first time, she began making detailed pencil studies of individual objects, apparently for use in her painted still lifes. Drawings for both the jug and vase (Fig. 36) in *The Birdcage* have survived and probably came from the same sketchbook, made around 1928.[70] The colour notes on the drawings correspond to the finished painting and the objects themselves reappear in an almost identical manner. The eight pencil studies which remain from the sketchbook are of isolated objects with no outside reference apart from the recurrent indication of a table to define the space. As Matisse did similar pencil studies for his still-life paintings, drawings such as *La Coupe de Raisin* where the objects seem to float on the paper, he may have suggested the practice to Hodgkins.[71] The image in the pencil study of *Vase with Flowers* recurs in *Still Life in a Landscape* (Fig. 35), but the vase is removed from an interior to be placed on a table in the landscape. The table in *Still Life in a Landscape* is treated in a similar way to that in *The Birdcage*, viewed from above with a cloth hanging over the edge, which suggests that they were both done at around the same time.

A Country Window (Fig. 37) is another early still-life landscape, containing objects resembling those in the sketchbook drawings. It was done probably in 1929 at Haywards Heath and shows a characteristically English landscape and buildings. No individual drawings for the still life have survived, but two finished compositional studies in London (see Pl. 22) and Wellington contain many of the objects in the painting, rearranged in a somewhat different way. Hodgkins's treatment of the still life in the drawings, however, is much more fluid than in the painting. In the Wellington drawing the still life is integrated into the landscape, the curve of the table repeated in the distant hills, whereas *A Country Window* has a clear separation between still life and landscape. The flowers of the Tate drawing invade the landscape area but in the painting the still life is defined spatially by the edge of the tablecloth. By contrast with the rhythmic movement of the flowers and patterned tablecloth in the drawing, the painted still-life objects have a more independent and palpable quality. The original rhythm of the drawing has gone, to be replaced by a variety of individual viewpoints and a more awkward handling of the still-life elements, now clearly detached from the picture space.

A constant concern for Hodgkins was the relationship between the two elements of still life and landscape. Sometimes, as in *The White House* (Pl. 21), the still life acts as a barrier through which the landscape is only partly visible. She now composes her still life from flowers and plants arranged on two tables and a chair in the foreground. The effect is of a richer and more luxuriant vegetation, spreading across the picture surface. This may indicate a shift away from the household objects of *A Country Window,* but whether her attitude to still life is any more than formal is difficult to establish. Certainly her selection of still life elements is closer to the approach of members of the Seven and Five Society than that of Picasso or Gris, and their treatment more traditionally naturalistic.

The White House, though painted very thickly, is rather more fluid than *A Country Window*. There is another version of the subject in a private collection, which includes the same white house but a different still life, now arranged on a table in the foreground.[72] *A Country Window* also exists in two examples, and from this date Hodgkins began to make multiple variants of the same subject, probably executing them at the same time. In this she once again followed a practice more common in French painting than British, for Picasso, Matisse and Braque often executed works in series. The trees in the background of the painting and the style of architecture of the house suggest that *The White House* was painted in France, and from a reference by Howell it can be dated to 1930.[73]

In other still-life landscapes Hodgkins seems more interested in integrating landscape and still life into one continuous space. *Berries and Laurel* (Pl. 22) is an example of this approach; it also dates from around 1930, and was first exhibited at the Seven and Five Society in January 1931. Painted in a similar manner to *The White House*, the still-life arrangement of plants and berries suggests autumn. The still-life objects are now treated from a consistent viewpoint and occupy their own distinct space. The horizon is high with just a narrow strip of blue sky visible, flattening the picture space. This is one of three versions of the subject in which certain objects such as the white vase recur in differing combinations. The view is from the window of Geoffrey Gorer's cottage at Bradford-on-Tone, where Hodgkins stayed towards the end of 1930.[74] The versions in Adelaide and ex. Gorer Collection have a lower horizon than *Berries and Laurel*, giving a sense of looking through the still life to the landscape, which unfolds in a series of planes into depth.

Yet another variation of the still-life landscape is where the still life is arranged on a table either within the landscape or suspended above it. Many of the works in this category were carried out in watercolour, some at St Jeannet in southern France, where she worked from January to April 1930. The St Jeannet watercolours share a common structured approach to landscape and can be dated together on stylistic grounds because of their similarity to *St Jeannet No. 1* in Salford.[75] *Still Life in a Landscape* (Wakefield Art Gallery) (see Pl. 23) is a typical example; the viewpoint is from above, embracing in one continuous space the still life on a transparent table and the landscape visible beneath. The transition from still life to landscape is blurred by the bowl of fruit on the crumbling garden wall. This type of transparent layering of space is particularly suited to watercolour, remaining rather more suggestive and atmospheric than her contemporary work in oils.

FIGURE 36
Vase with Handles, c.1928
Pencil, 305 x 228mm
Auckland City Art Gallery

FIGURE 37
A Country Window, c.1929
Oil, 555 x 675mm
Dunbar Sloane, Wellington

Raoul Dufy also did many watercolours in the St Jeannet region, works in which the structure of the landscape is given special prominence.[76] A similar concern is evident in Hodgkins's watercolour *Still-Life Landscape* (Pl. 23), where the patterns made by the fields and lanes continue into the decorative arrangement of the still life. Space is treated as a flat surface, allowing the rhythmic movement of the design to cover the entire work. In these watercolours the still life has a greater role, the large objects viewed in close-up dominating the often tiny details of the landscape, its fields, lanes and trees.

In her oil paintings Frances Hodgkins gradually moved towards the more unified treatment of the picture surface already apparent in her drawings and watercolours. Perhaps the culmination is *Wings over Water* (Pl. 25), executed probably towards the end of 1931 and depicting the view from her window at Bodinnick, Cornwall.[77] As a comparison with the two preparatory drawings reveals, she is now able to translate the rhythm and flow of her drawing style into the medium of oil paint. Hodgkins retains the window-view format but space is flattened across the whole painting, blurring a distinction between interior and exterior space. *Wings over Water* is one of the last of her landscape still lifes based on an actual place. Henceforth her landscapes were to be more abstract and imaginary, and she was to enhance the mysterious aspects of her still lifes, the objects becoming increasingly more symbolic under the influence of Surrealism.

At the end of 1930 Frances Hodgkins was sixty-one years old. She had come through her years of experimentation; the art for which she was to become acclaimed largely lay before her but the course of her work was determined. Hers was an essentially French attitude to art based on beauty of form and colour, a direct response to nature and a willingness to experiment. From now on her inspiration was to be Mediterranean light and colour, as she continued to produce a range of major paintings in her characteristic themes of still life and landscape.

---

1. Wyndham Lewis, 'The Art of the Great Race', *Blast*, 2, 1915, p.71.

2. For Garstin, Stanhope Forbes and other members of the Newlyn School, see *Painting in Newlyn*, exhibition catalogue, Barbican Gallery, London, 1985.

3. Norman Garstin, 'West Cornwall as a Sketching Ground', *Studio*, 47, 1909, pp.109-21.

4. FH to her mother, 17 Feb. 1915, St Ives, Cornwall.

5. The main articles are as follows: C. Hay Thomson, 'An Artist of the Moderns', *Everylady's Journal* (Melbourne), 6 Jan. 1913, p.12; Anne Cornstalk, 'Miss Frances Hodgkins', *Lone Hand* (Sydney), 2 June 1913, pp.xxviii-xl; A. G. Stephens, 'Frances Hodgkins', *Bookfellow* (Sydney), 1 May 1913, pp.ix-x (repr. in a slightly different version in *Otago Daily Times*, 3 May 1913, p.5); 'Miss Frances Hodgkins's Work', *Sunday Mail* (Adelaide), 28 June 1913, p.9. All the above are discussed (and partly quoted) by E. H. McCormick, 'Frances Hodgkins: The Path to Impressionism: 1892–1912', *Art New Zealand*, 16, 1980, pp.28-35, 66.

6. A useful discussion of Fry's two Post-Impressionist exhibitions of 1910 and 1912–13 is given by Frances Spalding, *Roger Fry: Art and* Life, London, 1980, pp.131-41, 156-63. For British Post-Impressionism, see *Post-Impressionism*, exhibition catalogue, Royal Academy of Arts, London, 1979–80, pp.178-217.

7. Sickert's use of tempera is discussed by Wendy Baron, *Sickert*, London, 1973, p.153.

8. John Salis, review, *New Witness*, 24 Feb. 1916 in Press Cuttings International Society's exhibitions at the Grosvenor Gallery (National Art Library, Victoria & Albert Museum, London).

9. See Belinda Thompson, *Vuillard*, Oxford, 1988, reproduced in Pl. 59.

10. The original title of this painting was *The Victorians*. It was first exhibited at the nineteenth exhibition of the Women's International Art Club in March 1920 at the Grafton Galleries as *The Victorians*, along with *My Landlady* (Fig. 17), and was subsequently shown at the November 1926

Hodgkins Exhibition at All Saints, Manchester as *Victorians* (lent by Mrs Skinner). It later entered Lucy Wertheim's collection and is listed in Arthur R. Howell, *Frances Hodgkins: Four Vital Years*, London, 1951, p.112 as 'The Edwardians (Mr and Mrs Skinner)'.

11. International Society Autumn Exhibition, Oct. 1916, Grosvenor Gallery, No. 239, Frances Hodgkins, *Unshatterable*, oil. The painting was included in Hodgkins's exhibitions at Sydney and Melbourne in 1919 and was described by the art critic of the *Argus* as follows: '"Unshatterable" — is a good presentation of Belgian refugees' (Press Clippings Book, Jan. 1905 to June 1921, Art Gallery of New South Wales Library).

12. The contacts between Cedric Morris and Hodgkins are examined in E. H. McCormick, *Portrait of Frances Hodgkins*, Auckland, 1981. Their artistic relationship is discussed by Richard Morphet, *Cedric Morris*, exhibition catalogue, Tate Gallery, London, 1984, pp.21-22, 36-37.

13. Cedric Morris, notes for his address, Hodgkins Exhibition, Bournemouth Art Society, 1948, in Cedric Morris Ms. Papers, Tate Gallery Archive, London.

14. For Laura Knight, see *Painting in Newlyn* and Caroline Fox, *Dame Laura Knight*, Oxford, 1988.

15. Norman Garstin, 'The Art of Harold and Laura Knight', *Studio*, 57, 1913, pp.183-96.

16. Reproduced ibid., p.195.

17. FH to her mother, Aug. 1915. The subject was also treated by the American painter Thomas Eakins in *The Swimming Hole*, 1883.

18. For an account of the exhibition, see Spalding, pp.156-63.

19. Sickert's views are given in his review of the 1910 Post-Impressionist Exhibition in the *Fortnightly Review*, 89, Jan. 1911, pp.79-89.

20. For *Ennui* (Tate Gallery), see Baron, pp.357-8, and reproduced in Fig. 223.

21. Nina Hamnet's *Portrait of a Landlady* (private collection) is reproduced in Spalding, Pl. 76.

22. FH to Hannah Ritchie, c.Aug. 1917, St Ives, Cornwall. The six versions by Hodgkins of Ritchie's sketches are in the Auckland City Art Gallery.

23. For Vorticism, see Richard Cork, *Vorticism and Abstract Art in the First Machine Age*: vol. 1: *Origins and Development*; vol. 2: *Synthesis and Decline*, London, 1976.

24. FH to G. F. Mann, 23 Oct. 1917, St Ives, Cornwall (Art Gallery of New South Wales, Australia).

25. See Morphet, p.22.

26. Reproduced ibid., p.21.

27. FH to her mother, 9 June 1920, St Ives, Cornwall.

28. The five drawings, all in black chalk, are *Mediterranean Landscape* (private collection, Auckland); *Hilly Landscape, with Village* and *Landscape, South of France* (Whitworth Art Gallery, Manchester); *Cassis* (Auckland City Art Gallery); *Olives, St Tropez* (Hocken Library, Dunedin).

29 FH to her mother, 4 Feb. 1921, Martigues, Bouches du Rhône, France. Frank Rutter was a well-known critic and had been an editor of the magazine *Art and Letters*. He wrote the foreword to the catalogue of her one-woman exhibition at the Hampstead Gallery in February 1920.

30. The term 'significant form' was employed by Clive Bell in *Art* (1914) but originated with Roger Fry and had been used by him with reference to Cézanne in a review in the *Fortnightly Review* (1 May 1911). See the discussion by Frances Spalding in *Roger Fry*, pp.163-5.

31. Ibid., pp.197-8; Fry's painting *The Harbour, Cassis* (Glasgow City Art Gallery) is reproduced in Pl. 73. The Fauve painters, Marquet, Derain, Braque and Matisse, all worked at Cassis between 1904 and 1909. See *The Fauve Landscape*, exhibition catalogue, Los Angeles County Museum, 1990.

32. Charles Ginner, 'The Cézanne Stunt', *Art and Letters*, July 1917, pp.41-43.

33. See the reproduction of Muirhead Bone's *Outskirts, Marseilles* in *Colour*, Feb. 1922, p.11.

34. FH to William Hodgkins, 28 Feb. 1921, Martigues, Bouches du Rhône, France.

35. *Colour*, June 1922.

36. Myfanwy Evans, *Frances Hodgkins* (Penguin Modern Painters), Harmondsworth, 1948, p.11.

37. Juan Gris, *Bottle of Wine and Water Jar* (1911, Rijksmuseum Kröller-Müller, Otterlo), reproduced in Douglas Cooper, *The Cubist Epoch*, London, 1970, in Pl. 220.

38. For a discussion of the distinction between analytic and synthetic Cubism, see John Golding, *Cubism: A History and an Analysis, 1907-1914*, London, 1968, pp.114–16. Golding's book is the standard account of analytic Cubism. Synthetic Cubism emerges after the First World War in the paintings of Picasso, Braque and Gris; see the recent accounts by Kenneth E. Silver, *Esprit de Corps: The Art of the Parisian Avant Garde and the First World War, 1914–1925*, Princeton, 1989, pp.299-361; and Christopher Green, *Cubism and its Enemies*, New Haven & London, 1987.

39. See the brief account in McCormick, *Portrait*, pp.100-103.

40. Evans, *Frances Hodgkins*, p.14.

41. The literature on the 1925 Paris exhibition is extensive; the most important document is the twelve-volume catalogue of the fair: *Encyclopédie des Arts Decoratifs et Industriels Modernes au XXième Siècle*, Paris, 1925. Useful surveys of the exhibition are given by Tim Benton, Charlotte Benton & Aaron Scharf, *Design 1920s*, Open University, Milton Keynes, 1975, pp.62-66; and Silver, *Esprit de Corps*, pp.362-90.

42. For Dufy's designs, see Dora Perez-Tibi, *Dufy*, New York, 1989, pp.83-114: Sonia Delaunay's fabrics are discussed in Jacques Darnase, *Sonia Delaunay Fashion and Fabrics*, London, 1991, which includes some contemporary photographs taken at the 1925 Paris exhibition.

43. Dufy's hangings are discussed and reproduced by Perez-Tibi, pp.71-83.

44. FH to Isabel Field, 29 Aug. 1925, Platt Abbey, Rusholme, Manchester.

45. FH to Duncan Macdonald, 19 July 1945, Studio, Corfe Castle, Dorset.

46. It was discovered recently that the reverse of *Adoration* (Whitworth Art Gallery) has a pencil study for *The Yellow Houseboat* (watercolour, Whitworth Art Gallery), which dates both works to around 1924–25, as The *Yellow Houseboat* was certainly executed in France. Her interest in family groups at this date can be confirmed by the unfinished painting *Child in a Pram* (Auckland City Art Gallery), which according to Hannah Ritchie was executed in Provence around 1925

(Hannah Ritchie Ms. notes on works by Frances Hodgkins, Auckland City Art Gallery).

47. *Lancashire Mill Girls* (watercolour, Miss Janet Green Collection); *Lancashire Mill Girls* (watercolour, private collection, UK).

48. FH to Hannah Ritchie, c.21 Jan. 1923, Studio, Burford.

49. According to the transcript of a recording by Lett Haines for a documentary on Frances Hodgkins in 1969 (Cedric Morris Ms. Papers, Tate Gallery Archives).

50. See the discussion of the return to Classicism in French painting by Silver, pp.270-98.

51. For Wertheim's activity as a collector and dealer, see Penny Johnson & Judith Collins, *Adventure in Art: Modern British Art under the Patronage of Lucy Wertheim*, exhibition catalogue, Salford Museum & Art Gallery, 1992.

52. See her account of the meeting in Lucy Wertheim, *Adventure in Art*, London & Brussels, 1947, p.2.

53. See the list of works Wertheim lent to the 1947 exhibition *Pictures by Frances Hodgkins* at the City of Manchester Art Gallery. Reprinted in Howell, *Frances Hodgkins: Four Vital Years*, pp.126-7.

54. The four paintings by Hodgkins at Wertheim's October 1930 opening show were *Still Life in Front of Landscape*, *The Bridesmaids*, *The Farmer's Daughter* and *Margretta*.

55. Arthur R. Howell to FH, 5 March 1930. The contract is reproduced in McCormick, *Portrait*, Auckland, 1981, p.110.

56. FH to Lucy Wertheim, c.24 Feb. 1930, St Jeannet, Alpes Maritimes, France.

57. See Richard Morphet, *Cedric Morris*, exhibition catalogue, Tate Gallery, London, 1984, p.104, cat. no. 33.

58. According to a letter from Lett Haines to Mary Chamont, 14 Oct. 1963 (Tate Gallery Archive).

59. See Avenal McKinnon, *Frances Hodgkins 1869–1947*, exhibition catalogue, Whitford & Hughes, London, 1990, cat. no. 13.

60. *Two Sisters* (pencil, Hocken Library, Dunedin); *Village Girls* (oil, private collection, NZ), reproduced McKinnon, cat. no. 14.

61. For Marie Laurencin, see Daniel Marchesseau, *Marie Laurencin, Catalogue Raisonné de l'Oeuvre Peint*, Editions du Musée Marie Laurencin, Paris, 1986.

62. For the Seven and Five Society, see Marjorie Anne Kirker, 'The Last Years of the "Seven and Five" Society', MA Report, Courtauld Institute, University of London, 1979; and Mark Glazebrook, *The Seven and Five Society 1920–35*, exhibition catalogue, Michael Parkin Fine Art, London, 1979–80.

63. Ben Nicholson's account of meeting Wallis was first printed in *Horizon*, vii, 1943, which also contains the first important discussion of his work by Sven Berlin. See also Sven Berlin, *Alfred Wallis Primitive*, London, 1949, and Edwin Mullins, *Alfred Wallis, Cornish Primitive Painter*, London, 1967. There is a large collection of Wallis's paintings at Kettle's Yard, University of Cambridge, which was made by J. Ede.

64. FH to Dorothy Selby, 4 March 1945, Corfe Castle, Dorset: 'Have you seen a 2/- booklet of Childrens Art

(Tomlinson) get it if you haven't — awfully good'. The book in question is R. R. Tomlinson, *Children as Artists*, London, 1949.

65. For Ben Nicholson's paintings at this date, see Jeremy Lewison, *Ben Nicholson*, Oxford, 1991. For Christopher Wood, see *Christopher Wood*, exhibition catalogue, Minories Gallery, Colchester, 1979. The relation of Nicholson and Wood to Wallis is examined by Charles Harrison, 'The Modern, the Primitive and the Picturesque' in *Alfred Wallis, Christopher Wood, Ben Nicholson*, exhibition catalogue, Scottish Arts Council, 1987.

66. For the connections between Wood and Morris, see Morphet, pp.37-38. Lucy Wertheim was Wood's dealer and in a letter of 27 Aug. 1930 to her, Hodgkins recorded her views on his death.

67. See Green, *Cubism and its Enemies*, pp.20-21, 33-36, 77-78; and Silver, *Esprit de Corps*, pp.350-7.

68. For Winifred Nicholson's still-life landscapes, see Judith Collins, *Winifred Nicholson*, exhibition catalogue, Tate Gallery, London, 1987. Nicholson's two essays on colour ('Unknown Colour', 1937, and 'Liberation of Colour', 1944) are reprinted in *Unknown Colour: Paintings, Letters, Writings by Winifred Nicholson*, London, 1987, pp.99-103, 124-9.

69. See FH to Arthur Howell, 26 Sept. 1930, Flatford Mill, E. Bergholt: 'you are very good with titles retain that excellent title still-life landscape — it is just it.'

70. Eight drawings (six still lifes and two landscapes) of uniform size are in the Auckland City Art Gallery. They are reproduced and discussed by E. H. McCormick: 'Some recently acquired drawings by Frances Hodgkins', *Auckland City Art Gallery Quarterly*, 58. A further two still-life drawings in the Piper Collection appear to come from the same sketchbook as the Auckland set.

71. See John Elderfield, *The Drawings of Matisse*, London, 1984, cat. 38, Pl. 164.

72 See *Frances Hodgkins, Works from Private Collections*, exhibition catalogue, Kirkcaldie & Stains Ltd, Wellington, 1989, cat. no. 35.

73. Howell, p.85: 'Do please try to do something like those three pictures you painted towards the end of your show there with the white house in them . . .'.

74. See McKinnon, cat. no. 20, which reproduces the version ex. Gorer Collection.

75. See Johnson & Collins, *Adventure in Art*, cat. no. 20 (reproduced on the cover of the catalogue).

76. For Dufy's watercolours in the St Jeannet–Vence region, see Perez-Tibi, *Dufy*, pp.134-5.

77. According to a letter from Geoffrey Gorer of 22 Feb. 1955 (Tate Gallery Archive), *Wings Over Water* was bought by his mother, Mrs R. A. Gorer, from the studio of the artist, then in a Hampstead mews. This studio can be identified as the Mall Studios behind Parkhill Road, Hampstead, which Hodgkins used c.1930–31, alongside Henry Moore and Barbara Hepworth. See further Herbert Read, 'A Nest of Gentle Artists' in *Art in Britain 1930–40 centred around Axis, Circle, Unit One*, exhibition catalogue, Marlborough Fine Art, London, 1965, pp.7-9.

1931–1947 ELIZABETH EASTMOND

I feel pleasantly anchored . . . . I must look around for something fresh to which I can re-act — touch and see . . . . Something is really happening at last — and yet this, I feel, is only a half-way stage.

FRANCES HODGKINS, 19 OCTOBER 1930

THE EARLY THIRTIES 1931–33

Like ritual offerings of plenty Frances Hodgkins's still-life landscapes float pleasurable images of fecundity and delight before the eye. They form a persistent and intriguing strand in her artistic practice over the five or six years around the pivotal and prolific 1930: vases, urns, eggs, shells, berries, succulent melons, gourds and that especially favoured motif, the creamy-white arum lily, are set first on tables tilted, medieval fashion, towards the viewer, then on altar-like ottomans, or — in a beautifully inspired gesture — placed simply on the ground. The relationship of objects to setting continually shifts as the artist experiments with changes of focus and scale, the enchanting artifice of the whole affair lightly and wittily proclaimed by the use of a sprightly twist of drapery accompanying a table group here, twirling about a prop there or deftly whisked skywards to fall behind other arrangements in a gesture of mock drama.

Frances Hodgkins's experiments within this already inventive synthesis of genres continue in her later work alongside her various types of landscape and the more occasional figure subject, with the idea re-cast and transformed from 1937 on in the many works focusing on farm machinery and other agricultural implements in landscape settings.

Stylistically Hodgkins's still lifes, still-life landscapes and figure subjects of the 1930s and 1940s move through a succession of phases and demonstrate a continual sense of adventure in form, iconography and colour. A clear understanding of this has been complicated by considerable dating problems with many works from this period, but in general her work — always retaining its highly individualistic colour and painterly qualities — moves from responses to the lyrical naturalism and *faux-naïveté* associated with the Seven and Five Society, to 1920s New Classicism, to Surrealism, through to Neo-Romanticism, with constant and varied signs of her great admiration for the major artists of the French School like Matisse, Picasso and Dufy. There are also connections with specific British artists after the Seven and Five episode: with Paul Nash, with John Piper, and connections too with the aesthetics of other cultures and times: with Chinese art, with medieval art, with outsider and child art. At its best, her work of this period fuses an acute response to the experience of natural phenomena with its antithesis, where form and colour operate freely with a total lack of respect for appearances.

Frances Hodgkins's remarkable late phase can be usefully tracked through from the landscape still lifes of around 1929, when she became, at sixty, a prolific producer of works which form a vital and individual component of British modernism. It continues up until 1946, the year before she died at the age of seventy-eight: 'my aim, as you know, being to do higher things as time goes on — and as time goes on I compete against myself more & more . . .'.[1] This was written in 1942 (at seventy-two) after several successful solo and group shows in the 1930s and two years after her selection for the prestigious *Biennale di Venezia* in 1940.

After the fulcrum point of her successful solo exhibition at the St George's Gallery, when she presciently sensed herself at a 'half-way stage', 1931 in the south of France sees her consolidating the directions established in the 1930 still-life landscapes. *Arum Lilies* (Pl. 26), described by Eric Newton as a work of 'uncanny alchemy',[2] was almost certainly produced

FIGURE 38
Cut Melons, c.1931
Oil on canvas, 535 x 643mm
Museum of New Zealand,
Te Papa Tongarewa

there. It is first documented in the eleventh exhibition of the Seven and Five Society in February 1932. Twenty artists exhibited, with Frances Hodgkins, Ben Nicholson, Winifred Nicholson and Henry Moore each showing six works. *Arum Lilies* has close connections with three surviving oils, all on board, unfortunately never hung together: *Red Jug* (shown in the same Seven and Five exhibition),[3] *The Green Urn* (see Pl. 26) and *Cut Melons* (Fig. 38). In its *plein air* arrangement of large-scale objects including urn, vases, fruit and flowers against a distant landscape (more indistinct in the other three), it has iconographic connections with a number of watercolours also probably done in 1931.

These works can be associated with Frances Hodgkins's stay from February to August of that year at Martigues and at St Tropez. Here she was in the congenial company first of the sculptor Maurice Garnier, whom she had met at St Jeannet the year previously,[4] and then in St Tropez, with the expatriate New Zealand painter Maud Burge and her husband, who had a villa neighbouring Signac's where Maud 'arranges & collects still life & flowers for me w^h we do in the cool garden —'.[5] Here Frances Hodgkins also met another expatriate New Zealand painter, Gwen Knight, for the first time.[6] A letter from the Hôtel Moderne conveys a buoyant mood: 'Les Martigues is an old friend of mine — I find fresh things to paint on every visit . . . . Today is a blue day — like a cake of cobalt — I am looking — Tomorrow I will paint —'.[7] It continues to mention delights enjoyed en route in Paris: 'I saw some immaculate Matisses: a wall of them; each picture was painted with a different palette —'. And in a letter liberally laced with artists' names (Augustus John, Pascin, Hermine David, Christopher Wood, Léger, Garnier), she makes a special mention of 'a very exciting show of Picasso — Braque — Matisse etc.'.

Her obviously intense enthusiasm for French art has particularly strong expression in the oils of this period.[8] This group has a new simplification of shapes which may also owe something to 1920s New Classicism, while the particularly sensuous use of colour is Matissean with a Hodgkins subtlety. The paintings display that admired 'different palette': *Arum Lilies* held together by cool greens, blues, creams, *The Green Urn* by greens played off warm russets, *Red Jug* dominated by Matissean vermilion, and *Cut Melons* keyed within a range of rather un-English highly pitched pale greens, creams and yellows. Colour here, combining chromatic sensuousness with an emphasis on succulent fruit, links sight and taste in a highly suggestive and effective manner[9] and the works, with their images of abundance and fecundity — lilies, eggs, large-scale cut melons — are quite evidently those mentioned in a letter in which the artist recalls 'a sumptuos [*sic*] short period at St Raphael. I bought hundreds of melons in the market to paint in my room — melons give intense satisfaction'.[10]

These images are more than brilliant and subtle essays in expressive colour, however: they also make evocative play between motifs of abundance and of void: the tipped jug in *Arum Lilies* versus containers of eggs, fruit, lilies; the empty gourd in *The Green Urn* versus the exceedingly suggestive central cut melon; *Red Jug*'s pairing of an empty with a full jug of flowers. They also involve certain oddities of arrangement: a dish of apples sitting on top of an urn (*Arum Lilies*), a device used by Picasso in his classicising *Still Life with Pitcher and*

Apples (1919) (see Pl. 26); a single leaf poking out from under a similarly placed dish in *The Green Urn* and a blank dark window behind the scattered melons of *Cut Melons*. Surrealism probably provided Hodgkins with the liberty to upset the more staid arrangements of conventional still life, with the swathe of blue curtain and the slightly ominous window distant echoes of motifs in de Chirico's metaphysical paintings.[11]

The whole project of transporting, liberating, still life from a domestic setting into the landscape can of course be linked in a general sense with the surrealist theme of constructing irrational dialogues with the unexpected. It is particularly marked in *Cut Melons*, where the window, that ubiquitous framing device for still-life groups, becomes — in a complete reversal of normal procedure — an opaque object behind the group, eyeing it and us in a curiously eerie fashion.

At another, post-Freudian, level of response, the objects have inescapable connotations of the erotic, most blatantly in the melons split open to display their vulval centres. Unlike her British contemporary Matthew Smith or continental artists like Matisse, Dufy and Picasso, Frances Hodgkins never explored that major subject in modern painting, the female nude. Drawing on Meyer Schapiro's psychoanalytic interpretation of Cézanne's apples, where apples become symbols of the erotic,[12] it could be argued that the fulsome fleshiness of the cut melons, plus the motifs of lilies, eggs, urns (long understood as symbols of the feminine) operate as substitutes for the female nude, or at least as signifiers of sexuality and the feminine. Indeed, in Picasso's *Still Life with Pitcher and Apples*, recent commentators see a 'potent anthropomorphic presence, where it is almost impossible not to see a woman'.[13] Such associations in Hodgkins's work are supported by her characteristic emphasis on the objects' symbolic presence.

A lighter, more ethereal quality characterises the watercolours of this period. Despite Hodgkins's conviction that oils carried greater significance,[14] these paintings make a hauntingly effective group. *Pottery* (*Still Life in Landscape*)[15] and *Two Plates* (Fig. 39)[16] were exhibited with *Red Jug* and *Arum Lilies* in the 1932 Seven and Five Society exhibition. *Two Plates* has close iconographic and stylistic connections with *Pottery*: the jug with blue convolvulus is a common motif and convolvulus is similarly used in *Still Life/Still Life with Lilies*.[17] All three share that theatrical flourish of drapery and are set against a vague misty landscape of light washes enlivened by the repetitive accents of little Y-shaped cyphers for trees.

Closest to Hodgkins in British art in her work with still life at this time were Ben Nicholson, Winifred Nicholson and David Jones. But each had different preoccupations: Ben Nicholson moves from foreground still life against setting around 1930 to an overall planar emphasis with an increasingly geometric, abstract approach to form by 1932; Winifred Nicholson's beautifully simple still-life arrangements rarely take flight from the window sill and her particular concern is with the dissolving, luminous effects of light; David Jones may place objects with ritual associations on tilted tables but his febrile, linear fragmentation of form and light washes of colour share little with Hodgkins's more sensuously luxuriant approach to form and colour, especially in the oils done in the south of France in 1931.

FIGURE 39
Two Plates, c.1931
Pencil, pastel & watercolour, 395 x 575mm
Museum of New Zealand,
Te Papa Tongarewa

In August 1931 Hodgkins returned to Britain, eager for the response of her dealer, Arthur Howell, to her canvases. His enthusiasm is described in *Frances Hodgkins, Four Vital Years*, where he noted the works' 'spectral or surrealistic' tendencies.[18] But the future of the St George's Gallery was by now under a cloud as a result of the financial crisis, and for Hodgkins the ensuing six-month period was one of anxiety. It was not until signing up with the Lefevre Galleries in February 1932 that she could begin to enjoy artistic and financial security once more.

Despite these difficulties the letters she wrote from Cornwall from December 1931 to April 1932 mention a stream of work, and a smallish number of surviving watercolours, drawings and oils can be linked with this period.[19] It seems probable that the Leeds *Wings on Water* (see Pl. 25) was done at this time, and possibly the version in the Tate (P1. 25) already discussed. The former arranges objects on an ottoman fringed with berries and the ubiquitous arum lily before a diagonally divided landscape-seascape. Near the horizon are two Wallis-like ships sailing into the harbour. The parrot to the right makes a brilliant splash of colour against the pale green sea; the insertion of this exotic motif (which may be connected with a reference to a parrot in an April letter)[20] gives this complex work its special vitality, its characteristically Hodgkins sense of capturing the sparkling, evanescent moment, a feature too of the writing of her compatriot Katherine Mansfield. Stylistically there are more connections with the still-life landscapes done at The Croft in 1930 than with the St Tropez oils: perhaps Frances Hodgkins was consciously returning to 'paint "British"', as she had planned after the episode in the south of France.[21]

April at Lanteglos in Cornwall coincided with an exhibition at Zwemmers in London organised by Paul Nash: *Room and Book*, which prefigured Unit One in its grouping of artists and incorporation of different media.[22] Frances Hodgkins's *Cut Melons* was included. But the characteristics of *Cut Melons* were very unlike those of the next significant grouping of her works after the 1931 still-life landscapes: the predominantly watercolour paintings produced at Bridgnorth, Shropshire, near the Welsh border.

Frances Hodgkins was again in congenial company, this time her old friends from Manchester, Hannah Ritchie and Jane Saunders, and her long-standing friend, Dorothy Selby. She was also secure in her new arrangement with the Lefevre Galleries.

This group of watercolours, drawings and one surviving oil all feature a view over a stretch of water, as in the two versions of *Wings over Water*, except here the horizon is lower. Devices like scudding Dufyesque clouds or the wavy line of an awning serve to align distant images with the picture plane. A new overall unity is evident in the use of fluid, rhythmic, organic washes subtly merging and binding the various components of the painting together. This constitutes a marked stylistic break away from the more separate treatment of foreground objects and background setting seen in works of the previous few years. Dufy's work is a major inspiration. Frances Hodgkins had shown her customary sharp judgement when she proclaimed him 'slick', but added 'not that slick'[23] and the exhilarating *joie de vivre* and breathless surface tremor of his calligraphic style obviously struck a chord.

There is a slight shift in subject emphasis in this group of works. Still-life-related objects (seats, urns) are present, but they are on a smaller scale and presented as less significant components of the compositions. This shift could be taken as a sign of Hodgkins's continually experimental approach or it could be construed as the after-effect of Howell's discouraging letter stating that the Lefevre Galleries 'are getting a little tired of the same kind of still-life'.[24] Certainly, her reply from Cornwall appears to respond to this criticism when she mentions with some irony that she is embarking on landscape now, 'if only to show you that I do not flout your wishes'.[25]

However, the still-life-related objects in the Bridgnorth landscapes provide each work with a reminder of human presence. This is most wittily achieved in the distinctly anthropomorphic boat of *Pleasure Boat* (see Pl. 27). The boat's face — window/eyes, door/nose and step/smiling mouth — comically watches us from its mooring in a knowing play on the operation of the gaze, as the image, suspended before the picture plane, views the viewer.[26]

The obviously intentional humour of *Pleasure Boat* is not unique to this work. A general gleeful jauntiness characterises works like *Two Dogs*;[27] *Cat and Mousetrap* shows an obviously sly humour in the choice of subject;[28] while major oils like *Poet Resting under a Tree, Spain* (Fig. 45), with its decidedly phallic tree, or *Self-Portrait: Still Life* (Pl. 30), in its subtle play on strategies of self-image, add to a picture of an artist whose work can employ humour on various levels and in this respect stands refreshingly apart from much being done in Britain at this time.[29]

A human presence, or rather absence, is suggested by the wrought-iron seats of *The Lake* (originally *River Garden, Bridgnorth*)[30] and *Boathouse on the Severn*.[31] *The Lake* also has a foreground urn crowned with a sprinkling of little red flowers — perhaps the same urn which appears on a larger scale in *Enchanted Garden (A Cornish Garden)* (Pl. 27).[32] This Severn view (its houses are very like those in *Boathouse on the Severn* and its general composition like *Pleasure Garden*) is an outstanding work of this group, with its lightness of touch and overall organic washes in blues and greens with spots of orange coalescing in a brilliantly kinetic image.

Pleasure Garden's floating light sweeps of watercolour enlivened by a spry calligraphy (see Pl. 27) are suggestive of Chinese painting, which featured in that summer's *Studio*.[33] Its central table and its arrangement provides a connection with the still-life landscapes from 1928 on. Here, the table group is associated with a highly evocative wooden statue of two women, one holding a bunch of grapes.[34] These reappear in the one surviving oil, the classically titled *Sabrina's Garden* (Fig. 40, Sabrina is the Roman Severn), where the statue forms a major compositional counterpart to the table, with one of the figures making eye-contact with the viewer.[35] The statue and the unattended table, curiously placed cloth and oddly distinct black vase give this image both a classicising and a surreal quality, reminiscent of de Chirico. Interestingly, two drawings related to this work survive. One shares the same pro-

FIGURE 40
Sabrina's Garden, 1932/33
Oil on canvas, 645 x 920mm
Bristol Art Gallery

portions as the oil: *Sketch for Sabrina's Garden*, where the viewpoint is shifted to the right, the statue omitted and the focus is on the table — with different objects on it, as if an earlier filmic take.[36] The other drawing features only the two-figure statue.[37] This suggests that in the paintings the artist is imaginatively aligning two separately conceived motifs (and the placing of the statue to the right of the table in *Pleasure Garden* supports this) because of a special interest in the sensuously classicising image of the two women. Certainly it provides another variation on a motif much explored by Hodgkins: the double portrait or double image;[38] it provides the only opportunity to depict the female nude (at one remove) in landscape and it operates perhaps as a metaphor for the close female companionship so often enjoyed by Frances Hodgkins on painting excursions such as this.

A couple of months or so after the Bridgnorth sojourn Frances Hodgkins escaped the British winter by travelling south, this time to Ibiza in the Balearic Islands. In January she wrote to her friend, the painter and textile designer Karl Hagedorn: 'in this clear ivory light every common object looks important & significant . . . things appear in stark simplicity minus all detail — nothing corked up (bouchee) or hidden as in the grey, or brown light of the North'.[39]

A large number of works survive from this period, almost rivalling the highly productive 1930. Once again she was in the company of a close group of friends, continuing the St Tropez connection with Maud Burge and Gwen Knight and meeting up with another expatriate New Zealand artist, May Smith, at the Hotel Balear[40] — 'my three friends', as she described them.[41] In the letter to Karl Hagedorn she mentioned sending off 'my first batch of Aquerelles [*sic*] to Lefevres — they are mainly Cat and Dog subjects, something novel for me'. A number of watercolour studies of these subjects (some with body colour), done in broad brush strokes, with a tonality primarily in the rich umber/slate-blue range can be linked with this period.[42]

Technically and tonally related to these are some watercolour still-life/still-life landscape subjects, including the outstanding watercolour *Phoenician Pottery and Gourds* (Fig. 41).[43] This has a tipped-over urn (a device adopted earlier in still lifes of 1930 and used in *Arum Lilies*), gourds (as in *The Green Urn*) and jug, scattered with a brilliantly controlled spontaneity across a ground of broad brownish washes.[44] The image is perfectly enlivened by a small, inspired ripple of blue on the horizon above the jug — the whole kinetic arrangement caught in a dramatically taut image. A similar dramatic intensity is shared by *Two Heads* dated variously 1920–25 or c.1935, but whose style and technique appears much closer to these Ibizan works.[45] Its double-image motif is shared by a drawing from Hodgkins's stay on Ibiza: the delicate, arcadian *Flute Players* (Fig. 42).

The boldness of these paintings, often using the whitish tones of the paper for the effect of bright light, marks a change of emphasis from the more overall treatment and softer, more delicate tonality of the Bridgnorth works. This approach did not always meet with her dealers' approval, however: in a long and somewhat patronising letter Duncan Macdonald of Lefevres instructed her to look well at her earlier oils for guidance and reported that the

FIGURE 41
Phoenician Pottery and Gourds, c.1933
Watercolour, 406 x 542mm
Auckland City Art Gallery

Leicester Galleries (with whom the Lefevre Galleries were associated) showed 'no great enthusiasm' for a recent batch of works.[46] 'They still do not have any form', he commented. Perhaps he felt ill at ease with the admittedly somewhat sketchy, unfinished look of some of the works. But another clue to the rather critical tone may lie in developments hinted at stiffly later in this letter: 'I understand it is your intention to join a group called "Unit One" . . . . I gather their exhibitions are not to be held here but in a new gallery recently opened.' The new gallery was the Mayor Gallery, which re-opened in April that year with a surrealist show, and so became (with Zwemmers, Tooths and the Redfern) another competitor for the Lefevre and Leicester Galleries. The first exhibition of the new group Unit One was held at the Mayor Gallery in April 1934.[47]

Frances Hodgkins was pleased to be invited to join this avant-garde group,[48] a number of whom had been members of the Seven and Five Society[49] and had exhibited in the earlier, similarly Paul-Nash-inspired exhibition *Room and Book* of April 1932 at Zwemmers.[50] Unit One's philosophy, as outlined by Nash in his famous letter to *The Times*,[51] demonstrated a radical challenge to the now rather tepid avant-gardism of the Seven and Five, in its emphasis on 'the expression of a truly contemporary spirit', on 'Design . . . considered as a structural pursuit', and on a shared concern for 'an architectonic quality'.[52] Hodgkins, however, resigned from the group in October 1933 and before its first and only exhibition, evidently finding its programme too doctrinaire.[53] Her place was taken by Tristram Hillier, whose work clearly fell into the surrealist camp. But coverage of Unit One's artists and philosophy prior to October included Hodgkins, and (despite not showing in its one exhibition) this provided her work with a context in Britain's major avant-garde grouping of that time and helped consolidate her reputation.[54] Her painting *Arum Lilies* (Pl. 26) appeared on the first page of Herbert Read's article 'Unit One' in the *Architectural Review* (with Colin Lucas's distinctly international modern house The Hopfield). But strong as this painting is, in the company of the more radically abstract or surrealist works by the other members, Hodgkins was perhaps right in feeling this was not the most appropriate context for her. Interestingly, Eric Newton's appeal, in an article aptly titled 'The Centre Party', for appreciation of a broader spectrum of practices was published in May 1934,[55] soon after, and possibly as a result of the April Unit One exhibition and also soon after the Zwemmers March/April exhibition *Objective Abstraction*, which featured a grouping of artists then adopting a non-geometric, less dogmatic form of abstraction.[56]

The invitation to join Unit One arrived while Frances Hodgkins was in Ibiza in March. But worries about her work and her contract commitments,[57] followed by Macdonald's discouraging letter, together of course with her own scepticism about the suitability of any prescriptive grouping as a context for her work, may have all combined to effect her October resignation.

In Britain, 1933 also saw the publication of Herbert Read's *Art Now* (which did not include Hodgkins) and closer personal contacts being forged with European artists.[58] But Ibiza in 1933 was by no means entirely isolated from European artistic practice and debate. There were many migrants from other parts of Europe there, especially Germans fleeing Nazism, among them the philosopher-critic Walter Benjamin, the photographer Gisele Freund, the art historian Jean Selz, the Peruvian surrealist Andrea Gamboa, the Catalan poet Luis Frances, Maurice Garnier, and the German ex-Dadaist Raoul Hausmann.[59] 'There are more writers (of all nationality) [*sic*] than painters — I know a fair number of nice people whom I enjoy talking with — we meet in the cafes when we can — Swiss, Czechoslovakian Russian — Belge', she wrote to Dorothy Selby, mentioning also that she had decided to postpone her Lefevre show until the autumn.[60]

Hausmann, now turned anthropologist/photographer/architectural historian and theorist, produced a remarkable series of photographs of the local vernacular architecture of Ibiza.[61] Some of Frances Hodgkins's Ibizan landscapes also feature the indigenous architecture, emphasising its geometric forms and simplicity, as in the watercolour *Church at San Jose*[62] and *Ibiza, Study for Oil* (Fig. 43), where the cluster of sturdy, cubic buildings has something in common with Hausmann's *Maison Paysanne — Cal Tio — Ile d'Ibiza* (1933) (Fig. 44).

Two closely related panoramic oil landscapes from the vantage point of Dalt Vila, the old hill-top town of Ibiza, exist in New Zealand collections, both titled *Ibiza*, each with a

FIGURE 42
Flute Players, c.1933
Pencil, 533 x 393mm
Auckland City Art Gallery

FIGURE 43
Ibiza, Study for Oil, c.1933
Watercolour, 428 x 558mm
Auckland City Art Gallery

FIGURE 44
Raoul Hausmann, *Maison Paysanne — Cal Tio — Ile d'Ibiza*, 1933
Photograph, 127 x 180mm
Musée Départemental de Rochechouart,
Limoges, France

view across Ibiza harbour over the promontory of Sa Penya to the mountains beyond.[63] The rich purples and oranges in the Auckland version and the dark tones in the foreground of the Dunedin work suggest these may be evening scenes. Indeed May Smith remembered her working both early in the morning and again in the evenings after four to avoid the heat and harsh light of midday.[64] These superb landscapes have, however, a freer treatment of paint which may suggest completion at a later date, a frequent practice in Hodgkins's late work.

Two other surviving oil landscapes are *Spring in the Ravine (Spring in the Ravine, Ibiza)*[65] and *Poet Resting under a Tree, Spain* (Fig. 45).[66] The former has a medievally symmetrical arrangement of three hills and foreground central gush of river painted in broad curving brush strokes, the hills dotted with runic Y-shaped trees, as in the paintings done in the south of France. The intriguing *Poet Resting under a Tree, Spain* may well have been painted in the early months in Ibiza, but its most distinguishing feature is of course the comically phallic tree-trunk dominating the foreground. While composition and style connect with the neo-primitivist strand of the Seven and Five group, the focus on the truncated tree is obviously and humorously surrealist. It is almost reminiscent of some of Max Ernst's oddly anthropomorphic beings of the 1920s[67] and foreshadows the tree-stump motif in Paul Nash's 1934 *Event on the Downs* (Fig. 46).[68] Certainly Surrealism was getting a fair amount of coverage in the press at this time; it was a strong factor in Unit One; it was the theme for the re-opening show at the Mayor Gallery (Dali, Miró, Ernst), and it featured in *Cahiers d'Art* in 1933 (Ernst). But bizarre as this image may at first sight appear in Hodgkins's *oeuvre*, she had already of course experimented with the quirkily anthropomorphic and humorous in works like *Pleasure Boat*.

The beautiful oils, *Spanish Still Life and Landscape* (see Pl. 28) and *Evening* (Pl. 28),[69] are closely related to *Poet Resting under a Tree, Spain* in the treatment of landscape and the motifs of the small square houses. They are also interrelated in terms of *plein air* still life, stacked organisation of objects and the images of jar and goblet-shaped vase. Both have a highly ritualistic feel, with the objects symmetrically placed on tilted altar-like supports. These two powerful and suggestive still-life landscapes mark a high point in her exploration of this theme and in her Ibizan-based work as a whole, with *Evening*'s luscious pinks and creamy whites a major essay in superbly expressive colour. Like pagan offerings to some goddess of fertility and abundance, they once again effectively unite the chromatic and the sensual in their luxuriant colour and display of succulent fruits.

In these two works, as in earlier still-life landscapes, Frances Hodgkins's flowers, fruits and containers are given a strong symbolic presence and an effectively indefinable scale. She plucks still life from its usual associations with the interior, where it can operate as a sign of nature, of the outside, contained within the civilised inside space of the house; she exhilaratingly collapses this familiar dynamic.[70] She also frees the objects from any association with the feminine in a specifically domestic sense by removing them into this outside world where they are set against their source, the land, as fruits of the earth. This exterior setting can, however, signify, simultaneously, both an essential femininity (as land is generally gendered feminine in European culture), and, the outside world of male culture. Through these evocative ambiguities and by persistent and prolonged experimentation with the still-life landscape idea, Hodgkins constructs a distinctive, subtly transgressive series of images and significantly expands and alters conceptions of still life as a genre.

THE MID TO LATE THIRTIES 1934–39

Over the years 1934–39 Frances Hodgkins was based first in London and then in various country villages in Britain, with her longest and most productive spell abroad, once more in Spain, this time Tossa de Mar, from the autumn of 1935 until the spring of 1936. This period of her artistic practice evolved first against the later years of the Depression and then against the instability and threat of war in Europe. Her personal life saw the continuing support of key friends, old and new, but while artistically productive, these years — she was now in her late sixties — were intermittently interrupted by bouts of ill health. On a professional level her contract with the Lefevre Galleries continued, ensuring her regular exhibitions and a certain amount of financial security, but the relationship did have its difficulties and a renegotiation of the terms of the contract was arrived at in June 1938.[71]

A clear sense of Hodgkins having carved out a secure niche for herself in British art in the 1930s is expressed in a letter of 1932, in which she described an offer from Tooths to exhibit, as well as the support of the Lefevre Galleries: 'Funny how these favours come thick & fast when you are established in safety —'.[72] Her decision to resign from Unit One late in 1933 and from the Seven and Five Society when in April 1934, under the influence of Ben Nicholson, it had become the Seven & Five Abstract Group[73] are testimony to her independence of spirit, while her independent moral stance is shown by her withdrawal from the exhibition of contemporary British art organised by Arthur Lett Haines at the Anglo-German Club.[74]

The period 1934–39 sees two major one-woman shows: at the Leicester Galleries in February 1935 and at the Lefevre Galleries in October–November 1937. Another solo show — which did not altogether meet with her approval — was held at the Wertheim Gallery (while she was in Spain in January 1936).[75] She also showed in around thirty group exhibitions over this time, some of them outside Britain: in 1935 in the British section of the Universal International Exhibition at Brussels, in 1938 at the *Salon d'Automne* in Paris, in 1939 at the World's Fair in New York, in Brisbane and also at the Centennial Exhibition in New Zealand. Besides reviews in the major papers, coverage in *Apollo* and the *Studio*, her work was illustrated in *Cahiers d'Art*[76] and covered in a number of *Listener* articles, including those by Eric Newton and Geoffrey Gorer.

This six-year period — after the 'decisive years' of 1928–30 and the consolidation of her career between 1931 and 1933 — shows a confidence in the continuing inventiveness of her

FIGURE 45
Poet Resting under a Tree, Spain, c.1932/33
Oil on canvas, 560 x 685mm
Private collection, New Zealand

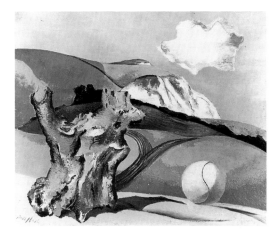

FIGURE 46
Paul Nash, *Event on the Downs*, 1934
Oil, 508 x 610mm
Government Art Collection, Department of
National Heritage, UK
Reproduced by permission of Paul Nash
Trust.

approaches to style, iconography and colour. Works generally fall more clearly into groups or sets of related subjects, almost always initially inspired by the perceptual excitement and experience of the specifics of place or object, which are then quite freely transformed. Landscape subjects dominate and in a letter of 1934 we can get a picture of that tension between experience and invention in her self-parodic 'I go out into the fields every day among the red cattle, strike an attitude and paint a composite picture — a sort of wish fulfilment of a picture —'.[77] There are also a number of notable still lifes, still-life landscapes and her unique self-portrait still lifes from this time, although the period is framed by two major figure subjects: *Spanish Shrine* (1933–34) (Pl. 29) and the *Double Portrait No. 2 (Katharine and Anthony West)* (1937/9) (Pl. 33).

Usually dated 1933 because of its Spanish subject, the large oil, *Spanish Shrine*, connects with other works of 1934–35: its style shares their looser treatment of oil paint and a vertical alignment of subject with setting. Therefore while probably conceived in Ibiza, it may well have been finished later.[78] *Spanish Shrine* was exhibited a number of times in Frances Hodgkins's lifetime and was Eric Newton's choice as the illustration to his 1941 *Listener* article on Hodgkins, in which he praised the work's balance between abstraction and repre-

FIGURE 47
Decorative Motif, c.1933/34
Oil on canvas, 492 x 590mm
Museum of New Zealand, Te Papa
Tongarewa

sentation — very much to his taste: 'both a symbol and a description and the two are inter-woven'.[79] The magic of this compelling, hypnotic image is bound up with the fine tension generated by a merging of the hieratic in the treatment of figures with the kinetic in the flickering, mobile effects of iridescent colour across the picture surface.

Although primarily a figure subject, *Spanish Shrine* is also in part another play on the Hodgkins still-life landscape combination, for it incorporates her favourite still-life motifs: containers, fruit and flowers, with landscape. But now she was back in urban London after the spell in Ibiza, works which can probably be linked to this time (1934–35) are not surpris-ingly mainly still lifes rather than still-life landscapes or landscapes. *Decorative Motif* (Fig. 47) was first exhibited in Hodgkins's February 1935 show and so was probably painted around 1933–34. Its distinctive methods of framing and linking major motifs against and within an inner enclosing irregularly rectangular shape are shared by *Spanish Shrine*. Its sensual colouring orchestrates pinks, beiges, creams and maroons, which, together with the generality of its title (a feature in common with other works of the time), makes this an effective exercise in formal and decorative values.[80] *Decorative Motif*'s bird ornament occurs again in the watercolour *Christmas Decorations* (Fig. 48), which is signed and dated 1935.[81] Because of stylistic and compositional features in common with these works Dunedin Art Gallery's beautiful *Still Life* (generally dated 1937–38) is more probably dated around this period.[82]

FIGURE 48
Christmas Decorations, 1935
Watercolour, 412 x 570mm
Private collection, New Zealand

Two other closely connected major oil still lifes probably date from around this period rather than later. They are *Self-Portrait: Still Life* (Pl. 30) and *Still Life: Self-Portrait* (see Pl. 30), the latter the more representational and probably the earlier. Although it is a more loosely treated watercolour, *Christmas Decorations* has much in common with this version in its piled-up arrangement of interconnecting objects around a central motif. The circular red shape of the bauble is even echoed in the oil's red beret. But the significance of the two oils lies in their radical merging of the genres of still life and portraiture. For in their choice of objects emblematic both of the personal tastes and appearance of the artist and also of self-image as a category of artistic practice (*Still Life: Self-Portrait*'s mirror), metaphor is inventively, sub-tly and wittily investigated through an ostensibly still-life project. The luminous, highly keyed colouring of the Auckland painting also connects with *Spanish Shrine* and the monu-mental, piled-up effect of the image within its island-like enclosure, particularly strong in the Auckland version, is reminiscent of *Spanish Shrine*, *Decorative Motif* and *Still Life*. In the two self-portrait/still-life paintings especially, Hodgkins achieves, in addition to her land-scape still lifes, another brilliant synthesis of genres and produces paintings which in formal terms move from the strategies of her earlier still-life arrangements into a new overall deco-rative emphasis linking objects and setting in an almost abstract manner.

Few other major works can be confidently assigned to this 1934–35 interlude; and in September 1935 she once more avoided the British winter and established herself in Tossa de Mar, where she had 'learnt the technique of Tossa and got a way of living that suits me'.[83] Here she began to experiment consistently with the technique of painting in gouache, a

FIGURE 49
Private Bathing, 1935/36
Gouache, 546 x 750mm
Private collection, UK

medium of major significance for the rest of her career. There is an increased emphasis from this period on the (modernist) practice of working on related groups of paintings, as she herself suggests by the use of the terms 'set, series, suite'.[84] But again not all works were completed in Spain: a letter from Corfe Castle explains that there is 'Plenty of work ahead of me' and that she is 'looking for a quiet corner where I can settle down & crystallize the after glow of my Spanish memories — before they grow dim —'.[85]

Two still lifes of vegetables on a table — a change from the earlier fruit and flowers — date from the time in Tossa and are similar in size and arrangement: *Pumpkins and Pimenti* (Pl. 31) and *Marrow*.[86] *Pumpkins and Pimenti* shows a decisive move towards a more fluid, calligraphic yet substantial style, probably arrived at through the special qualities of the gouache medium, with the colour, unlike that of the London still lifes of 1934–35, restricted to a particularly subtle, close range of streaky olive-green and grey tones, with the occasional note of deep blue and warm orange. *Pumpkins and Pimenti* is yet another brilliant play on the still-life landscape theme, as roughly described mountains seem to erupt through the table top and behind it in an irrational manner immediately suggestive of surrealist practice.[87] Indeed Surrealism was more consistently in the air in the British art scene at this time: the *International Surrealist Exhibition* (featuring some British artists alongside the main continental contingent) was held in London in June 1936, and Herbert Read's *Surrealism* and David Gasgoyne's *A Short Survey of Surrealism* were published that year.

The overall calligraphy and close tonal range of *Pumpkins and Pimenti* also characterises *Private Bathing* (Fig. 49), a major essay in Hodgkins's new, more boldly gestural language of pictorial signs facilitated by the gouache medium.[88] Another gouache, *Hill Landscape*, has close stylistic connections with these works and was probably done at this period.[89] It is also interesting as one of the early versions of a subject much explored later in works done in Wales and particularly in the Isle of Purbeck: the rounded hill shape enclosing a central building.

Other surviving Spanish landscapes display a brighter palette[90] and rich colour combinations are explored in *The Road to Barcelona* (oranges, pinks), a painting which Myfanwy Evans described as having 'all the drama, all the emotion, all the intensity' in its colour;[91] in *In Perspective* (reds, pinks) (Fig. 50) and in *The Return of the River* (blues, whites).[92] All these works also show a new interest in a sharp, geometric emphasis with odd distortions. *In Perspective* overlays the images of buildings with a kind of grid, playing on the ambiguous relationship between two disparate pictorial conventions, a device also seen in recent art practice and one which was explored in the 1930s in a more surrealist fashion by Paul Nash in his *Landscape from a Dream* (Fig. 51). This free play with formal elements plus the intensity of the colour of these works may owe something to Hodgkins's continuing interest in Matisse. Indeed Matisse described his approach for a British audience in a 1935 issue of the *Studio*, explaining that 'For me, the subject of a picture and its background have the same value', while 'the picture is formed by the surfaces, differently coloured, which results in the creation of an "expression".'[93] The new angular distortions may also be a response to Picasso,

FIGURE 50
In Perspective (En Perspective), 1936
Gouache & watercolour, 510 x 655mm
Victoria & Albert Museum, London

whose paintings Hodgkins saw exhibited in Barcelona: 'I was lucky to see a Picasso Show in Barcelona (good) a most purifying experience', she reported to Macdonald.[94]

Other works which share this angular emphasis include *Phoenician Ruins*[95] and *Ruins*,[96] both exhibited in the 1937 Lefevre Galleries exhibition. *Ruins* was probably painted on the Dorset coast later in the English summer. The still life *Chairs and Pots*, usually dated c.1939 but first exhibited in 1938, appears to relate stylistically to this group of Spanish gouaches, in particular to *The Return of the River*, both in its geometric tendencies and in its spatial ambiguities.[97] Its predominantly blue colouring and the rather surrealist effect of the swirling linear ripples on the floor, also prominent features of the Christchurch work, recall the sea's invasion of Paul Nash's hotel room in *Harbour and Room* (1932–36), exhibited in the 1936 *International Surrealist Exhibition*.[98]

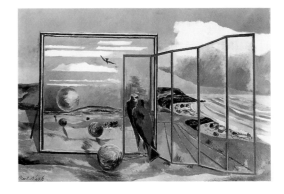

FIGURE 51
Paul Nash, *Landscape from a Dream*, 1936–8
Oil on canvas, 679 x 1016mm
Tate Gallery, London

After the period in Corfe in 1936 recapturing the 'after glow' of her time in Spain, Frances Hodgkins made for Wales, which provided the inspiration for the next significant grouping of works. Late August saw her first at Llangenith near Swansea, then at the little fishing village of Solva, with Dorothy Selby as her companion. 'I have been working moderately

FIGURE 52
Solva, 1936
Gouache, 545 x 753mm
Birmingham Museums & Art Gallery

hard, moderately successful in a landscape of steep valleys speedy rivers & castles looking like their own mountains', she later wrote to Macdonald.[99] This visit, together with subsequent excursions to Wales in 1938 (when Graham Sutherland was there) and 1942, yielded a cluster of motifs which recur with minor variations in a group of at least six particularly closely related works in gouache and oil. The rather mundane motifs are houses against hills, cows in meadows, double bridge and foreground river.

The intensity of the focus on this cluster of images is belied by the deceptively simple, free, brisk handling of paint in individual works. *Solva* (1936) (Fig. 52) is a major work from this group, with *House by a Stream* sharing the same basic layout.[100] *The Calf* is an almost filmic close-up of the standing animal in *Solva* and *House by the Stream*, with the foreground river shrinking, as in *Study for Pembrokeshire Landscape*,[101] into a finite tongue-like shape reminiscent of medieval art's sign language for 'river'.[102] Two oils exist on the same theme: *Solva (A Country Landscape)*[103] and *Middle Mill, Solva*, dated 1942, a rather stilted studio version of these earlier works.[104] Another work variously titled *Farmyard Scene* or *Llangenith College Farm* shares the sectional treatment of space in these gouaches and *Solva*'s cow placed against a patch of darker colour.[105]

What was it about these motifs that caught Hodgkins's imagination? Was the interest more than formal? Certainly the image of house/habitat set within an enveloping, rounded hill had already been seen in *Hill Landscape* and it occurs frequently in later landscapes painted in the Isle of Purbeck. The obsessive recurrence of a particular landscape image was a major characteristic of Paul Nash's work, of course, seen most famously in his numerous works featuring the twin, breast-like Wittenham Clumps: 'They were the pyramids of my small world', he wrote.[106] A keenly associative reading of Hodgkins's hill/house motifs might consider them suggestive of the feminine, the maternal, and in a general sense landscape at this time was associated with these ideas, as David Mellor has shown.[107] Frances Hodgkins herself could make gender-linked references to landscape: writing in August 1939 from Northumbria, she described the view which 'stretches as far as the Border . . . with the graceful feminine looking [inserting here a wavy sketch for emphasis] Cheviots half encircling the view'.[108] But even if this provides a useful slant on these paintings, they do not share Nash's feeling for the mysterious and hermetic spirit of place. Rather, having found a collection of motifs with an, arguably, special resonance for her, Hodgkins uses these as the skeletal — yet recognisable — basis for free formal play with colour, shape and a variety of gestural marks. The images, discretely treated, have become simplified, almost child-like signs of themselves as in a kind of symbol language.[109] This effect — in *Solva*, cows against an enclosing patch of dark blue paint, green houses haloed by whitish blue — had already been investigated in paintings like *Private Bathing*, with its use of pockets or compartments of space.

It is also worth remembering that medieval art, with its symbolic, anti-representational aesthetic and its compartmentalising devices, was enjoying some vogue in various publications over the 1930s. John Piper's essay 'England's Early Sculptors', for instance, celebrates 'this free play of the artists' impulse working within ordered limits', a notion which strikes a particular chord with Hodgkins's approach in these landscapes.[110]

From May 1937 until early 1939 Frances Hodgkins's base was Worth Matravers, a village near Corfe Castle overlooking the English Channel. She had an ex-cowshed studio there and made forays into neighbourhood farmyards, across to nearby Kimmeridge Bay (the inspiration for a number of Paul Nash paintings and photographs) and into Wiltshire, where she stayed with the painter Katharine Church (Kitty West) and her husband Anthony West, the writer, later in 1937. Worth was home to Paul Nash at times over the period 1935–37.[111]

The Wests rented Quarry Farm near Tisbury in 1936–37.[112] Frances Hodgkins stayed with them around August 1937. A later letter mentions 'the happiest long week end with the Wests & have painted 3 quite attractive canvases inspired by objects observed by me out of the corner of my subjective eye, when *really* looking for black berries'.[113] A solo exhibition was coming up at Lefevres in October and a group exhibition in January 1938 (with Ivon Hitchens, Winifred Nicholson, Julian Trevelyan, and Katharine Church among others). 'I shall be bitterly sorry if you do not show some of the new ones I have sent you, particularly the oils of Anthony West's Farm — please do include them', she wrote.[114] *Quarry Farm, Wiltshire*[115] was shown in both exhibitions and other works also exhibited are linked to this location in various ways: by title, in the case of *Wiltshire Farmyard*, or by recent identification: *The Colonel's House* and possibly *Entrance to a Tunnel*.[116] *Quarry Farm, Wiltshire* presents an almost aerial map-like treatment of its farmyard subject, recalling Piper's observations on the flattened effects obtained from the air in his 1937 *Axis* article, 'Pre-History from the Air'.[117] It is one of the first securely dated works from Frances Hodgkins's late phase to focus on agricultural implements. (Hodgkins painted a number of threshing scenes around 1920.) The same exhibition featured the oil *The Wheelwright's Shop*, which concentrated on a farm cart to the exclusion of other objects.[118]

Besides the carts, *Quarry Farm, Wiltshire* also includes the central motif of a water tank, seen at an angle so that two sides are equally visible. Just this object and view of it appears in the superb oil *Tanks, Barrels and Drums*, also in the 1937 Lefevre Galleries exhibition.[119] This suggests the possibility that this work and the numerous other related studies in drawings and in gouache are related to Quarry Farm visits, or that the 1937 visit suggested exploration of this new motif, which could, of course, be seen in most farmyard settings. *Tanks, Barrels and Drums* is a major essay on a grouping of objects which, in its emphasis on a strong overall design of simple curved and geometric shapes, veers on the abstract. Patches of pinks, plums, mauves, russets, flatly painted here, over-painted there with flecks of pale green or indian red, bring to mind Myfanwy Evans's expressive comments on Hodgkins's paintings of the late thirties as 'marvellous agglomerations of colour and shape . . .'.[120]

Here is the still-life landscape project in another guise. The arrangement of these objects

FIGURE 53
Empty Drums and Barrel, 1939
Gouache, 420 x 560mm
Private collection, New Zealand

FIGURE 54
Kimmeridge Foreshore, c.1938
Oil on canvas, 760 x 1015mm
Victoria University of Wellington

in one of the Tate Archive drawings[121] even recalls an earlier still-life landscape like *Pottery (Still Life in Landscape)*, except that the conventional jugs — one upright, one placed on its side — are replaced by an upright and a prone barrel and drum, empty containers. The new 'still-life' objects, as in *Empty Drums and Barrel* (Fig. 53), are the more usually overlooked detritus of the farmyard scene. They seem to be a consciously non-picturesque choice in comparison with earlier subjects, although similar motifs are treated in a more melancholy and associative fashion by the neo-romantics, a movement with which Hodgkins's work is more closely linked in the 1940s. In the focus on the monumentality of these simple cubic, cylindrical and rounded shapes, Hodgkins arrives at an effect which has some similarities with Paul Nash's groups of geometric objects in landscape settings, such as *Objects in Relation* (1935) and *Equivalents for the Megaliths* (1935).[122] The latter may have been inspired in part by the monuments of Avebury, but by Nash's own testimony his interest here was less antiquarian than in 'shapes equivalent to the prone or upright stones, simply as upright or prone, or leaning masses, grouped together in a scene of open fields and hills . . .'.[123]

The sturdy objects of *Tanks, Barrels and Drums* and *Empty Drums and Barrel* also, paradoxically, appear to float weightlessly in a vertical arrangement in space. Similarly arranged are the more conventional still-life motifs of jugs, vases and dishes in the lithograph commissioned by Contemporary Lithographs Ltd:[124] *Arrangement of Jugs* (Pl. 32), which draws closely on two watercolours of c.1936–38: *Still Life* and *Arrangement of Jugs* (see Pl. 32). Like the watercolours, Hodgkins's lithograph is characterised by crisp, floating shapes held in tension with patches and sweeps of clear colour: a brilliant cadmium yellow singing out next to a primary red contributes to a particularly light, buoyant image. Its colouring and emphasis on sharpish vertical shapes has something in common with John Piper's contribution to the series, *Abstract Composition*.[125]

After the production of the lithograph and with the notable exception of *Double Portrait No. 2 (Katharine and Anthony West)*, the bulk of Hodgkins's work from 1938 to around 1940 was mainly landscape-related. The considerable time at Worth, and then (after some months at Bradford-on-Tone in 1939) back again in the Isle of Purbeck (Corfe this time from mid July) provided Hodgkins with the motifs for a group of landscapes which are closely linked in style, although precise dating is uncertain. These are the oils *Kimmeridge Foreshore* (Fig. 54), *Dairy Farm, Houses and Outhouses, Purbeck* (Fig. 55) and the similarly titled gouache.[126] The July 1938 visit to Kimmeridge may support the usual dating of 1938 for *Kimmeridge Foreshore*, although it was not exhibited until the October 1941 Leicester Galleries Hodgkins exhibition, like the oil *Houses and Outhouses, Purbeck*. But again exhibition appearance is not an infallible guide to dating — except as a *terminus post quem* — especially when this one included the much earlier *Sabrina's Garden* and *Spanish Shrine*. *Kimmeridge Foreshore* and the oil version of *Houses and Outhouses, Purbeck* share an overall emphasis on clusters and swathes of often baffling shapes, making them some of the most abstract yet in Hodgkins's *oeuvre* — 'in each folded space a life of colour', as Myfanwy Evans put it.[127] The rich colouring is in patches, swoops and ripples of mainly greens, some earth tones and intense blues, suggesting an exotic camouflage whose muted, close tones foreshadow the neo-romantic tendency in her art prominent in the 1940s.

A comparison with an earlier landscape like *Solva* shows how far Hodgkins had moved towards abstraction. However, a commentator could interpret the oil *Houses and Outhouses, Purbeck* and certain other works as inflected by current events, namely the outbreak of war: 'This is Frances Hodgkins' war art. They are paintings that are urgent, tragic comments on dereliction and wreckage. They are not of war subjects, but humanity at war is the emotional background for these rubbish heaps among the out-houses of a south Dorset farm.'[128] A contemporary response like this is intriguing in its confirmation that the objects chosen by Frances Hodgkins — as in the still-life landscapes and in works like *Tanks, Barrels and Drums* — can operate for many viewers on associative as well as purely formal levels. A number of letters of 1938–39, particularly those to Willie, her brother in New Zealand, speak in some detail of political events leading up to the war, of the 'awful time of strain and tension',[129] of blackouts, of 'sitting in darkened rooms, gas mask handy'.[130] But Frances Hodgkins still managed two productive painting excursions before returning to Corfe by the outbreak of war on 1 September.

The first of these, in August, was to Northumbria, to her old friend Jane Saunders, where she did 'quite a lot of painting in the farm barns & in Jane's very pleasant Studio'.[131] The gouaches *Northern Barn*, *Barn Interior* (both dated 1939) and *Circular Barn* were almost certainly produced at this time.[132] These works focus on farm machinery in barns, the interior settings allowing for further exploitation of an overall formal emphasis. The shapes are harshly angular, jagged; objects are boldly distorted and the colouring limited to stern greys and browns with a liberal use of black. There is an conscious lack of interest in pictorial pleasantries. This, together with the prominence of motifs like upright shafts (*Northern Barn*) and the grindstone, for sharpening tools like hay knives (*Circular Barn*), done just as the machinery of war was grinding into action, can also suggest a 'war art' reading here as well as presenting further experimentation with abstraction.

If these works do indeed express something of the atmosphere surrounding the build-up to war, such a coincidence of the aesthetic with the social was hardly a constant feature of Hodgkins's work and the warm, luscious Mediterranean tones of the gouache *August Month (Walls, Roofs and Flowers)* (Pl. 34), first exhibited in the April 1940 Lefevre Galleries exhibition, may also have been painted during that Northumbrian August visit, when the sombre 'Barns' were conceived or while she was with the Wests in Berkshire at the end of the month.

The stay at the Wests' provided Hodgkins with the subject of her major pre-war figure subject, the dramatic, Picassoesque *Double Portrait No. 2 (Katharine and Anthony West)* (Pl. 33). Although actually dated 1937, it may have been signed later and Katharine Church herself remembers Frances Hodgkins working on the preparatory drawing of Anthony West and the watercolour of herself in the first week of the war.[133] The watercolour and sketch survive (see Pl. 33), providing an obvious basis for the oil. That the studies were produced separately, the oil's 'double' take obviously a pictorial fiction, repeats the probable situation

FIGURE 55
Houses and Outhouses, Purbeck, c.1938
Oil on canvas, 1285 x 1025mm
British Council

with *Sabrina's Garden*.[134] As a double portrait it follows a long-standing tradition in Hodgkins's *oeuvre*, from works like *Loveday and Ann* (1915) to *Double Portrait* (1922–25) and *The Brides-maids* (1930).

In her letter to Willie on 1 September — 'All is confusion . . . and *now* it *is* war' — Frances Hodgkins described her time with the Wests, their preparations for evacuees, and the dark-ening of her studio windows at Corfe. Over the final months of 1939 the letters express constant anxieties over the war and over producing work for her upcoming April 1940 exhi-bition at the Lefevre Galleries. The uncertainties of this period were exacerbated by the can-cellation of her contract with the Lefevre Galleries in response to which she wrote gallantly and not without some irony, 'C'est la guerre . . .'.[135]

But as in the past, a period of difficulty and stress was transformed into a newly confi-dent and productive stage in her career. The agent for the transformation this time was the welcome December invitation to represent Britain at the *Biennale di Venezia*. This was un-doubtedly major confirmation of her prominent status in British art and it marks the begin-ning of the final phase of Frances Hodgkins's career: the war years.

THE WAR YEARS 1940–46

During the war years Frances Hodgkins's art was increasingly associated with Britain's neo-romantic movement in terms of exhibition groupings and contemporary writing. A key to this period as a whole, however, lies in the merging of the neo-romantic tendency in her art with her continuing, subtle response to French art and an aesthetic in which her highly individual use of colour was prominent. She herself articulated the latter concerns clearly in 1943 when she wrote of 'that universality I ever strive after . . . between the Ecole de Paris & FH'.[136]

She was seventy-one in 1940 when she was selected as one of a small group of artists to represent Britain at the *Biennale di Venezia,* a significant endorsement of her achievement.[137] This event launched the years of welcome but time-consuming attention from admirers and pressing requests for more work, for old work and — now that her position was quite be-yond doubt — for signatures on works old and new. She had made a name for herself. On a personal level there were difficulties associated with intermittent illness, age and the often desperate strain of living under war conditions. But the period was surprisingly productive, seeing both continuities and intriguing new shifts and experiments in her art. Four major solo exhibitions were held (in addition to the *Biennale*) and her work appeared in around thirty group shows, including two in Paris and one in the United States.[138]

She could no longer continue the pattern of restorative and productive trips to Europe: she made Corfe Castle her base, working in a studio which was once a nonconformist chapel.[139] The early months of 1940 in Corfe were dominated by the task of gathering together the twenty-six works for the *Biennale* and completing work for the April exhibition at Lefevre's. However, because of war conditions the works were shipped back from Paris and shown — to acclaim — at Hertford House in London (present home of the Wallace Collection). The selection certainly had its strengths: it showcased major oils like *Spanish Shrine* and gouaches like *Solva*, but the inclusion of modest watercolours like *Boy and Girl*,[140] seems, in retrospect, to lessen the overall impact.[141]

Among the most recent works in the two spring exhibitions was the 'Barns' series done in Northumbria just before the outbreak of war. The next cohesive grouping of her work has connections with the 'Barns' paintings in terms of subject: they were again studies of farm machinery, but now placed outside in landscape settings. These tangled heaps of machinery done frequently in dark, close tones like mauves, greys, moss greens, black, can be associated with neo-romantic art practice in their choice of subject, expressive interpretation and sombre tonality.

An emergent neo-romanticism had been a strand of British art practice in the 1930s in the landscape paintings of Nash and Sutherland. It was stimulated by — and expressed in — projects like Nash's *Shell Guide to Dorset* (1936) and Piper's writings in *Axis* and in *The Painter's Object* (1937), where he called for a return to nature as a source of inspiration.[142] Later, as an official war artist, his recordings of bombed buildings encouraged him to combine his interest in the specifics of place with an emotive romantic response to their ruined condition. And of course his book *British Romantic Artists* (1947) was a major attempt to reinscribe the parameters of a major British tradition and give it contemporary currency by presenting Nash, Sutherland and Hodgkins as the most recent exponents. This gave them the added authority of a place in what seemed at the time an appropriately nationalist historical tradition. Piper's return to nature after working in abstraction in the mid thirties, plus Nash's metaphysical/surrealist-inflected landscapes and connections with Dorset — obviously a neo-romantic county *par excellence* — provide some of the context for Hodgkins's war-period landscapes. In the 1940s her work and that of other Neo-Romantics featured in the literary magazines *Penguin New Writing* and *Horizon*, where John Piper introduced his essay on her with a suitably romantic picture of Corfe's castle poking its 'silver-grey ruined walls into the thinning mist'.[143]

Later in the forties Hodgkins's work was often shown in the company of both the established and the new wave of Neo-Romantics, which included John Craxton, John Minton,[144] and the 'two Roberts', Colquhoun and MacBryde. But a particularly interesting grouping in 1945 at the Lefevre Gallery had her alongside Moore and Sutherland (as major Neo-Romantics), Matthew Smith (clearly aligned with the School of Paris) and Francis Bacon, who was to become a major exponent of figure painting in 1950s Britain.[145] (One of the two works by Bacon was his seminal *Three Studies for Figures, at the Base of a Crucifixion*.) Hodgkins's paintings included her much earlier, French-influenced *Cut Melons* as well as recent oils and gouaches, a strategy which in retrospect has the effect of articulating the gulf between her

FIGURE 56
Broken Tractor, 1942
Gouache, 381 x 571mm
Tate Gallery, London

FIGURE 57
John Piper, *All Saints Chapel, Bath*, 1942
Watercolour, 425 x 559mm
Tate Gallery, London

work of the early thirties and that of the forties, and, at the same time, of reminding the viewer of her allegiance to French art, to notions of 'pure painting' which were still, together with the neo-romantic connection, a factor in her recent work.

The shift from the motifs of *Cut Melons* and other paintings of the thirties — the jugs, urns, fruit, flowers in landscapes — to the very different associations of farm machinery in the later thirties and forties is of course more than simply a sign of the artist's seeking fresh ideas. In the 1940s Neo-Romantics saw imagery like this as appropriate to their interest in the specifics and 'spirit' of place, where the romantic allusions of disused and rusting man-made objects in the rural scene could be exploited and also adopted as metaphors for the tortured war-embattled psyche within the sheltering — and now urgently fetishised — English landscape. French School artists like Picasso responded in ways which are well known to the horrors of the contemporary situation, while even in a still-life artist like Braque prevailing conditions provoked a transition to *vanitas* themes.

Surrealism was a major factor in the development of Neo-Romanticism and while the broken tractors are of course perfectly appropriate to their rural settings, their sometimes ambiguously anthropomorphic appearance has surrealist overtones. This is especially the case with the major gouache of this series, *Broken Tractor* (1942) (Fig. 56), which, interestingly, was shown in the exhibition *World War Two* at the Tate Gallery, Liverpool in 1989. The mangled tractor's wheel hubs look like grotesque, anguished eyes and the cutter's jagged teeth are presented as an erect, aggressive motif, an effect which was first explored in some of the Northumbrian 'Barns'. The suggestion of a church or even churchyard setting adds to the potent levels of meaning suggested by this work. Stylistically it has links with Piper's war paintings of ruined buildings, such as *All Saints Chapel, Bath* (1942) (Fig. 57): ruins are also suggested in Hodgkins's painting and treated in a particularly graphic way similar to Piper's approach, with much scoring over and through the paintwork. But the connections between the two artists at this time by no means flow one way: Piper was a great admirer of Hodgkins's art, as both his critical writing and personal letters testify. 'Thank you for the enormous pleasure and instruction that these new works give, your humble admirer J.P.', he wrote in one letter.[146] Both artists shared an interest in Dufy and it can certainly be argued that, in a general sense, Piper found Hodgkins's exhilaratingly free experimentation with form, colour and animated surface effects a liberating and inspiring influence.[147]

Related to *Broken Tractor* are a gouache sketch of a broken-down tractor,[148] *The Elevator*[149] and *The Reaper*.[150] The latter is close to *The Elevator* in style and presentation of subject although its tonality is more sombre. The reaper's upright shaft is also prominent in *Farm Implements (Farm Piece)*,[151] shown in the same 1940 Lefevre Galleries exhibition as *The Elevator*. The pictorial focus on this part of the machine is further accentuated in *Farm Implements* by a hazy halo of green paint around its central, assertively hornlike features and by their emphasis in black in *The Reaper*. Given the context and treatment of this subject, it is difficult not to infer associations here with that other, grim, reaper, of war.

There are two other closely related surviving gouaches on the tractor theme which are both dated 1941: *Landscape with Engine* (Fig. 58) and *Motor Transport*.[152] Both focus on the side view of a traction engine prominently placed in the middle ground of a landscape surrounded by trees and other more ambiguously described objects. Typical of Hodgkins's approach to related works, the use of colour gives each similarly organised work a different mood. The potentially incongruous effect of the focus on the machine is softened by her assured range of painterly gesture. This was a type of subject taken up later by John Minton in his *Farm Machine* (1944),[153] while the general treatment with its scattering of staccato brush marks in the foreground and depiction of the rounded, muscular curves of the hills has connections with Robert Colquhoun's work of this time.[154] Like Minton, he was a protégé of the Lefevre Galleries and like other Scottish Neo-Romantics was generally more influenced by the School of Paris than his English counterparts. Despite the painterliness of Hodgkins's image, however, its ancestry can also be traced in part to Surrealism, to images like the photograph of a creeper-covered train in a landscape setting which the Surrealist magazine *Minotaure* featured in the 1930s.[155]

There is also a related context for these images in a sphere of contemporary discourse that focused on the machine, on its impact, its significations, its representations. In the *London Bulletin*, platform for Surrealism in Britain, a whole issue in 1938 focused on the theme of the machine in conjunction with the exhibition *The Impact of Machines*.[156] Humphrey Jennings's article 'The Iron Horse', positing the machine as a pseudo-animal, appeared in this magazine, as well as his painting *The Locomotive*.[157]

In all of these works by Hodgkins, wheels are prominent motifs. They become *the* motifs in an extraordinary painting titled *Smithy* (Pl. 35), where two sets of interlocking bright pink spokes appear to dance and spin dizzily together over the picture surface. Again, like *Landscape with Engine*, this work has its pair, *Farmyard* (see Pl. 35). With their freely twirling spokes, minimal 'house' signs and dot/dash shorthand landscapes these are among the most adventurous and experimental of Hodgkins's late works.

Smithy was exhibited in Hodgkins's solo show at the Leicester Galleries in October 1941 but it appeared earlier in the group Summer Exhibition at the same venue in 1940, with one other major painting: *Window Group (Window Piece)* (Fig. 59). Like *Smithy* this work breaks now ground in Hodgkins's *oeuvre*. It may connect with Neo-Romanticism in the atmosphere generated by its sombre tonality, but equally significant is its complex formal play on that subject of long-standing interest to Hodgkins from the late 1920s on, the still-life landscape. The new, more boldly gestural, graphic technique plays over the whole picture surface and the background houses are described in abbreviated fashion as in *Smithy* and *Farmyard*. Particularly arresting is the play on inside/outside relationships: the sketchy grid (of the window panes) allows for a treatment of discrete areas, but its more usual role as a definer of near and distant spaces is constantly manipulated and defied as Hodgkins has background, houses and the finial of the roof below erupting into the room itself. Objects seem to swim in and out of focus in a rather hallucinatory fashion although their motion is anchored by the animate, almost surrealist, presence of the central, circular fruit bowl.[158]

FIGURE 58
Landscape with Engine, 1941
Gouache, 437 x 568mm
Ministry of Foreign Affairs & Trade, New Zealand

FIGURE 59
Window Group (Window Piece), c.1940
Gouache, 485 x 684mm
Private collection, New Zealand

In a later still-life landscape, *Walled Garden with Convolvulus* (Pl. 36), shown in the March–April 1943 Lefevre Galleries solo exhibition, a lighter, almost Mediterranean, palette supplants the neo-romantic tonality of other works, while jugs and other objects move into the outside environment, apparently on the ground, as in those paintings of the early thirties. However, two other beautiful still-life landscapes dating from the early forties see Hodgkins enmeshed in the evocative gloom of 'romantic valley':[159] *Mushrooms* (1941) and *Wild Violets and Honesty* (1941).[160] Both float their respective motifs across the whole picture surface in a highly dreamlike fashion. The amorphous, organicist imagery was shared by other surrealist and neo-romantic artists: works like Eileen Agar's *The Light Years* (1938) or Paul Nash's *Swan Song* (1929) also present floating visionary arrangements which include mushrooms, leaves and shells within a mysterious ambience.[161] In Hodgkins's two gouaches spectral objects have a kinetic effect as they sink into and gently emerge from mysterious hollows and cocoons of space. The lightly worn pictorial complexities of these paintings, together with their magical, twilight colouring confirm yet again that in her best work Frances Hodgkins's poetic sensibility was of a very high order.

The way these paintings encourage the viewer to move in and explore their dark, mysterious recesses — totally at odds with the presentation of subjects a decade earlier — is further explored in many of the paintings associated with Hodgkins's most productive foray over this period: to Dolaucothy in Wales in the autumn of 1942. As she wrote to Eardley Knollys, with whom she struck up a friendship on this visit: 'I have done masses of work . . . in and about the woods & river of Dolaucothy and have even seriously made pictures of the funny chimney ornaments . . .'.[162] It was Eardley Knollys who introduced her to the china-ornament collector whose collection formed the inspiration for another tightly knit group of images which, with the Welsh landscapes, were shown in her March–April 1943 solo exhibition at the Lefevre Galleries in tandem with the exhibition *Picasso and his Contemporaries*. This was one of the most cohesive shows of Hodgkins's work over the period from 1931 on: it focused consistently on very recent work and all fifteen paintings were in gouache.[163]

The China Shoe (Pl. 37) was a gift to Eardley Knollys, 'a token of my friendship', and has the shoe, wittily adorned with a prominent heart, in the centre foreground. Other vases of flowers with a somewhat ghostly presence are arranged above and behind, the whole image described in a dark greenish-blue tonality. This, together with the suggestive, sketchy style, links it with the earlier *Mushrooms* and *Wild Violets and Honesty*. The two other works based on the same objects, subtly shifted, are *Ornaments* and *Ornaments with Flowers* (see Pl. 37), with *Ornaments* sharing *The China Shoe*'s dark tonality, while *Ornaments with Flowers* is by contrast suffused in light airy whites, pinks and pale blues.

Two other gouaches from this series shown in 1943 include the wheel as a prominent motif. *Green Valley, Carmarthenshire* has it as a central foreground image,[164] while *The Mill Wheel* (Fig. 60) has the large wheel dominating the left side of this lush, almost abstract composition. Both works were selected for the 1945 Paris exhibition organised by the British Council, *Quelques Contemporains Anglais*, a grouping with an emphasis on neo-romantic art-

FIGURE 60
The Mill Wheel, 1942
Gouache, 362 x 560mm
Ministry of Foreign Affairs & Trade, New Zealand

ists like Colquhoun, Jones, Moore, Nash, Piper and Sutherland. *The Mill Wheel*'s interlocking of verticals and horizontals with curved shapes and the wonderfully animated foreground pile of dots and dabs are also features of *Root Crop*, a major gouache from this group, where a particularly fine tension is held between perceived scene and totally free formal and colouristic reconstruction of it.[165]

Frances Hodgkins was also in 1942 using motifs close to home: Corfe Castle's spectacular hilltop ruins and the local parish church of St Edward the Martyr. However, unlike the Romantic artists' treatment of such a scene, or even more recent representations of Corfe Castle itself by artists like Paul Nash in the *Shell Guide to Dorset*,[166] or Christopher Perkins,[167] Hodgkins does not focus on this image and all the romantic associations it carries: her paintings have the church and castle as small-scale, sketchy, graphic — but just legible — motifs crowning complex arrangements of form, line and colour.

The New Rick (see Pl. 38) has the castle perched at the top left, while the rest of the image is dominated by the haystack and other equipment associated with the subject.[168] It overlays large patches of colour with vivid dark linear accents, a method pushed even further in *Church and Castle, Corfe* (Pl. 38). This fine gouache pairs church with castle above an assortment of objects including a sharpening wheel, in a shadowy, possibly moonlit, setting. The subtle tonality and inclusion of motifs like the church link it with certain studies of Piper's like his *Farmyard Chapel, Near Launceston* (1943),[169] but Hodgkins's veil of flickering painterly signs and her de-emphasising of the two buildings avoids Piper's more literally romantic project and again achieves that fine balance between representation and abstraction.

Other paintings have the castle in the background as a minor motif: the oils *Corfe Castle*, its dense, rich greens similar to the earlier Purbeck landscapes,[170] *The Wheelwright's Shop*,[171] and the gouache *Courtyard, Corfe Castle*, with its tall foreground plants reminiscent of Nash's foreground sunflowers.[172] The gouache *Corfe Castle* (see Pl. 38) pairs church and castle as does *Church and Castle, Corfe*, but in this case behind the dominant motif, an old barn: is the title an intentional irony? Tones are again dark and shadowy — here greys and mauves — as in *Church and Castle, Corfe*. Both gouaches construct a fictional symmetry in their twinning of the two structures emblematic of church and state: another indicator of Hodgkins's free adaptation of her source material, since the castle in fact easily dominates the village, the church and the whole of the surrounding countryside.

It was in 1942 that the proposal was mooted to include Frances Hodgkins in the Penguin Modern Painters series edited by Sir Kenneth Clark. Myfanwy Evans was to be the writer. Frances Hodgkins was delighted: 'As far as pictures can be described no one could to it better', she wrote.[173] But partly due to war conditions the project was delayed although Myfanwy Evans had produced a draft of the text by about March the following year. The postponement became something of a burden for both artist and writer, but the book was finally published in 1948.

Despite the inevitable distractions such enterprises presented, and major problems with her studio (the roof collapsed in June and was not repaired until later in the year), two

FIGURE 61
The Weir, 1943
Oil, 640 x 760mm
Glasgow Art Gallery & Museum

FIGURE 62
Abandoned Cottage, Cerne Abbas, 1943
Gouache, 380 x 520mm
Private collection, New Zealand

groups of work on related subjects survive from this time. One of these was based on the subject of the weir, a motif which had featured in earlier works like *Pastorale* (1929) (see Pl. 24) and in *The Weir, Bradford-on-Tone* (c.1934).[174] Each of the three paintings from this closely related group is titled *The Weir* and each has the artist exploring the graphic and abstract pictorial possibilities offered by a close-up, tilted view of rushing weir waters.[175] As a motif there is a sense of Hodgkins moving right in for a close focus on one of the components — a stretch of water — that dominated the foreground of the pre-1940 Solva group of Welsh landscapes. Her treatment of the image has other connections with those landscapes in that Glasgow's *The Weir* (Fig. 61) also has the curve of the river shrinking into a finite loop shape, testimony yet again to Hodgkins's ability to transform the perceived specifics of natural phenomena into a more abstract and symbolic presence.

The other group of related works stem from Frances Hodgkins's stay, with her dear friend Dorothy Selby, at Cerne Abbas in the autumn of 1943: 'that cosy little village which we wrung dry in our search for subjects'.[176] *The Tithe Barn, Cerne Abbas*[177] and *Abandoned Cottage, Cerne Abbas* (Fig. 62) see Hodgkins staging a central dwelling, like *Corfe Castle*'s barn, and choosing again a recurring topos of neo-romantic artists: a dilapidated structure within the English landscape. John Piper's moonlit *Ruined Cottage* (1940) is another such work.[178] However, Hodgkins's treatment is again more concerned with the painterly possibilities inspired by such a structure than with a particularly associative interpretation of it. *Abandoned Cottage, Cerne Abbas* appears to use the same elements as *The Tithe Barn, Cerne Abbas*, but it is treated in a much freer manner so that structures and their substance fade away, leaving their residues in an image where colour, shape and line float, wriggle and dance in controlled abandon over the picture surface.

Frances Hodgkins was seventy-six in 1944, affected by the stress of war conditions — 'the planes overhead bringing back wounded from Normandy have scared all art out of me'[179] — up against the obstacle of periodic illness, and lacking that supportive 'body' about the house: much-needed domestic help.[180] Nevertheless, she did produce a group of three important oils that year.

These are the three works inspired by a location particularly close to hand: the courtyard beside her cottage and studio in West Street, Corfe Castle. John Wesley had preached there in 1774. Courtyard, cottage and chapel studio survive; and as with other known locations for late Hodgkins paintings, it is possible to gain a fairly precise insight into the variety of syntheses the artist manages so effectively between adaptation and manipulation of the idiosyncrasies of place with a quite freely inventive formal approach. Although dated 1944, some of these may have have been finished in 1945, since mention of 'subjects at my doorway' in May that year could well refer to completion of one or more of them.[181] All are of a similar size and painted on board and each in its title and colour is related to a specific time of day, recalling an interest explored in earlier work.

Purbeck Courtyard, Early Afternoon (see Pl. 39) is painted in close tones — predominantly greens and tans — from a viewpoint which appears to be looking down Well Court (the courtyard) towards the opening through to the garden and studio. *Purbeck Courtyard, Morning* (see Pl. 39), predominantly sepia, gold and peach tones, looks across and up the courtyard from the artist's studio, substituting for a sense of the structures' substance subtle skeins of colour and line. With its foreground 'still life' of cat and jars on a ledge absorbed pictorially into the spaces beyond, Hodgkins makes play yet again on that recurring theme in her late work, the still-life landscape, although here the setting is architectural rather than natural.

The most memorable of the group is the painting Hodgkins called *Courtyard by Night* but now known as *The Courtyard in Wartime* (Pl. 39).[182] Various elements of the courtyard — studio, cottage porch, steps — are disengaged from their context and transformed into mysterious signs of place which merge into dramatic areas of expressive colour. The choice of an emotive night scene places this work in the context of the wartime nocturne, where night could be used in a specifically apocalyptic sense when the subject was something like Sutherland's *Devastation 1941 — East End Street* (see Pl. 39). Hodgkins liked his work, but as with Piper, the admiration was mutual, as Sutherland made clear when he visited Hodgkins in April and 'said he had come to call on Sir Joshua Reynolds'.[183] Although the difference in their aesthetics is of course substantial, in that interesting April 1945 grouping at the Lefevre Gallery it was Sutherland she was closest to in terms of commitment to a notion of landscape.[184]

In May 1945, after a long winter with fuel problems affecting her studio work, and hard on the heels of this exhibition, there was relief and joy at hand: it was spring — always inspirational to Hodgkins — work was selling, she was taking down the depressing black-outs and above all it was the end of the war. It meant a great release of tension and a burst of new work: 'My Muse has returned to me —'.[185] She might not have tended to those domestic tasks she so abhorred, but she was working again and 'the very air is different — the trees & sunshine *know* —'.[186]

A British Council exhibition in Paris marking the liberation of France, *Quelques Contemporains Anglais,* included Hodgkins with a grouping that was again predominantly neo-romantic.[187] Philip Hendy's accompanying essay emphasised her strengths as a colourist, with Matthew Smith as the only other *'coloriste sans peur'*.

Indeed, her remarkably subtle and expressive use of colour, exceptionally *'sans peur'*, is seen in her last surviving oils, which date from this year: *Still Life — Zipp* (see Pl. 30) continuing the theme of personal belongings seen in the two earlier self-portrait/still lifes, with its purples, mauves and golds glowering out from a grey-black ground; and *The Spanish Well, Purbeck* (Pl. 40), with its intricate arrangement of gleaming shafts of oranges, pinks, mauves, aquamarines and a range of greens dominating the grey-black shadows and sky. The renewed, although subtle, brilliance of colour in *The Spanish Well, Purbeck* reverses the balance of *Still Life — Zipp*, contrasts with much other work of the war years and seems to hark back to the warm colouring of paintings inspired by those earlier visits to Spain and the south of France. It seems oddly appropriate that this softly exultant use of colour should be linked to a subject whose title has such strongly associative qualities.

One of her last gouaches, done in 1946, *Spring at Little Woolgarstone*, refers to the Corfe home of Hodgkins's friends David Brynley and Norman Notley.[188] The light fresh greens, the whites, are again in a quite different key from so many of her works of the war years. But the central motif, a tunnel-like entrance, immediately conjures up neo-romantic associations: as David Mellor put it, 'It was that same vortex of the organic, that opening to the body, that dark passage to a hide, which had haunted Neo-Romanticism since Sutherland's *Entrance to a Lane* (1939).'[189] Hodgkins's image shares with Sutherland's a central focus, partly defined in mustard yellows. Painted at this juncture in her life, the dark central shape's womb-like haven could also be read as foreshadowing Hodgkins's own imminent return to mother earth, her death in 1947.

However, early 1946 saw her enjoying time with the Pipers and her February visit to the Gorers in Hampstead allowed her to review a range of her work in their substantial collection: 'I have been feasting phoenix wise on my own pictures', she wrote to Eardley Knollys.[190] It was probably around then that the November Retrospective at the Lefevre Galleries began to take shape.[191] It was fortunate that Hodgkins could enjoy this small foretaste of that major exhibition, for by June she was writing to Dorothy Selby, 'The Zest of life has left me —'[192] and although she did make the Retrospective itself (on the last day), by November she had become increasingly frail.

In March 1946 she visited Bradford-on-Tone for the last time and produced two spirited gouaches: *The Croft House, Bradford-on-Tone* and *Cherry Tree at the Croft*.[193] Whether these, *Spring at Little Woolgarstone* or two other gouaches done in Dorset are her last works it is difficult to gauge. In the staccato stabbing brush marks around a central arched shape — here a bridge — in *Farm Bridge, Dorset* (Fig. 63) there are close connections with *Spring at Little Woolgarstone* and again the colouring is fresh and vital. *Farm Bridge, Dorset* employs the motifs of bridge and river, dwelling and trees within an enveloping hillside. Just this arrangement is found in an oil of 1945, *To the Castle, Corfe*,[194] as well as in the other 1946 gouache, *Dorset Farm*, chosen as the most recent example of her work for the 1948 Penguin Modern Painters *Frances Hodgkins*.[195] Again there is that concentration on an interplay of quite mundane subjects whose shapes, relationships and perhaps significations intrigued her, an interplay which was first established in the Welsh landscapes like *Solva* in 1936. In these two gouaches especially, however, with reductive brilliance, lines suggestive and baffling float over and under blurry washes, vigorous paint marks and bare ground. The images hang together by the skin of their teeth: their nonchalant poise and deceptive simplicity the result of an idea of at least ten years' standing.

Late gouaches like *Dorset Farm, Farm Bridge, Dorset* and oils like *Spanish Well*, together with the cream of Frances Hodgkins's works of the thirties and forties have the artist operating with a consistently high degree of invention within those 'ambiguous borderlands':[196] that

FIGURE 63
Farm Bridge, Dorset, 1946
Gouache, 455 x 535mm
Private collection, New Zealand

fertile gap between representation and abstraction. Never formulaic, Hodgkins constantly reworks the possibilities of that terrain in a highly imaginative transformative act underpinned by the intense pleasures of perception. As she herself wrote, 'Myself, I would say that I, my medium and my subject act & react to produce new & vital creations &, if possible, achieve a perfect balance —'.[197]

Now, fifty years on, and within a culture freer from the pressure to privilege a narrow notion of the avant-garde at the expense of other related art practices, it is possible to assess Hodgkins's important late work with greater clarity. In its avoidance of a total identification with dominant movements like Surrealism or abstraction it emerges as a project determinedly independent yet intelligently alert to and subtly inflected by such movements. It is precisely the dynamic generated by this relationship in tension with an inventively idiosyncratic exploration of such themes as the still-life landscape and, most importantly, a constantly evolving personal language of form and colour, which makes hers an individual and substantial achievement within the context of British art of this period.

1. FH to Alex. Reid of the Lefevre Galleries, 10 May 1942.

2. Eric Newton, 'The Centre Party', *Listener,* 23 May 1934, p.863.

3. Auckland City Art Gallery. Evans, *Hodgkins,* Pl. 10.

4. E. H. McCormick, *Late Attachment, Frances Hodgkins & Maurice Garnier,* Auckland City Art Gallery, 1988.

5. FH to Dorothy Selby, 25 June 1931.

6. Gwen Knight: audio tape, 'Frances Hodgkins', Pt. II, Radio New Zealand. I am grateful to Avenal McKinnon for this reference. Gwen Knight was the subject of Frances Hodgkins's *Under the Pines,* Museum of New Zealand, and *Gwen,* private collection, New Zealand.

7. FH to Arthur R. Howell, 14 Feb. 1931.

8. Hodgkins's enthusiasm for French art clearly evolves from direct contact with works of major contemporary artists in France (as well as those seen in dealer gallery exhibitions in London), so countering Charles Harrison's opinion of her exposure to second-rate French paintings of the 1920s: *English Art and Modernism 1900–1939,* London, 1981, p.196. She also read *Cahiers d'Art,* which over 1928–31 gave generous coverage in its large-scale plates to Derain, Braque, Rouault, Picasso, Matisse, Lurçat etc. In a letter from Martigues, 30 Jan. 1928, to Lett Haines FH apologised for not 'sending the Paris "Cahiers" as I said —' (Tate Gallery Archive).

9. A contemporary colour theorist, Manlio Brusatin, links the effects of colour with the essentially physical domains of breathing and taste: *A History of Colors,* Boston & London, 1991, p.5.

10. FH to Eardley Knollys, 4 March 1944.

11. De Chirico's work had some exposure in Britain around this time in, for example, 1928 and 1932 exhibitions at Tooths and in Paul Nash's article 'Giorgio di [*sic*] Chirico, the Columbus of the Unknown', *Listener,* 29 April 1931, p.720.

12. Meyer Schapiro, 'The Apples of Cézanne, An Essay on the Meaning of Still-Life', in *Modern Art, 19th and 20th Centuries,* London, 1978, pp.1-38.

13. Elizabeth Cowling & Jennifer Mundy, *On Classic Ground, Picasso, Léger, de Chirico and the New Classicism 1910–1930,* Tate Gallery, London, 1990, p.209.

14. FH to Lilian (Miss) Harmston, 14 April 1931.

15. Manchester City Art Gallery. *Frances Hodgkins 1869–1947, A Centenary Exhibition,* Queen Elizabeth II Arts Council of New Zealand, 1969, Fig. 59.

16. Evans, *Hodgkins,* Pl. 24.

17. Private collection, New Zealand. Avenal McKinnon, *Frances Hodgkins,* Whitford & Hughes exhibition catalogue, 1990, Pl. 10.

18. Arthur R. Howell, *Frances Hodgkins, Four Vital Years,* London, 1951, p.83.

19. *Documentary of Frances Hodgkins*: taperecorded interviews by June Opie, NZBC, 1969, transcripts Auckland City Art Gallery. Winifred Nicholson was at nearby Marazion, recalled meetings with FH and was 'very grateful for the help she gave me'. Another contact was Daphne du Maurier (FH to Dorothy Selby, 21 Dec. 1931).

20. FH to Dorothy Selby, c.April 1932.

21. FH to Lilian (Miss) Harmston, 15 Oct. 1931.

22. *Room and Book,* 2–25 April 1932. The painters and sculptors were: John Armstrong, Edward Bawden, John Bigge, Ivon Hitchens, Frances Hodgkins, David Jones, Ben Nicholson, Paul Nash, Eric Ravilious, Edward Wadsworth, Barbara Hepworth, Gertrude Hermes, Maurice Lambert, Henry Moore.

23. FH to Arthur R. Howell, 14 Feb. 1931.

24. Arthur R. Howell to FH, 28 Nov. 1931.

25. FH to Arthur R. Howell, c.10 Dec. 1931.

26. The confrontational placing of the pleasure boat's face is a feature, like some others in Hodgkins's art, which can be traced back to very early works: see, for example, *A Dutch Girl*, c.1907, Museum of New Zealand. It appears in figure groups of the late 1920s and and early 1930s and is a dominant feature of *Double Portrait No. 2 (Katharine and Anthony West)* (Pl. 33).

27. Private collection, New Zealand. *Frances Hodgkins, Works from Private Collections*, Kirkcaldie & Stains Ltd, Wellington, 1989, Pl. 26.

28. Private collection, New Zealand. *Frances Hodgkins, Works from Private Collections*, Pl. 30.

29. A gleeful sense of humour is frequently expressed in Frances Hodgkins's letters and is often remarked on in reminiscences of the artist: May Smith commented on her 'keen sort of repartee' and her delight in being 'mischievous' ('Frances Hodgkins', Pt II, audio tape, see note 6); Ben Nicholson remembered how, on seeing an illustration of his (of a horse's head on one side of a hill, its rump on the other side), she went straight for it and laughed like a horse . . . she was a card' (Opie interviews, see note 19).

30. Tate Gallery. *Frances Hodgkins — The Late Work*, exhibition catalogue, Minories Art Gallery, Colchester, 1991, p.26.

31. Private collection, New Zealand. *Frances Hodgkins*, Whitford & Hughes exhibition catalogue, Pl. 18.

32. Exhibited as *Enchanted Garden* in the Arts Council's *Frances Hodgkins Memorial Exhibition*, 1953. See commentary to Pl. 27.

33. Jiro Harada, 'Masterpieces of Chinese Painting', *Studio*, Jan.–June 1932, pp. 140-7. For British artists like Hodgkins an overall decorative approach was sanctioned not only by the work of continental colleagues, but also by the aesthetics demonstrated in other contemporary exhibitions such as *Flemish Tapestries* (1932), *English Medieval Art* (1932) and *Persian Art* (1931).

34. In New Zealand *Pleasure Garden* has been one of the best-known, or more precisely, notorious, of Frances Hodgkins's works. It was the focus of a major controversy over its acquisition by the Christchurch City Council for the Robert McDougall Art Gallery. Initially rejected as a purchase offered by the British Council in 1948, then refused even as a gift in 1949, and only accepted in 1952, the lengthy, highly public and extremely vigorous debate on the issue really marked the New Zealand public's belated exposure to modernism. See especially Margaret Frankel, 'The *Pleasure Garden* Incident at Christchurch', *Year Book of the Arts in New Zealand*, no.5, 1949, pp.10-21; T. H. Scott, 'The Frances Hodgkins Controversy', *Landfall*, 12, Dec. 1949, pp.360-74; T. H. Scott, 'The *Pleasure Garden*. A Postscript', *Landfall*, 20, Dec. 1951, pp.311-13; 'It Can't Happen Here?', *Image: A Quarterly of the Visual Arts*, London, Spring 4, 1950, pp.2-4. The incident had something in common with the 1933 controversy in Britain over the Tate Gallery's refusal of Picasso's *Profile* (1927), with the time lapse between the two incidents perhaps roughly indicating the relative time differences in the reception of modernist ideas by these two non-continental countries. The unsuccessful bid to buy Picasso's *Profile* for the Tate had the effect of forcing the public to 'face modernism': Marjorie Anne Kirker, 'The Last Years of the Seven and Five Society', Report, Courtauld Institute of Art, London, 1979, p.44. At the beginning of the 1930s there were no works by Picasso at the Tate Gallery.

35. Supporting a later dating for *Sabrina's Garden*, Hannah Ritchie wrote, 'while I was at work at Bridgnorth in 1932 Frances Hodgkins made drawings *further along the river bank*

. . . . It seemed to me that it is a picture done in her studio after a good deal of thinking round the material she gathered on the 1932 visit to that inspiring bit of the riverside in Bridgnorth': letter to Mary Chamot, 6 Aug. 1951, Tate Gallery Archive. 'The original painting of Sabrina's Garden with its 2 wooden figures is, incidentally my favourite of that vintage 1930–40 . . .', FH to Peter Watson (of *Horizon*), 14 Nov. 1941.

36. Robert McDougall Art Gallery, Christchurch. Evans, *Hodgkins*, Pl. 8.

37. Private collection, New Zealand. *Frances Hodgkins, Works from Private Collections*, Pl. 29.

38. The numerous double portraits and works such as *Two Dogs, Two Plates*, etc.

39. FH to Karl Hagedorn, 29 Jan. 1933, Hotel Balear, Ibiza.

40. May Smith: audio tape, 'Frances Hodgkins', Pt. II.

41. FH to Dorothy Selby, 29 Jan. 1933.

42. E.g., *Cat and Dog*, private collection, New Zealand; *Cat and Mousetrap*, private collection, New Zealand; *Siamese Cats*, private collection, New Zealand; *Yudi-y-Moro: Two Dogs*, Dunedin Public Art Gallery.

43. *Phoenician Pottery and Gourds* was exhibited in the thirteenth Seven and Five exhibition, March 1934. *Pottery and Gourds, Ibiza*, Rugby Collection, University of Warwick, is a closely related work. Other watercolours from this group include *Fish and Shells* and *Spanish Pottery*, both British Council. The former, continuing that earlier motif of the twist of drapery, was exhibited (as *Still Life, Fish, Shells*) in the Oct.–Nov. 1933 Lefevre Galleries Hodgkins exhibition, *New Water-colour Drawings, Frances Hodgkins, the Late Work*, p.28; the latter, its misty landscape setting sprouting gigantic arum lilies, was a purchase recommended by Herbert Read for the British Council.

44. The Phoenician pottery of this work's title relates to the artifacts made by the Phoenician colonists of Ibiza. Pottery and vases of many kinds had long been a favourite motif of Hodgkins, particularly over the period 1928/9–1933. The possible symbolic connotations of these objects as signifiers of abundance and of the feminine operate alongside a context for this interest in other artists' practice: classically shaped pitchers and amphorae were a stock motif for the New Classicists; ceramic arts were practised extensively by Picasso and Dufy; the Seven and Five exhibitions frequently included pots by Hodgkins's friend, the ceramic artist W. Staite Murray. Hodgkins's friend in Corfe Castle, Amy Krauss, was a potter; her French colleague Maurice Garnier, with whom she was in contact in 1930, 1931 and again in 1932–3, had a great interest in and wrote on the ceramics of his home region of the Saintonge: McCormick, *Late Attachment*, pp.22-23.

45. Museum of New Zealand. Richard Shone, *The Century of Change: British Painting Since 1900*, London, 1977, Pl. 94.

46. Duncan Macdonald to FH, 20 May 1933.

47. Unit One combined constructivist and surrealist tendencies in British vanguard art. The members were the architects Wells Coates and Colin Lucas, the sculptors Henry Moore and Barbara Hepworth, and the painters Edward Wadsworth, Ben Nicholson, Paul Nash, Edward Burra, John Bigge and John Armstrong. The inclusion of the two women artists, Hepworth and Hodgkins, signalled that Coates's earlier preference for an all-male grouping ('I favour a "Male" group, at any rate for a start': Wells Coates to Paul Nash, 29 Jan. 1933, Tate Gallery Archive) had been relaxed.

48. The invitation: letter from Paul Nash to FH, 13 March 1933, Tate Gallery Archive. The response: May Smith: audio tape, 'Frances Hodgkins', Pt. II. May Smith also recalled FH's surprise: 'I am so much older than they are.'

49. Ben Nicholson, Paul Nash, Frances Hodgkins, Barbara Hepworth, Henry Moore.

50. Paul Nash, Henry Moore, Ben Nicholson, Barbara Hepworth, Edward Burra, John Armstrong, John Bigge, Frances Hodgkins.

51. 2 June 1933.

52. Later, those members of Unit One who practised a consistent abstraction were to be associated with *Circle, International Survey of Constructive Art*, 1937.

53. Paul Nash to FH, 19 Oct. 1933: 'May I send my personal regrets.' Tate Gallery Archive.

54. The *Times* letter included Frances Hodgkins in its list of Unit One artists; Paul Nash, 'Unit One', *Listener*, 5 July 1933, pp.14-16, included FH; a Unit One advertisement included FH in the Oct. 1933 exhibition catalogue, *Art Now*, Mayor Gallery; Herbert Read, 'Unit One', *Architectural Review*, v. 74, Oct. 1933, pp.125-8, discussed FH's work.

55. 'The Centre Party', p.863.

56. *Objective Abstraction* included Ivon Hitchens, Ceri Richards, Graham Bell, Rodrigo Moynihan, Victor Pasmore.

57. FH to Dorothy Selby, 2 May 1933.

58. Ben Nicholson and Barbara Hepworth, for example, had visited France in 1932 and met several major artists, including Picasso and Braque. In 1933 they met Mondrian and were invited to join the Paris-based group of abstract artists, 'Abstraction–Creation'. Europeans Gropius, Gabo and Mondrian stayed in Britain in the thirties (Frances Spalding, *British Art since 1900*, London, 1986, pp.110-2).

59. Benjamin, Selz, Gamboa, Frances and Garnier are mentioned in Jean Selz, 'Benjamin in Ibiza', in Gary Smith, ed., *On Walter Benjamin, Critical Essays and Recollections*, Cambridge, Mass., 1991, p.362; Freund's visit is cited by Michel Guerrin, 'Freund's love affair with photography', *Guardian Weekly*, 19 Jan. 1991, p.15; for Hausmann's life and work on Ibiza, see *Raoul Hausmann Architecte Ibiza 1933–1936*, Fondation pour l'Architecture, Bruxelles, 1990.

60. FH to Dorothy Selby, 2 May 1933.

61. See *Raoul Hausmann*.

62. Dartington Hall Trust, Britain. *Frances Hodgkins, The Late Work*, p.40. Other Ibizan watercolours with architectural motifs include *Almond Tree*, present location not known, which features what is probably the hilltop church of San Miguel de Balansat, Evans, *Hodgkins*, Pl. 7.

63. Auckland City Art Gallery; Dunedin Public Art Gallery, *Frances Hodgkins, A Centenary Exhibition*, Fig. 73. A group of watercolour landscapes were also based on the view from the Dalt Vila. Three survive in New Zealand collections, each from a slightly different vantage point, by now an established practice for Hodgkins: *Terrace Garden, Ibiza*, private collection, New Zealand; *Ibiza — Balearic Islands*, Museum of New Zealand; E. H. McCormick, *Works of Frances Hodgkins in New Zealand*, Auckland, 1954, Pl. 29a; *Courtyard in Ibiza*, University of Auckland Art Collection, *The University of Auckland Art Collection*, Auckland, 1983, illustration inside front cover.

64. Audio tape, 'Frances Hodgkins', Pt II.

65. National Gallery of Canada, Ottawa. Exhibited Feb. 1935, Leicester Galleries, *Paintings and Water-colours by Frances Hodgkins*.

66. Exhibited in *British Art and the Modern Movement 1930–1940*, National Museum of Wales, Cardiff, 1962.

67. E.g., *Ubu Imperator*, 1923, Musée National d'Art Moderne, Centre Georges Pompidou, Paris.

68. The tree-trunk motif in *Poet Resting under a Tree, Spain* is evidently also the subject of *The Tree Stump* (present location not known), listed as 1932 in the St George's Gallery exhibition, *Homage to Frances Hodgkins*, 1949.

69. Shown in the twelfth Seven and Five Society exhibition, Feb. 1933.

70. A strategy in marked contrast to Norman Bryson's notion of a major 'technical curiosity' of the genre (still life): 'its disinclination to portray the world beyond the far edge of the table', Norman Bryson, *Looking at the Overlooked, Four Essays on Still Life Painting*, London, 1990, p.71.

71. FH to Duncan Macdonald, 25 June 1938; FH to Dr. T. J. Honeyman, 6 July 1938. The new contract involved FH producing work exclusively for the Lefevre Galleries, with 'the guarantee of £200 p.a. with percentage'.

72. FH to Dorothy Selby, c.April 1932.

73. John Piper to FH, 4 May 1934: 'I read your letter at the General Meeting of the 7 & 5 last night and everyone expressed regret at your resignation.'

74. FH to Lett Haines, c.11 Dec. 1933: 'I do not wish to identify myself with a movement aimed at benefitting English Art at a moment when such atrocious cruelty & hardship has been shown to Germany's own cultured classes.'

75. FH to Duncan Macdonald, c.15 Feb. 1936: 'It leaves me with a blank outlook as regards my real show with you for I suppose it wont do to have another one, at any rate till the Autumn.'

76. Herbert Read, 'L'Art Contemporain en Angleterre', *Cahiers d'Art*, no.1, 1938, p.34.

77. FH to Duncan Macdonald, 10 July 1934, from Geoffrey Gorer's cottage, The Croft, Bradford-on-Tone, Somerset.

78. *Spanish Shrine* was not shown in the Lefevre Galleries Oct.–Nov. 1933 exhibition. It first appears in FH's Feb. 1935 Leicester Galleries exhibition. Support for a later dating for completion of some Ibizan works is provided by a letter from FH to Miss Miller (secretary, Lefevre Galleries), n.d. 1934, requesting the return of '2 of the Spanish unfinished canvases'.

79. Eric Newton,'Frances Hodgkins', *Listener*, 2 Oct. 1941, p.473.

80. *Composition*, on loan to the Scottish National Gallery of Modern Art, Edinburgh, is a related work using the motif of the ostrich feather.

81. The same ornament appears in *Christmas Tree*, usually dated c.1945, private collection, New York.

82. Michael Dunn, *A Concise History of New Zealand Painting*, Sydney, 1991, Pl. 21. *Still Life*'s cut melons, jugs and grapes are shared by the St Tropez and Ibizan works, but the looser paint and piled-up effect, with the vase silhouetted against its island of table and drapery, have important similarities with *Spanish Shrine* and *Decorative Motif*.

83. FH to Rée Gorer (Geoffrey Gorer's mother), 7 Dec. 1935.

84. FH to Duncan Macdonald, c.15 Feb. 1936.

85. FH to Duncan Macdonald, 23 May 1936.

86. *Pumpkins and Pimenti* was probably *Still Life*, no.5 in the 1937 Oct.–Nov. Leicester Galleries exhibition. *Marrow* was probably *Marrow and Peppers, Tossa* in the same exhibition. It was selected by Kenneth Clark for the 1939 New York World Fair with *Still Life* (probably *Pumpkins and Pimenti*).

87. *Pumpkins and Pimenti* was exhibited (as *Still Life*, no. 13, with *Solva*, no. 14) in the London Gallery's group exhibition with a surrealist emphasis: *Living Art in England*, 18 Jan.–11 Feb. 1939, catalogue: *London Bulletin*, no.8–9, Jan.–Feb. 1939, p.57.

88. It is almost identical in composition with *Ruins, Cadaques* (private collection, New Zealand), shown in the 1937 Oct.–Nov. Leicester Galleries exhibition.

89. Private collection, UK

90. The titles of the two gouaches demonstrate the crucial role of colour for the works' meaning: *Spanish Landscape in Orange, Brown and Green* and *Spanish Landscape with Stooks in Grey and Pink*, both private collection, on loan to the Scottish National Gallery of Modern Art.

91. Auctioned Sothebys, 13 May 1992; Evans, *Hodgkins*, Pl. 15. Myfanwy Piper, 'The Life and Art of Frances Hodgkins', *Listener*, 21 Nov. 1946, p.705.

92. Robert McDougall Art Gallery, Christchurch. The 'River' returning is mentioned in a letter from FH to Dorothy Selby, c.Nov. 1935 and again FH to Rée Gorer, 7 Dec. 1935: 'The River has come back bringing new life to the village —'.

93. Henri Matisse, 'Modernism and Tradition', *Studio*, Jan.–June 1935, p.238.

94. FH to Duncan Macdonald, c.15 Feb 1936. FH later recommended a Picasso exhibition to Dorothy Selby: 24 June 1942.

95. Robert McDougall Art Gallery, Christchurch.

96. Museum of New Zealand.

97. Scottish National Gallery of Modern Art, Edinburgh. *Frances Hodgkins — The Late Work*, p.30.

98. Tate Gallery, London.

99. FH to Duncan Macdonald, c.12 Nov. 1936.

100. Private collection, UK, on loan to the Scottish National Gallery of Modern Art. *House by a Stream* was a dated gift from the artist — 1937 — so probably painted on the 1936 visit.

101. Auckland City Art Gallery.

102. Private collection, UK, on loan to the Scottish National Gallery of Modern Art. *The Calf*'s dimensions are similar to those of *The Cow*, listed in Howell as collection Amy Krauss, c.1938, shown in *An Exhibition of Pictures*, sponsored by the Isle of Purbeck Arts Club, 1948, no. 39.

103. Also titled *Middle Hill, Solva*. Auctioned Sothebys, May 1988. Probably one of the 'two square Welsh landscapes — painted this Spring' which FH suggests for a group exhibition at Agnews organised by Duncan Grant. FH to Duncan Macdonald, 20 May 1937.

104. Private collection, New Zealand.

105. Present location not known. John Piper, 'Frances Hodgkins', *Horizon*, vol. 4, no. 24, Dec. 1941, illustration opp. p.414; also illustrated in John Piper, *British Romantic Artists*, London, 1942, 2nd imp. 1946, opp. p.40 and in *Penguin New Writing*, 28, July 1946, between p.96 and p.97. Although *Llangenith College Farm* is dated 1940 in *Horizon*, its connections with the gouaches of 1936 and 1938 suggest it was painted around this time.

106. Paul Nash, *Outline, An Autobiography and Other Writings*, London, 1949, p.122.

107. David Mellor, *A Paradise Lost, The Neo-Romantic Imagination in Britain 1935–55*, Barbican Art Gallery, 1987.

108. FH to Dorothy Selby, 7 Aug. 1939. Anthropomorphising the landscape/natural objects was a characteristic of Nash's and Sutherland's art. Moore's sculptures associated woman with the landscape.

109. Child art was featured in various publications from the 1920s to the 1940s. Roger Fry championed it. There were numerous exhibitions of children's art, including, around this time, *Paintings by Children at Langford Grove*, Zwemmers, 1938. The sculptor, Mary Spencer Watson, took FH to view a class exhibition at the Old Malt House Preparatory School, Dorset (Mary Spencer Watson to author, 1992). As cited in '1914–1930. The Decisive Years', note 64, FH recommended R. R. Tomlinson's book, *Children as Artists*.

110. Myfanwy Evans, ed., *The Painter's Object*, London, 1937, p.122.

111. Earlier in the thirties Nash had stayed at Swanage and from these two points set out on the many exploratory journeys around Dorset which culminated in the informative and idiosyncratic *Shell Guide to Dorset* (1936).

112. Kitty West (the painter Katharine Church) to author, 1992.

113. FH to Duncan Macdonald, 20 Sept. 1937.

114. FH to Alex. Reid, 19 Oct. 1937.

115. Museum of New Zealand.

116. *The Colonel's House* is linked to Spain or France in McKinnon, *Frances Hodgkins*, cat.no. 21. However, Kitty West identifies the house as a neighbouring house at Quarry Farm that the Wests called 'the Colonel's house'. *Entrance to a Tunnel*, Manchester City Art Gallery, is stylistically related and probably refers (according to Kitty West) to the tunnel under the road at Quarry Farm. Letter to author, 23 June 1992.

117. *Axis*, 8, Early Winter 1937, pp.4-9.

118. Ministry of Foreign Affairs & Trade, New Zealand. McKinnon, *Frances Hodgkins*, cat. no. 26.

119. Present location not known. Ex-Leicester Galleries. Howell, *Frances Hodgkins*, Pl. IV, p.50.

120. Evans, *Hodgkins*, p.17.

121. Tate Gallery Archive, 846.33, untitled.

122. St Paul's School, London; Tate Gallery, London.

123. Paul Nash to Lance Sieveking, 3 May 1937, quoted in *Art in Britain 1930–40 Centred around Axis, Circle, Unit One*, Marlborough Fine Art, London, March–April 1965, p.59. There is also a surrealist dimension to FH's presentation of these empty containers in the landscape: they function a little like the 'Found Objects' (bricks, pipe etc.) in the exhibition *Surrealist Objects and Poems*, Nov. 1937, London Gallery, and can also be associated with Conroy Maddox's notion of 'the peculiar poetry of an object that has ceased to function', 'The Object in Surrealism', *London Bulletin*, Nos 18-22, June 1940.

124. The aim of Contemporary Lithographs Ltd was 'to introduce the work of living artists to the general public *in the original*' and it has been described as a 'landmark in British print publishing in the twentieth century': Anthony Griffiths, 'Contemporary Lithographs Ltd', *Print Quarterly*, vol. viii, no. 4, Dec 1991, p.400. While published with others in March 1938, *Arrangement of Jugs* appeared with the whole series in a September–October show at the Leicester Galleries.

125. Griffiths, 'Contemporary Lithographs Ltd', Pl. 227.

126. *Dairy Farm*'s present location is not known: Evans, *Hodgkins*, Pl. 28; the gouache *Houses and Outhouses, Purbeck* is illustrated in John Piper, 'Frances Hodgkins', *Horizon*, vol. 4, no. 24, Dec. 1941, opp. p.415.

127. Evans, *Hodgkins*, p.17.

128. John Piper, *Spectator*, 17 Oct. 1941.

129. FH to W. Hodgkins, 15 Oct. 1938.

130. FH to W. Hodgkins, 28 Sept. 1938.

131. FH to Dorothy Selby, 7 Aug. 1939.

132. Private collection, New Zealand; private collection, New Zealand; Dunedin Public Art Gallery.

133. Kitty West (Katharine Church) to author, May 1992. The Wests were at Quarry Farm in 1936–7 and Kitty West's distinct memory of the preparatory watercolour and pencil drawing being produced at Chisbury Manor, Berkshire at the outbreak of war in 1939 makes a persuasive case for the later dating of 1939. See commentary to Pl. 24.

134. This also foreshadows future events: the couple later separated.

135. FH to A. Reid, 12 Nov. 1939.

136. FH to Duncan Macdonald, 11 April 1943.

137. The other artists were Duncan Grant, Glyn Philpot, Alfred Munnings, Edward Wadsworth and Frank Dobson.

138. See pp. 172–4 for list of solo exhibitions and important group exhibitions.

139. Although based at Corfe Castle, FH visited Geoffrey Gorer's cottage The Croft, Somerset, May 1940, settling back at Corfe by September 1941; Henley-on-Thames, where she was taken seriously ill and Berkshire, where she convalesced, in the summer of 1941; a fruitful period in Wales in the autumn of 1942; Cerne Abbas in September 1943 and finally some short visits to Somerset in the early months of 1946, the year before she died.

140. Laing Art Gallery, Newcastle-upon-Tyne.

141. There is a parallel here with the occasionally less than rigorous selection of work in some recent exhibitions of Hodgkins's paintings. Apart from the *Frances Hodgkins Centenary Exhibition* of 1969, no recent exhibitions have combined a consistently high standard of work with full representation from *both* major sources of Hodgkins's work: New Zealand and Britain.

142. See especially John Piper, 'Lost, A Valuable Object', in *The Painter's Object*, London, 1937, pp.68-73. In the concluding paragraph Piper claims 'it will be a good thing to get back to the tree in the field'.

143. John Piper, 'Frances Hodgkins', *Horizon*, Dec. 1941, pp.413-6.

144. Craxton and Minton were both admirers of Hodgkins's work: Craxton initially through his art teacher, a close friend

of Hodgkins's (see Malcolm Yorke, *The Spirit of Place, Nine Neo-Romantic Artists and their Times*, London, 1988, p.300); and Minton through gallery visits c.1939–40, 'admiring the work of Frances Hodgkins, John Piper, Paul Nash and Henry Moore' (see Frances Spalding, *Dance till the Stars Come Down, A Biography of John Minton*, London, 1991, p.37).

145. *Recent Paintings by Francis Bacon, Frances Hodgkins, Henry Moore, Matthew Smith, Graham Sutherland*, April 1945, Lefevre Galleries.

146. John Piper to FH, c.Sept. 1941.

147. Anthony West brings Hodgkins into focus as an important colleague of Piper's in terms of shared interests and influence: *John Piper*, London, 1979, pp.87-88.

148. Tate Gallery Archive, 846.33.

149. Auckland City Art Gallery.

150. Private collection, New Zealand. The oil *Farmyard, Essex*, private collection, New Zealand, is based on the same farm machinery and setting.

151. Private collection, New Zealand.

152. Private collection, New Zealand.

153. Private collection, UK. Spalding, *Dance till the Stars Come Down*, Pl. III.

154. E.g. Robert Colquhoun's *Church Lench*, 1941, Arts Council of Great Britain.

155. *Locomotive in a Forest*, *Minotaure*, no.10, 3rd series, 1937, p.20.

156. *London Bulletin*, 4-5, July 1938.

157. *London Bulletin*, 3, June 1938, pp.22, 27-28. *London Bulletin*, 6, Oct. 1938, p.23, illustrated Jennings's *The Locomotive*, positioned similarly to Hodgkins's *Landscape with Engine* and *Motor Transport*.

158. The oval, animate form of the fruit-stand is reminiscent of Graham Sutherland's or even Ceri Richard's organic, ovoid forms of the forties. A similar object appears in a gouache still-life sketch by Hodgkins, which also explores the possibilities of the window-pane grid in a related manner: Tate Gallery Archive, 846.7.

159. The description is from Graham Bell, 'Art in the "Island Fortress", a review of Contemporary British Painting', *Studio*, 120, 1940, p.105: 'Francis [*sic*] Hodgkins is another artist . . . whose obscurities have something in common with poetry. Here it is the mood of Swinburne that is evoked . . . . It is a strange art, a blend of the decorative and the visionary. If we turn from this to the work of Ben Nicholson we must cross from romantic valley to the classical upland . . .'.

160. Cecil Higgins Art Gallery, Bedford; *Frances Hodgkins*, Centenary Exhibition catalogue, Fig. 92.
Present location not known; Evans, *Hodgkins*, Pl. 23.

161. Private collection, UK. Agar first met Nash in 1935 in Dorset and subsequently collaborated with him on a number of projects: Eileen Agar, in collaboration with Andrew Lambirth, *A Look at My Life*, London, 1988, pp.108-113.
Private collection, UK. Andrew Causey, *Paul Nash*, Oxford, 1980, Pl. 210. *Swan Song* was illustrated in *Axis* (ed. Myfanwy Evans), vol. 8, 1937, p.11.

162. FH to Eardley Knollys, 31 Oct. 1942. Eardley Knollys had been a co-director of the Storran Gallery in 1935–39. He was working for the National Trust when FH met him in Wales.

163. Besides the works discussed, the exhibition also included works such as *Welsh Emblem*, private collection, New Zealand; *Kitchen Range*, private collection, New Zealand; *Barn Interior*, Museum of New Zealand; *Green Valley, Carmarthenshire*, Dunedin Public Art Gallery; *Walled Garden with Convolvulus*, private collection, New Zealand (Pl. 36); *Broken Tractor*, Tate Gallery, London (Fig. 56).

164. Dunedin Public Art Gallery.

165. Auckland City Art Gallery.

166. *Corfe Castle from the Heath*, Fig. 5. 'Corfe alone is implaccable. No mood of nature or human intrusion can affect that terrific personality. It dominates the country like a calvary, a symbol never less than its history.' Paul Nash, *Shell Guide to Dorset*, n.d. but 1936, p.1.

167. Christopher Perkins, *Corfe Castle*, private collection, New Zealand. Roger Blackley brought this work to my attention.

168. *The New Rick* can possibly be connected with summer 1942 at Corfe, when FH wrote of 'working out of doors doing some hay making scenes'. FH to Isabel Field, 23 July 1942.

169. John Betjeman, *John Piper* (Penguin Modern Painters), Harmondsworth, 1944, Pl. 31.

170. Dunedin Public Art Gallery.

171. National Gallery of Victoria, Melbourne.

172. Art Gallery of New South Wales, Sydney.

173. FH to Myfanwy Evans, c.March 1943.

174. Exhibited Feb. 1935 in *Paintings and Water-colours by Frances Hodgkins*, Leicester Galleries.

175. *The Weir*, Glasgow Art Gallery and Museum; *The Weir*, Dunedin Public Art Gallery; *The Weir*, private collection, on loan to the Scottish National Gallery of Modern Art. These probably all derive from the weir at Bradford-on-Tone, Somerset, where Frances Hodgkins stayed intermittently in Geoffrey Gorer's cottage over these years and certain features of the view in the paintings are still apparent at that location; the Dunedin version was exhibited in 1948 as *Geoffrey's Weir*: Exhibition of Pictures sponsored by the Isle of Purbeck Arts Club, no. 93.

176. FH to Dorothy Selby, 16 Oct. 1943.

177. Tate Gallery, London.

178. Present location not known. Betjeman, *Piper*, Pl. 9.

179. FH to Dorothy Selby, 26 June 1942.

180. FH to Jane Saunders, c.30 June 1942. Piper, Moore and Sutherland were in stable relationships (as Nash had been), with Sutherland's wife described as 'the greatest human inspiration and encouragement of his career': Edward Sackville-West, *Graham Sutherland*, The Penguin Modern Painters, Harmondsworth, 1943, p.4. As noted by Malcolm Yorke, *The Spirit of Place*, p.157: 'Nash, Piper and Sutherland each had a strong-minded and supportive wife. They also had settled home lives and little need to play the bohemian artist —'. The bohemian life-style was associated with most of the younger, predominantly male, gay, neo-romantics. Frances Hodgkins, through gender, age and marital status, benefited from neither of these supportive contexts for inter-personal relationships.

181. FH to Jane Saunders, 3 May 1944.

182. FH to Eardley Knollys, 23 Nov. 1944.

183. FH to Jane Saunders, 3 May 1945.

184. *Recent Paintings by Francis Bacon, Frances Hodgkins, Henry Moore, Graham Sutherland*.

185. FH to Eardley Knollys, 28 May 1945.

186. FH to Myfanwy Piper, 12 June 1945.

187. *Quelques Contemporains Anglais* included Edward Bawden, Robert Colquhoun, David Jones, Henry Moore, Paul Nash, John Piper, Graham Sutherland, John Tunnard.

188. Museum of New Zealand. Linda Gill, ed., *Letters of Frances Hodgkins*, Auckland, 1993, Pl. 12.

189. David Mellor, *A Paradise Lost*, p.44.

190. FH to Eardley Knollys, 5 Feb. 1946.

191. FH to Eardley Knollys, 6 Feb. 1946, where the artist describes ideas for an exhibition of works 1930–45 from Mrs (Rée) Gorer's collection. The November retrospective at Lefevre's quite possibly derived from this.

192. FH to Dorothy Selby, 10 June 1946.

193. Private collection, UK. McKinnon, *Frances Hodgkins*, Pl. 31.
Private collection, UK. McKinnon, *Frances Hodgkins*, Pl. 32.

194. Robert McDougall Art Gallery, Christchurch.

195. Present location not known. Evans, *Hodgkins*, Pl. 31.

196. Peter Davis, *Modern Paintings and Drawings from the Collection of Dr. Peter Davis*, Scottish National Gallery of Modern Art, 18 April–17 May, 1964, introd. P. H. Davis, n.p. His collection included a number of paintings by FH.

197. FH to John Piper, c.Sept. 1941.

COLOUR PLATES

The Girl with the Flaxen Hair

1893
WATERCOLOUR, 485 x 381mm
SIGNED BRUSHPOINT LOWER RIGHT: F.H. '93
MUSEUM OF NEW ZEALAND, TE PAPA TONGAREWA

Girolamo Pieri Nerli, *Ruby*, c.1897
Oil on canvas, 480 x 330mm
Private collection

Frances Hodgkins painted this study in 1893, a year when she was taking lessons from the Italian artist Girolamo Pieri Nerli (1860–1926). Her father was an admirer of Nerli's works, several of which he owned. He too went to classes conducted by Nerli at that time. Because Nerli was a skilled portrait and figure painter his services as a teacher were much in demand in Dunedin.

The painting is comparable in its intimacy with Nerli's studies of young girls and women. Hodgkins has shown the girl's face close up without distracting background detail. Her watercolour technique has the casual effect produced by allowing the paint to run, wet on wet, down the paper in a manner similar to Nerli's use of watercolour. In the hair she has lifted some of the paint with a sponge to suggest highlights. In academic terms the head is drawn weakly, with the nose, for example, out of alignment with the lips and the eyes not adjusted to the curve of the face. Despite these flaws, Hodgkins has captured the innocent charm of the girl who also served as a model in other works of that year, such as *A Goose Girl* (private collection). Comparatively Nerli's heads of young girls seem to be more sensuous and knowing. The positioning of the head against the white surface of the paper adds to the informality of relationship between viewer and sitter. In choosing to paint this subject Hodgkins showed her independence from the preference for landscape shown by her father and sister, Isabel.

Mountain Scene

1897
WATERCOLOUR, 191 x 315mm
SIGNED BRUSHPOINT LOWER RIGHT: F.H. '97
HOCKEN LIBRARY, DUNEDIN

Unlike her father, Frances Hodgkins rarely painted alpine landscapes. When she did, as in *Mountain Scene*, the emphasis is quite different from her father's more conventional presentation, as in *The Southern Alps of New Zealand: An Evening Glow*, 1885. In contrast with the formula of a detailed, dark foreground with trees to frame the view, Frances left the foreground imprecise and open. The effect is to give the sketch a more modern feel by making it seem less artificial and contrived. In technique the watercolour has the direct, improvised quality of wet-on-wet painting she had learnt from Nerli. James McLachlan Nairn (1859–1904), the Scottish painter then based in Wellington, was one of the few landscapists to use this approach in watercolour at that time. Hodgkins allows blobs and runs of colour to have some freedom to shape themselves as if by accident on the paper. She uses calligraphic strokes in the foreground to suggest grass and plants rather than describe them exactly. In some places the white of the paper enters the drawing to indicate light and reflections on the snow and river water. The tilting of the imagery up the picture plane shows a consciousness of the surface and of two-dimensional design suggesting her debt to Nerli and possibly to Japanese prints. There is so little topographical emphasis in the work that there has been doubt expressed about its location. It is now thought to be a view of the Dart River.

William Mathew Hodgkins, *The Southern Alps of New Zealand: An Evening Glow*, 1885
Watercolour, 564 x 984mm
Dunedin Public Art Gallery

Orange Sellers, Tangier

1903
WATERCOLOUR, 510 x 395mm
SIGNED BRUSHPOINT LOWER RIGHT: F.H. 03
THEOMIN GALLERY, OLVESTON, DUNEDIN

When Frances Hodgkins visited Morocco in the winter of 1902–03 with her friend Mrs Ashington she was given a commission to paint this watercolour by Mr David Theomin, a wealthy Dunedin businessman. She had completed it by March 1903 and refers to it in a letter of that time to Dorothy Kate Richmond. 'I wish I could have sent you my large picture of the market — it is the apple or rather the onion of my eye — much the same sort of subject a jumble of onions melons & oranges. It is going tomorrow to Mr Theomin — I am going to eschew vegetables after this with a comfortable feeling I have done my duty by them . . . . ' In choosing to visit Morocco, Hodgkins was following in the footsteps of many major artists, such as Delacroix. Also, she was well aware of the colourful watercolours of exotic subjects painted by Frank Brangwyn (1867–1956) and Arthur Melville (1855–1904). Like Melville Hodgkins has used blobs of colour to suggest the fall of strong sunlight on the oranges and onions in the foreground. She has exaggerated their colours by reducing tonal modelling. To give the effect of strong sunlight, Hodgkins has indicated the figures and architecture by sketchy blue-mauve shadows. This helps to give a convincing feeling of glare, as if the forms are corroded by the sun's heat.

Ayesha

1904
WATERCOLOUR, 750 x 495mm
SIGNED WITH MONOGRAM AND DATED BRUSHPOINT
LOWER RIGHT: F.H. 1904
DUNEDIN PUBLIC ART GALLERY

*A*yesha was painted in Wellington from a posed model. In this elaborate watercolour Hodgkins has tried to use the colourful headscarf and costume, as well as the musical instrument and title to suggest an exotic location. She had been in Morocco not long before and we know that she painted a number of Moroccan subjects in Wellington based on studies made on the spot. In this work she pursues the richer, fuller colour effects the Moroccan experience had inspired. Although the work has recently been criticised for being contrived, it was bought by the Dunedin Public Art Gallery in 1904 for the rather high price of £21. This indicates that the ambition and technical confidence that *Ayesha* displays did not go unnoticed at the time. It was normal practice for artists in Britain and France to pose models in the studio in this way. An obvious precedent for this kind of subject can be found in the figure studies of Camille Corot. Hodgkins also painted some Dutch subjects in Wellington at about the same time. In retrospect it is possible to see that she found it difficult to adjust to living in New Zealand after her exciting years overseas. *Ayesha* allowed her an escape from the tedium of Wellington life. Soon she was to travel to Rotorua to paint the Maori, more evidence of her need for stimulus outside that which the capital had to offer.

Red Sails

1906
WATERCOLOUR, 686 x 448mm
SIGNED WITH MONOGRAM AND DATED BRUSHPOINT
LOWER RIGHT: F.H. 1906
DUNEDIN PUBLIC ART GALLERY

Frank Brangwyn, *Chioggia*
Oil on canvas, 620 x 750mm
Dunedin Public Art Gallery

Red Sails was exhibited at the Otago Art Society annual exhibition in 1906, with the title *The Orange Sail*. It was probably painted at Chioggia, a fishing port near Venice where Hodgkins was based for a time in June 1906. In a letter to her mother dated that month she wrote, 'The red and yellow sails of course are the feature of Chioggia, otherwise it would be quite uninteresting' — she had found the spectacle of Venice somewhat overpowering and not entirely adapted to her approach. Chioggia, by contrast, suited her purposes better.

Fishing boats in harbour were a popular subject for *plein air* painters in Britain and France. Newlyn artists like Norman Garstin (1847–1926) painted at fishing villages in France, as did the expatriate New Zealand artist Sydney Lough Thompson (1877–1973), who specialised in scenes of the sardine fleet at Concarneau. Hodgkins would also have been aware of the works of Sir Frank Brangwyn (1867–1956), who sometimes depicted boats and sails in a colourful and decorative manner. In fact, Hodgkins's watercolour recalls Brangwyn in the way she has positioned the viewer seemingly below the subject, so that the sails and masts rise dramatically above the viewer with an effect of grandeur. Throughout the work Hodgkins has achieved an effect of breadth and immediacy. It shows her growing confidence as an outdoors painter.

97

The Window Seat

1907
WATERCOLOUR, 645 x 515mm
SIGNED BRUSHPOINT LOWER RIGHT: F. HODGKINS
ART GALLERY OF NEW SOUTH WALES

The Window Seat was bought from Hodgkins's solo exhibition at Anthony Hordern's Gallery, Sydney, in 1913. It had been awarded a joint first prize at the Franco-British Exhibition in the Australian Women Artists' section in 1908. The two women depicted are Maud and Una Nickalls, English friends and supporters of Hodgkins. She was staying with them at their country house, Wispers, at Stedham, Sussex, when she painted the work. She refers to the painting in a letter to her mother dated 19 December 1907: 'Did I tell you I painted a portrait of Maud & Una at Wispers — in evening dress pale mauve & blue, in the window seat by lamp light & faintest moonlight — a very good thing I say . . .'.

Hodgkins here shows a sensitive study of two women engaged in intimate conversation. The subdued and unusual lighting effects can be found in quite a few works of this period. There is perhaps a recollection of the *Intimiste* interiors of French painters such as Vuillard whose works she could have seen in Paris. Her technique here has become less direct and involves layers of washes and lifting of paint by sponging out to suggest the softness and flicker of lamplight. There is considerable colouristic sensitivity in the contrast between the mauve tints and the cool blue of the sky. This was the first work of hers to be acquired by an institution outside New Zealand.

The Bridge

c.1907
WATERCOLOUR, 410 x 475mm
SIGNED AND DATED LOWER RIGHT: F. HODGKINS' 07?
PRIVATE COLLECTION

Norman Garstin, *Purple and Gold, Canal Scene*
Watercolour, 535 x 370mm
Theomin Gallery, Olveston, Dunedin

Frances Hodgkins spent quite a lot of time in Holland during 1907. It was a popular country for sketching classes of the kind Hodgkins herself took, as did her friend Norman Garstin. In fact, Garstin made a watercolour not dissimilar to this in composition now in the Theomin Collection, Olveston, Dunedin. Part of the appeal of Holland, as of Brittany, was the opportunity to paint figures in distinctive regional costume. The group of children in traditional Dutch costume at the bridge shows Hodgkins's response to this kind of picturesque detail. She admired the works of artists such as Lucien Simon or Stanhope Forbes, who often depicted village life where traditional values and costumes persisted. The painting is pitched in a low key suggestive of an evening light where visibility is reduced and forms begin to merge together and lose their sharpness. She made quite a few watercolours with this kind of lighting in Holland and also at Concarneau. Her receptivity to light effects reveals her continuing interest in impressionistic concerns and observation from nature. The date of this work is partly obscured but is probably 1907.

Dordrecht

c.1908
WATERCOLOUR, 680 x 455mm
SIGNED BRUSHPOINT LOWER RIGHT: F. HODGKINS
DUNEDIN PUBLIC ART GALLERY

This powerful watercolour showing the town of Dordrecht, Holland, with an effect of grey, wet weather, was purchased from the artist's exhibition at the Dunedin Public Art Gallery in 1913. Hodgkins was in Dordrecht in December 1907 and stayed there until March the following year. The weather was extremely cold and bleak, forcing her to paint indoors looking out the window for her subjects, as appears to be the case here.

Despite the subdued tonal range, the watercolour has a deep resonant colour which includes an ultramarine blue and umber combination. Hodgkins has introduced children into the foreground whose actions and reflections in the wet paving add to the interest of the subject. The subdued palette of this work recalls some of the Newlyn painters, especially her friend Norman Garstin, who had painted urban subjects of this type with wet weather and reflections. Hodgkins's approach, though, is freer and more impressionistic. Her feeling for the architecture of the town is more pronounced here than before and may be a response to the architectural dimension of Frank Brangwyn or John Singer Sargent's painting, with which she was familiar. She specifically mentioned her admiration for the nineteenth-century Dutch painters Anton Mauve (1838–88) and the Maris brothers Willem and Jacob at this time.

Summer

c.1912
WATERCOLOUR AND CHARCOAL, 586 x 498mm
SIGNED BRUSHPOINT LOWER RIGHT: F. HODGKINS
DUNEDIN PUBLIC ART GALLERY

This appealing study of childhood was purchased by public subscription from the art-ist's exhibition at the Dunedin Public Art Gallery in 1913. The outdoor setting with an effect of sunlight dappling over the figures of the nursemaid at left, the baby at the centre and the young girl at the right, shows her continuing interest in Impressionism. In this work Hodgkins has evolved a style of painting with long strokes and streaks of paint overlaid by some calligraphic lines which suggest movement and the quiver of light falling through the leaves of the overhead trees. The composition is focused on the baby's head, which is the centre of the nurse's and girl's attention. Their heads are less distinctly rendered and are in shadow, so that they become subordinate to the infant. Subjects of this nature are common in French Impressionist painting, especially in the works of major women artists such as Mary Cassatt. Hodgkins was also familiar with the works of French contemporary artists like Lucien Simon who had painted scenes of mothers with babies in intimate domestic situations. In Hodgkins's own painting there is an ongoing interest in the depiction of women and children during these years. She seems to celebrate the pleasures and confidences of women as a theme in her painting. There is probably also a response to the works of the French *Intimiste* painters Vuillard and Bonnard in this and related watercolours. In their paintings the small, everyday incidents of domestic life become subjects of consequence, as happens in Hodgkins's works.

At the Window

c.1912

WATERCOLOUR, 653 x 628mm

SIGNED BRUSHPOINT LOWER RIGHT: F. HODGKINS

ART GALLERY OF SOUTH AUSTRALIA, ADELAIDE

In this watercolour, purchased by the Art Gallery of South Australia in 1913, Hodgkins introduces a theme which was to occupy her for many years, a still life set in front of an open window with a view into the landscape or garden beyond. Here the treatment is very much centred on the play of light and shadow in an Impressionist manner. She employs the long, streaky strokes of paint, typical of this period, to convey light and movement as well as draw the imagery together. There is a conscious contrast of the curving shapes of the tabletop and plates with the rectangular panes of the windows of the French doors. The young woman is seated at the intersection between indoors and outdoors, providing the viewer with an added interest at this point.

It is easy to find prototypes for this kind of usage in French painting of the period, for example in the works of Pierre Bonnard. Hodgkins greatly enjoyed the simple things in life and especially the warmth of the sun. This small image captures perfectly the mood of optimism and buoyancy in her work done in France during her highly successful years before her return to New Zealand in 1912–13. Such works bring her Impressionistic paintings to a high point in quality before she changed direction.

Loveday and Anne

1916
OIL ON CANVAS, 670 x 670mm
SIGNED BOTTOM LEFT: F. HODGKINS
TATE GALLERY, LONDON

Frances Hodgkins described *Loveday and Anne* as her earliest oil painting in a 1945 letter, written shortly after it entered the Tate Collection. It was carried out at St Ives in early 1916, just in time to be included in the February 1916 exhibition of the National Portrait Society. The picture has a spontaneous and lively appearance, conveying an intimate domesticity quite removed from more formal portraiture. In this sense it is nearer to the work of French *Intimiste* painters such as Bonnard than to comparable English painting. Although in oils, the painting technique remains close to that of her contemporary watercolours. Hodgkins uses a very dilute oil paint, which she lets run and merge like watercolour. It is applied over a thin white ground, so uneven that in several places the bare canvas appears. She handles the paint in a free and sketchy style, creating different light effects through the use of bright, pure colours. There is very little modelling of form; the colours, applied in a single layer, have no real tonal range and the brush marks are clearly visible, contributing to the fresh and spontaneous feeling of the work. The lively stripes and checks further enhance the decorative treatment of colour. Hodgkins was quite prepared to modify the painting during the process of execution, and she seems to have wiped out and repainted the head of the woman on the left, whose arm is also very cursorily treated.

Mr and Mrs Moffat Lindner and Hope

1916
TEMPERA ON LINEN, 2000 x 1022mm
SIGNED BOTTOM RIGHT: F. HODGKINS
DUNEDIN PUBLIC ART GALLERY

Painted at St Ives in 1916, this is the largest of Frances Hodgkins's surviving paintings and one of her best documented works. First exhibited in February 1916 at the National Portrait Society, the painting was described by Hodgkins in a letter to her mother of January that year, while it was still being executed:

> Mr Lindner & his little girl Hope are posing for me against his great Studio window — open, with the wind tossing her brown hair, the sea beyond. They wear such jolly tweed clothes, he snuff coat, check waistcoat & orange tie with black spots — & his jolly pink face & white curls — same colouring as Father — you may remember he always reminds me of him, a younger edition — very dapper. Hope in grey tweed, berry red buttons & bright blue Tam, white stockings. This is a 4ft.x3ft. canvas in oil — and so far it shapes well.

This description shows that Hodgkins made a number of important changes during the course of the painting's execution. The most significant was the introduction of Mrs Lindner, not mentioned in the letter. She seems partly to be painted over Hope, and her presence gives a more informal quality to the figure group. The other major change was to Hope's clothing — perhaps to make a greater contrast with her father. The tempera paint is thinly applied over a very uneven white gesso ground. In places, such as under the figure of Mrs Lindner, the gesso is heavily built up; elsewhere, as at the top of the painting, the bare canvas reappears. Hodgkins may have used the gesso to cover earlier applications of paint while she progressively changed the picture. Such modifications, also seen in *Loveday and Anne*, formed part of her current practice. The tempera paint is similar to watercolour in appearance; in some places it is brushed on quite vigorously, in others the ground tends to absorb the pigment completely and no brush marks can be seen.

Moffat Lindner was a St Ives artist, a friend of Hodgkins's who encouraged her work. He also owned *Loveday and Anne* as well as paintings by Wilson Steer and Sickert.

Belgian Refugees

c.1916
OIL AND TEMPERA ON CANVAS, 710 x 800mm
SIGNED BOTTOM RIGHT: F. HODGKINS
ROBERT MCDOUGALL ART GALLERY, CHRISTCHURCH

Probably identical with the painting *Unshatterable*, exhibited in 1916 at the International Society, this is a rare example of a propagandistic subject from among Hodgkins's wartime paintings. In her rendition of a piled-up figure group, boldly outlined against a stormy sky, she is clearly influenced by the British painter, Frank Brangwyn, who treated the theme in a recruiting poster for the London Underground. The figure group is quite simplified with a greater unity than in her previous work. But, unlike Brangwyn's, it is composed only of women and children. During the war Hodgkins often painted ordinary working-class people and she showed great sympathy for children as subjects. However, there are also reminders here of the Madonna and Child and Holy Family paintings found in Renaissance art, which Hodgkins could have seen on her 1914 visit to Italy. *Belgian Refugees* is more subtle in colour than *Mr and Mrs Moffat Lindner and Hope*, and it seems that she deliberately restricted her palette for expressive effect. This is most obvious in the sky, which is quite thickly and vigorously painted in oils. By contrast, the clothing of the figures is mainly rendered in thin oil paint with the addition of some tempera.

Frank Brangwyn, Recruiting poster, 1914

Threshing Scene

c.1919
WATERCOLOUR, 535 x 688mm
SIGNED BOTTOM RIGHT: FRANCES HODGKINS
PRIVATE COLLECTION, AUCKLAND

Threshing in the Cotswolds, c.1919
Watercolour, 491 x 580mm
Dunedin Public Art Gallery

Watercolour continued to be of importance to Hodgkins and during the Great War she painted some of her largest watercolours. Gradually, she moved away from her earlier Impressionist-influenced emphasis on light effects and animated paint surface, towards a more reduced colour and structured composition. *Threshing Scene* is one of a number of such subjects, usually executed in the Cotswolds or at Great Barrington, where she held her summer painting classes. *Threshing in the Cotswolds* is another such work, closely related in style. In both paintings the dramatic diagonal, formed by the belt of the steam threshing machine, is balanced by the rounded forms of the ricks and the jutting elevator. The monochromatic colours are applied thinly and evenly, subordinated to the dominant structure of the composition. The figures, though animated, remain simple neutral shapes and her main interest seems to lie in the farm machinery. This fascination recurs in her landscapes of the Second World War, when the machines are transformed into symbolic and mysterious presences.

Three Children

c.1923–24

OIL ON CANVAS, 560 x 660mm

SIGNED BOTTOM LEFT: FRANCES HODGKINS

PRIVATE COLLECTION, AUCKLAND

This painting was probably executed in the south of France around 1923–24. Originally it was owned by Jane Saunders, a pupil and friend of Hodgkins, and it is also known under the expanded title, *Three Children (French Children)*. Only a small number of paintings have survived from late 1923 to early 1925, when Hodgkins lived in France. She remained in regular contact with Ritchie and Saunders, who both visited the south of France in 1924. Hodgkins at this time was experimenting with her art, as she attempted to introduce a more contemporary idiom, largely under the influence of Cubism. The three children, though Cubist in form, are painted in bright, lively colours and this innovation may be indebted to Matisse, who was based nearby in Nice. *Three Children* introduces a theme which later became of great importance in her work — informal portrait compositions of two or three figures. In this early example the approach is still experimental and, as yet, the formal and psychological relations remain somewhat unresolved.

The Red Cockerel

1924

OIL ON CANVAS, 707 x 914mm

SIGNED BOTTOM RIGHT: FRANCES HODGKINS 1924

DUNEDIN PUBLIC ART GALLERY

André Derain, *Still Life with Dead Game*,
c.1924

Oil, 1320 x 1960mm

Museum of Art, Carnegie Institute,
Pittsburgh

Painted in France, this still life may be the work she exhibited at the 1924 *Salon d'Automne* in Paris under the title *Nature Morte*. The subject of dead game is traditional to French still-life painting and often occurs in the work of the eighteenth-century artist Jean Baptiste Oudry. Usually Cubist still-life paintings do not include dead animals, but the theme had been revived by André Derain, whose *Still Life with Dead Game* of around 1925 is close in colour and treatment to Hodgkins's work. Hodgkins, though still working within a Cubist style, had by now mastered the Cubist treatment of space: the way in which object and space are conceived as a series of interlocking planes, the distinction between figure and ground removed, and different, often contradictory, views combined. She now uses a thicker layering of paint, blending the various parts of the composition together as she applies one colour over another. The central red cockerel is quite identifiable, but the forms of the hanging game to the left become a complex, more abstract pattern. Colour is reduced to a few significant accents — the red head of the cockerel, the blue plants. The overall monochromatic brown-green colour found elsewhere in the painting is indebted to analytic Cubism of the pre-war period.

119

Double Portrait

c.1922–25
OIL ON CANVAS, 610 x 770mm
SIGNED LOWER LEFT: HODGKINS
HOCKEN LIBRARY, DUNEDIN

Hannah Ritchie and Jane Saunders, c.1922
Watercolour, 284 x 380mm
University of Auckland Collection

The sitters in *Double Portrait* are Hannah Ritchie and Jane Saunders, two pupils and friends of Hodgkins who had assisted her financially during the Manchester years, and remained in contact until the end of her life. The painting was probably begun in October 1922, when Hodgkins made a brief visit to Manchester, but it remained unfinished in 1925. In March of that year Hodgkins wrote to Hannah Ritchie from London, 'I have your portrait group with me — it wears well. It needs *so* little to both faces to make it a fine thing — I'll bring it with me to finish it — I bequeath it to you both if you like it *when* finished.' As the letter reveals, the picture arose from Hodgkins's own initiative; it was completed in 1925 and given to Ritchie and Saunders.

An earlier version of the subject in watercolour has a quite different composition. It is not really a portrait group, but the simplification of the figures, linked in a rhythmic pattern, prefigures the later oil. Hodgkins retains the settee from the watercolour, extending her decorative treatment to the women's clothes, which now seem quite fashionable. The sitters' heads are almost abstract — flat, simple shapes — though still recognisable as individual portraits. In its simplification of form and intense colouration, the painting has much in common with the works of Modigliani and Matisse, whose own *Plumed Hat* of around 1919 has the same bright, flat colour.

Lancashire Family

c.1927
OIL ON CANVAS, 685 x 705mm
SIGNED LOWER RIGHT: FRANCES HODGKINS
AUCKLAND CITY ART GALLERY

Boy with a Boat, c.1927
Oil, 545 x 515mm
Dunedin Public Art Gallery

First exhibited in 1927 at the London Group show, *Lancashire Family* was purchased the following year by Hodgkins's friend, Arthur Lett Haines. It was painted towards the end of Hodgkins's stay in Manchester and shows her contemporary fascination with family groups of local mothers and children. The subdued colours, reduced to subtle variations of green and ochre, tend to emphasise the tonal aspect of the group, which is close to her surviving charcoal drawings. Indeed, drawing rather than painting is her dominant concern, and the only strong colour accent is the blue stripe of the boy's toy yacht. The figures are conceived as quite simple forms, unified by the strongly geometric composition. This is most obvious in the zig-zag pattern set up by the figures' hands and the diagonals of the almost square composition. Such an approach is quite classical in feeling and corresponds to the revived neo-classicism of painters such as Picasso and Léger in the 1920s. *Boy with a Boat* is closely related in formal terms, but the colours are now richer and the paint worked in a smoother manner.

Frances Hodgkins

Lancashire Children

c.1927
OIL ON CANVAS, 740 x 610mm
SIGNED LOWER LEFT AND LOWER RIGHT: FRANCES HODGKINS
PRIVATE COLLECTION

*L*ancashire Children was probably painted by Hodgkins in Manchester around the same time as *Lancashire Family*, but in her new, richer painting style. Although she keeps the dominant ochre colouration of *Lancashire Family*, the paint is much more thickly applied: layered and impasted so that the gestural brush marks carry an expressive force. This style becomes increasingly apparent in her works of the late 1920s, such as *A Country Window* and *Still Life in a Landscape.* The children are framed by a window with still-life objects in the foreground, a format that anticipates her still-life landscapes of the 1930s. This was a theme already in use among members of the Seven and Five Society, which she was to join in 1929. The intense blue sky with its striated pattern of clouds also becomes a feature of her later Mediterranean landscapes. Originally the sky extended to the top of the canvas, where the blue paint can still be seen under the brown layer, indicating that this framing device only entered at a late stage of the painting's execution.

The Bridesmaids

1930
OIL ON CANVAS, 737 x 597mm
SIGNED BOTTOM LEFT: FRANCES HODGKINS
AUCKLAND CITY ART GALLERY

*T*he Bridesmaids was owned originally by Lucy Wertheim, a wealthy Manchester art collector, who first met Hodgkins around 1926 and later opened her own picture gallery in London. *Bridesmaids* was one of four Hodgkins paintings included by Wertheim in her inaugural group exhibition of October 1930. Over these years portraiture again became an important part of Hodgkins's production, and *Bridesmaids* is one of her most accomplished double portraits. Hodgkins places the two figures close together in a frontal manner, identically dressed and posed, so that they merge together in outline. The background trellis with its climbing branches sets up a further rhythm which is carried into the sitters' hats and reinforced by lines scratched through the paint surface. Hodgkins continues to use paint thickly but here the application is less laboured and the colour variations more subtle. Indeed, by means of slight modifications to the eyes, mouth, and hand positions of the sitters, Hodgkins is able to characterise them as two quite distinct individuals, calm and self-possessed in feeling.

Two Sisters, c.1928
Pencil, 345 x 532mm
Hocken Library, Dunedin

126

127

The White House

c.1930

OIL ON CANVAS, 635 x 610mm

SIGNED BOTTOM LEFT: FRANCES HODGKINS

ART GALLERY OF NEW SOUTH WALES

Garden View, c.1930

Pencil, 405 x 299mm

Tate Gallery Archive, London

The White House was painted between November 1929 and April 1930, when Hodgkins was based in France. A pencil drawing (Tate Gallery Archive) shows the same house but from the closer viewpoint of an adjoining garden. The house reappears once again in another oil painting (private collection, Wellington), though the foreground still life is replaced by a different group, displayed instead on a round table. The combination of landscape and still life was a frequent theme in Hodgkins's work from the late 1920s onwards. At this date, she often places the still life directly into the landscape, contrasting the still-life objects with their natural surroundings. Here she attempts to integrate two quite different views: the still life seen from above and the distant house with its surrounding trees. The house itself almost disappears behind the giant plants in a curious form of subject reversal. The work is executed in seven to eight thick layers of paint, applied one over the other, sometimes wet on wet, the colours merging. Some changes in the composition are still visible on the paint surface — most notably the reworking of the chair, and the green pot plant, which was introduced at a late stage, painted over a cloth still visible beneath.

Berries and Laurel

c.1930
OIL ON CANVAS, 640 x 763mm
SIGNED BOTTOM RIGHT: FRANCES HODGKINS
AUCKLAND CITY ART GALLERY

Landscape with Still Life, c.1930
Oil, 635 x 762mm
Art Gallery of South Australia

Still Life, c.1929
Pencil, 378 x 445mm
Tate Gallery, London

Painted around 1930, *Berries and Laurel* was first exhibited in January 1931 at the Seven and Five Society. It is closely related to two almost identical still-life landscapes which show the view from Geoffrey Gorer's cottage at Bradford-on-Tone. Hodgkins stayed there towards the end of 1930 when the three paintings were probably done. All have the same white vase and berries, but arranged in somewhat varied groupings. Hodgkins's usual practice was to make both studies of individual objects and more elaborate compositional drawings in pencil, which she then used as the basis for her oil paintings. In *Landscape with Still Life* still life and landscape are integrated into a unified, continuous space. By contrast, in *Berries and Laurel* the still life dominates the foreground and the landscape is now reduced to a kind of backdrop. The absence of sky heightens this effect and tends to concentrate attention on the central image.

Hodgkins's sense of decorative pattern emerges in the formal transitions between the flowers in their narrow vases and the shapes of the distant trees. All three paintings have a brown–green–blue colour progression with green dominant. This is very characteristic of her English still-life landscapes: as she observed in a letter of 9 July 1930, '. . . anywhere in England is unsympathetic & difficult for an artist — The sea of green everywhere — The red brick — & the stoney paths & the stoney stares of the villagers — Oh Lord!'

Still-Life Landscape

c.1931
WATERCOLOUR, 359 x 471mm
SIGNED BOTTOM RIGHT: FRANCES HODGKINS
PRIVATE COLLECTION, AUCKLAND

Frances Hodgkins also painted many still-life landscapes in watercolour. By contrast to her oils, the still-life objects in these works are less dominant and more integrated into the landscape. When using the more transparent medium of watercolour, Hodgkins treats the picture space as a series of interesting layers. Drawing still remains of major importance in defining the structure of the work and usually she begins by outlining the design lightly in pencil before applying the watercolour paint. On the basis of its similarity to other dated watercolours, this painting was executed in the south of France around 1931.

The still life is suspended above the landscape so that the rhythm of the crockery and fruit is carried into the pattern of fields, trees and houses far below. There is a concentration on detail and a very precise treatment of form in her watercolours of this time.

Still Life in a Landscape, c.1931
Watercolour, 500 x 595mm
Wakefield Art Galleries & Museum

132

Pastorale

1929–30
OIL ON CANVAS, 630 x 730mm
SIGNED BOTTOM LEFT: FRANCES HODGKINS
PRIVATE COLLECTION, AUCKLAND

Pastorale, c.1929–30
Oil, 763 x 635mm
Auckland City Art Gallery

Pastorale is a mountain region in the Alpes Maritimes near St Jeannet where Hodgkins was based in the winter of 1929–30. Another painting with the same title is in the Auckland City Art Gallery, but it shows a quite different view, and the landscape is rendered in a more sombre range of blue-green tones. Another closely related painting is *The Valley Mill* (Art Gallery of Ontario), which represents the same location and where the buildings, trees and mountains are rendered is a similar vibrating manner. Hodgkins's treatment is still quite naturalistic in *Pastorale,* though in places she flattens and softens the forms, often blending together quite different spatial areas to give a fluid rhythm to the work. This effect is enhanced by the decorative marks she applies on the path by the bank and in the river itself, all of which intensify the suggestion of a strongly moving stream.

Wings Over Water

1931–32
OIL ON CANVAS, 710 x 910mm
SIGNED BOTTOM RIGHT: FRANCES HODGKINS
TATE GALLERY, LONDON

Wings Over Water, c.1931
Pencil, 514 x 610mm
Private collection

One of Hodgkins's most elaborate still-life landscapes, *Wings Over Water*, is based on the view from her window at Bodinnick in Cornwall, where she was painting in the winter of 1931–32. However, according to a letter written by Geoffrey Gorer in 1955, the picture was carried out in London and bought directly from Hodgkins's Hampstead studio by his mother, Rée Gorer. Another painting entitled *Wings on Water* has a different view but shares such features as the high horizon and the exotic parrot, and was certainly painted about the same time. There are two preparatory drawings: one in the Museum of New Zealand, Wellington and the other in the Piper Collection. The Piper drawing is the more complex of the two and, while it is close to the finished painting in the Tate, there are some significant modifications. Hodgkins changes the distant view of Fowey to relate it more formally to the interior space and she eliminates the decorative pattern of the wallpaper and tablecloth, probably to enhance the importance of the shells. Whereas in the Leeds painting she makes a direct contrast between the foreground still life and the landscape beyond, in the Tate version the relation between interior and exterior space is much more complex and ambiguous. The still life composed of shells is unique in Hodgkins's work, the elaborate enfolded shapes of the shells suggesting a rhythm which is carried through the whole painting.

Wings on Water, 1931–32
Oil, 686 x 965mm
Leeds City Art Gallery

137

The Green Urn, c. 1931
Oil on board, 630 x 540mm
Private collection, New Zealand

Pablo Picasso, *Still Life with Pitcher and Apples*, 1919
Oil on canvas, 650 x 435mm
Musée Picasso, Paris

Arum Lilies

c.1931
OIL ON BOARD, 640 x 540mm
SIGNED LOWER RIGHT: FRANCES HODGKINS
PRIVATE COLLECTION, UNITED KINGDOM

Set in the lush olive and dark greens of a Mediterranean landscape, the images and arrangement of *Arum Lilies*: lilies, leaves, eggs and jug, all arranged about the central motif of the urn, bring to mind a kind of pagan offering to plenty, to fertility.

Arum Lilies is related to a small group of oils probably painted in the south of France in 1931. They include *Red Jug* (Auckland City Art Gallery), *Cut Melons* (Fig. 38) and *The Green Urn*, with *Arum Lilies* of a similar size and sharing the same support — board — as *Cut Melons* and *Green Urn*. The choice of the urn, together with the more substantial and stately approach to the depiction of objects in these paintings, responds, in a general sense, to the approach of the New Classicists, while both *Arum Lilies* and *The Green Urn* share the specific image of an urn supporting a platter of fruit, a conjunction of motifs explored by one of the major New Classicists, Picasso, in his 1919 *Still Life with Pitcher and Apples*. Hodgkins's paint treatment is, however, looser and more sensuous, her quirky distortions relating to the *faux-naïveté* of the Seven and Five Society, while her very personal colouring sings subtly and resonantly within an effectively limited range of greens, near blacks and creams lit up by clear notes of yellow and white.

First exhibited in the eleventh Seven and Five Society exhibition in February 1932, *Arum Lilies* was included in Frances Hodgkins's 1946 Retrospective and was illustrated a number of times in the 1930s: by Herbert Read in his 1933 *Architectural Review* piece on Unit One, in a 1934 *Listener* article by Eric Newton and in 1938 in Read's *Cahiers d'Art*, 'L'Art Contemporain en Angleterre', an overview of contemporary British art which also included reproductions of works by artists such as Eileen Agar, Edward Burra, Henry Moore, Paul Nash, Ben Nicholson and John Piper.

Pleasure Boat, 1932
Watercolour, 542 x 430mm
Private collection, New Zealand

Pleasure Garden, 1932
Watercolour, 530 x 425mm
Robert McDougall Art Gallery, Christchurch

Enchanted Garden (A Cornish Garden)

1932
WATERCOLOUR AND PENCIL ON PAPER, 546 x 451mm
SIGNED LOWER RIGHT: FRANCES HODGKINS
SHEFFIELD CITY ART GALLERIES

This magical painting plays on the still-life landscape idea by merging the foreground urn and pergola in a fluid whirl of linked and layered washes. Crisply accented green leaves articulate the centre foreground. The image as a whole is doubly framed: by the pergola and above that by the blurry remains of a scalloped awning shape, giving stability to the painting's highly mobile, kinetic effects. The lively, floating quality of the washes has something in common with Dufy, while the uptilted, overall decorative presentation may be a response to the aesthetics seen in certain exhibitions of non-European art of around this time, such as the huge *Persian Art* at Burlington House in 1931.

Enchanted Garden was painted at Bridgnorth, Shropshire, in the summer of 1932. The urn is similar to this motif in *The Lake (River Garden, Bridgnorth)*, the sunflower and awning to those in *Sabrina's Garden* (Fig. 40) and *Pleasure Garden*, while the view of distant houses suggests a vantage point like that used in other Bridgnorth paintings including *Boathouse on the Severn*, *Pleasure Garden* and *Pleasure Boat*.

Although exhibited as *A Cornish Garden* in the *Frances Hodgkins Centenary Exhibition* (1969) and more recently in the Minories Art Gallery's *Frances Hodgkins — The Late Work* (1991), this work is clearly a Bridgnorth painting and not 'a Cornish garden' and it was exhibited as *Enchanted Garden* in the Arts Council's *Frances Hodgkins Memorial Exhibition* of 1952. In the same year it was also included in two group exhibitions of women artists' work: *Famous British Women Artists* at the Graves Art Gallery, Sheffield and *Works by British Women Artists Executed during the Lifetime of the Queen*, Nottingham Castle Coronation Exhibition.

Evening

1932-3
OIL ON CANVAS, 535 x 640mm
SIGNED TWICE WITH INCISED SIGNATURE LOWER
RIGHT: FRANCES HODGKINS
PRIVATE COLLECTION, NEW ZEALAND

Spanish Still Life and Landscape, 1933/34
Oil on panel, 515 x 630mm
Robert McDougall Art Gallery, Christchurch

The luscious colouring of *Evening*, together with its ritualistic, iconic display of objects on an altar-like table, make this still-life landscape one of Frances Hodgkins's most suggestive variations on this theme. Succulent pinks effectively contrast with deep blues, russets and green, offering again that affective combination of sensuous colour and fruits. The vine, centrally placed goblet and also, perhaps, the closed jar to the left, mysteriously cocooned by the pinkish swirl of drapery, have religious associations, while the other, pre-Christian, significations of the vine — sensuous abundance, excess — add to the effective play of associations generated by this painting. The vine also has an important formal role in framing the foreground arrangement and in connecting it with the landscape setting, while enclosing the white house whose windows appear to eye the viewer cleverly from the centre of the painting.

Evening was almost certainly painted when Frances Hodgkins was in Ibiza from late 1932 to August 1933. It was exhibited in the twelfth Seven and Five exhibition in February 1933 — so probably painted late in 1932 — along with five other paintings by Hodgkins and works by David Jones, Winifred Nicholson, Henry Moore, Ben Nicholson, Ivon Hitchens and another expatriate New Zealander, Len Lye.

Evening's composition has much in common with that of *Spanish Still Life and Landscape*, sharing with it the motifs of goblet and jar, testimony yet again of Hodgkins's frequent use of the series. Interestingly, the colour range has altered dramatically, *Spanish Still Life and Landscape* emphasising greens, tans and creams, with *Evening*'s green goblet shifting to blue and the jar from blue to green, with a flourish of drapery rather than the vine's support framing the arrangement. Although clearly connected, the works appear never to have been shown together.

143

Spanish Shrine

1933–34
OIL ON CANVAS, 654 x 927mm
SIGNED LOWER LEFT: FRANCES HODGKINS
AUCKLAND CITY ART GALLERY

One of the few large-scale figure compositions from Frances Hodgkins's late phase, *Spanish Shrine* was exhibited a number of times in the 1930s and 1940s. Eric Newton singled it out for comment after a 1941 exhibition, praising the balance achieved between 'the world of her eye and the world of her mind's eye . . . . The picture is both a symbol and a description and the two are interwoven.'

Given its subject, and as a large oil first shown in February 1935, it was almost certainly conceived (if not begun) while on the island of Ibiza in 1933 and completed (as letters testify of unspecified Spanish works) on her return to Britain. This compelling painting has Hodgkins presenting her figures in iconic, neo-primitivising style against a roughly suggested rocky backdrop which frames and unites the group and sprouts a favourite motif, arum lilies, to the side. Landscape, fruit, flowers and containers connect with her landscape still lifes but here they are associated with the dominant presence of the three female figures, the central one a statue. Triads have featured before in Hodgkins's *oeuvre* — *Three Children* (Pl. 15) is one earlier example — while other artists like Picasso in his classicising *Three Women at the Spring* (1921) also used this grouping. However, the application of paint in slab-like shapes and the spiritual atmosphere of the image also have associations with Rouault, whom Hodgkins admired.

Other works by Hodgkins like *Sabrina's Garden* (Fig. 40), *Pleasure Garden* (see Pl. 27) and *The Urn* (private collection, New Zealand) use statues as suggestive motifs, while the direct frontal placing of these figures occurs in the other major late figure painting, *Double Portrait No. 2* (*Katharine and Anthony West*) (Pl. 33). But *Spanish Shrine* seems to be the only painting certainly from Hodgkins's stay in Ibiza which prominently features the local people and in this respect, as in the frontal presentation, it relates in a general way to the photographs of Ibizan women taken by the ex-Dadaist Raoul Hausmann, who lived there in 1933–36.

145

Self-Portrait: Still Life

c.1935
OIL ON CARDBOARD, 762 x 635mm
SIGNED LOWER RIGHT: FRANCES HODGKINS
AUCKLAND CITY ART GALLERY

Still Life: Self-Portrait, c.1935
Oil, 610 x 710mm
Private collection, UK

Still Life — Zipp, 1945
Oil on canvas, 615 x 740mm
Robert McDougall Art Gallery, Christchurch

Self-Portrait: Still Life is one of the best known of Frances Hodgkins's late paintings in New Zealand collections. In this unusual work Hodgkins imaginatively merges the two usually distinct genres of portraiture and still life, wittily challenging the usual parameters of both. The objects she chooses to speak for her presence — for this is a work of metaphor — are telling, a centrally placed bowl and pink rose, symbols of femininity; what is probably a belt in the 'foreground', suggestive of the body; a marvellously frivolous — if not fetishistic — pink high-heeled shoe, signifying the self, the feminine; and a mass of patterned scarves providing play for a disguise? of richly colourful and complex abstract, decorative effects. The closely related *Still Life: Self-Portrait* arranges similar motifs in a landscape format, but sets a mirror — stock tool of self-portraiture — in the centre. Here the personally expressive tendencies of the painting are enhanced by the addition of the artist's red beret and amusingly thwarted by the mirror's refusal to reflect conventional appearance.

Although usually dated 1941, *Self-Portrait: Still Life* appears to be more closely connected in terms of theme and style to paintings of around the mid thirties. *Still Life: Self-Portrait* has been dated c.1933 and both works cluster their similar motifs in an organic piled-up manner which is shared by still lifes like *Decorative Motif* (Fig. 47), first exhibited in February 1935, and *Christmas Decorations* (Fig. 48), dated 1935. *Still Life — Zipp* may well take up the theme of the still life of metaphor in 1945, but *Self-Portrait: Still Life* and *Still Life: Self-Portrait* are both closer to works of the thirties like *Spanish Shrine* and *Decorative Motif* in their warmer, more highly keyed colouring, markedly contrasting with *Still Life — Zipp*'s very dark, melancholy tonal range typical of Hodgkins's World War II paintings, and also with its different painterly techniques.

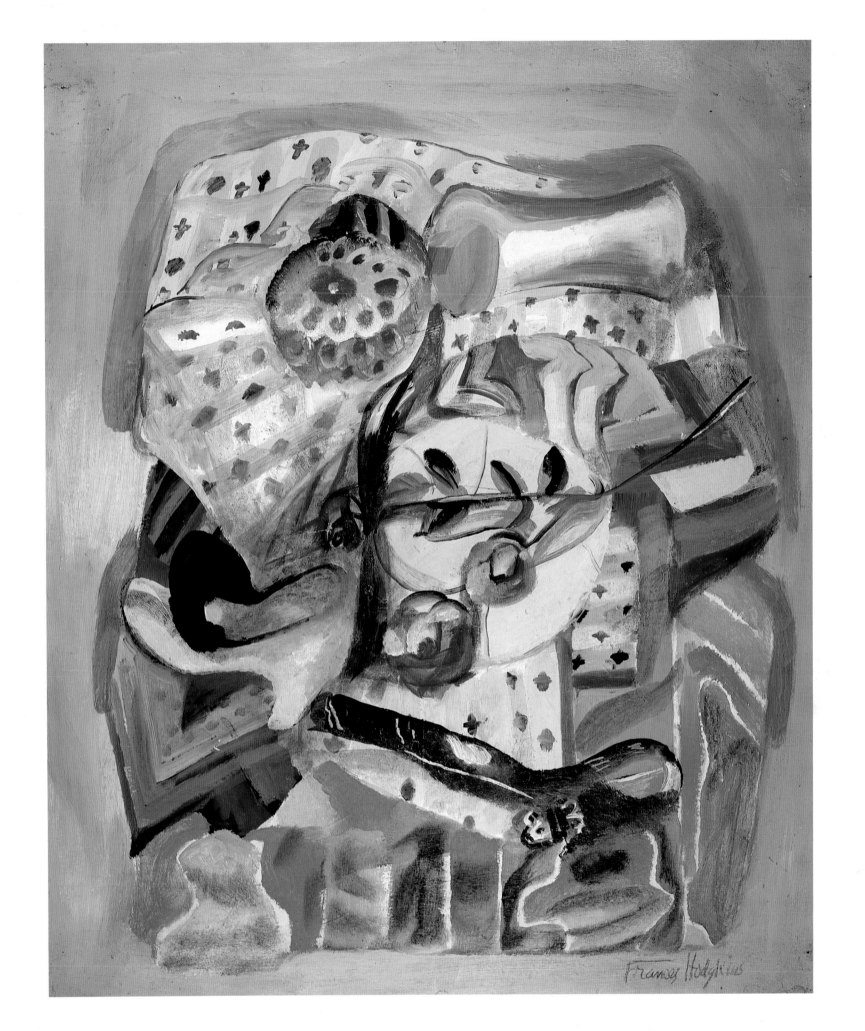

Frances Hodgkins

Pumpkins and Pimenti

c.1935–36

GOUACHE, PENCIL, CHALK, 510 x 710mm

SIGNED LOWER LEFT: FRANCES HODGKINS (AND INSCRIBED LOWER LEFT, BELOW MOUNT: STILL LIFE c.1935)

FLETCHER CHALLENGE ART COLLECTION

Pumpkins and Pimenti returns to the still-life landscape idea using vegetables instead of the fruit and flowers characteristic of earlier versions. It was owned by Sir Kenneth Clark, probably painted in Tossa de Mar where Frances Hodgkins spent the winter of 1935–36, and is related to *Marrow* (present location not known), which was exhibited at the 1939 World's Fair in New York probably with *Pumpkins and Pimenti* as *Still Life*. It was also exhibited in 1939 in the London Gallery's mainly surrealist exhibition, *Living Art in England*, as *Still Life*, alongside work by Eileen Agar, Naum Gabo, John Banting, Ithell Colquhoun, John Heartfield, John Melville and Edward Wadsworth.

Pumpkins and Pimenti sees Hodgkins working effectively in gouache, using a variety of brush marks, with parts of the work enlivened by the graphic qualities of pencil and chalk. From this time on gouache becomes the major medium for the artist, allowing her to experiment with a marvellous range of expressive, calligraphic marks. Colour in this painting is subtly muted — foreshadowing her work in the 1940s — yet with surprising accents as in the blues on the pumpkin and central pepper. The surrealist aspects of *Pumpkins and Pimenti* are clear, as distant hills appear to be in the process of forming around the table arrangement, an interesting development from her earlier still-life landscapes. But while the conjunction between landscape and still life is bizarrely close in appropriately surrealist fashion, Hodgkins's seemingly spontaneous painterly effects, together with the effectively vague definition of the landscape, provide a particularly haunting image informed by Surrealism but by no means in thrall to a textbook application of its tenets.

Arrangement of Jugs

1938
LITHOGRAPH, 610 x 457mm
SIGNED LOWER RIGHT: FRANCES HODGKINS
PUBLISHED BY CONTEMPORARY LITHOGRAPHS LTD,
LONDON

Still Life, c.1937
Inscribed 'For Kitty and Anthony from
Frances Hodgkins'
Watercolour, 623 x 477mm
Private collection, UK

Arrangement of Jugs, c.1937
Watercolour & pencil, 470 x 622mm
Private collection, UK

*A*rrangement of Jugs is Frances Hodgkins's only surviving print. It was commissioned by Contemporary Lithographs Ltd, a venture founded in 1936 by Robert Wellington and John Piper with the intention of providing a wide public with quality, reasonably priced, 'original' works. Printing was done at the Curwen Press, where the artists drew their designs, with some — like Ivon Hitchens and Frances Hodgkins — new to the medium given technical assistance by John Piper. *Arrangement of Jugs* was one of the fifteen prints in the second series, launched in March 1938, which included artists such as Vanessa Bell, Duncan Grant, Edward Wadsworth, John Piper and Edward Ardizzone.

Arrangement of Jugs successfully adopts and extends Hodgkins's mid-thirties approach to colour and form. The objects are simplified to outlines or silhouettes, with bright splashes of colour sometimes floating freely in space and effectively disregarding allegiance to particular objects. Some of the stone is left unworked, the resulting light paper tones contributing towards a particularly buoyant image. Both Wellingon and Piper were enthusiastic about Hodgkins's print, the former finding 'the medium is used in quite a fresh way', the latter seeing it as 'the best in the series'. Hodgkins herself found the project 'interesting and remunerative as a side line' and was pleased when the British Museum purchased the series which included her print.

Two watercolours in private collections are very close to *Arrangement of Jugs* and appear to be studies for it: the identically titled *Arrangement of Jugs* and *Still Life*. Hodgkins re-arranges similar objects, including the rectangular 'modernist' vase which also occurs as the receptacle for *Mimosa* (private collection, New Zealand) and appears in *Wild Violets and Honesty* (present location not known).

Double Portrait No. 2 (Katharine and Anthony West)

1937/39
OIL, 690 x 825mm
SIGNED: FRANCES HODGKINS (AND DATED LOWER RIGHT: 1937)
MUSEUM OF NEW ZEALAND, TE PAPA TONGAREWA

Katharine Church (Kitty West), 1939
Watercolour, 480 x 580mm
Private collection, UK

Anthony West, 1939
Pencil, 356 x 267mm
Private collection, Britain

While this large oil double portrait is titled *No. 2* in relation to *Double Portrait* (Pl. 17), Frances Hodgkins used the double image motif quite frequently in figure subjects (*The Bridesmaids*, Pl. 20, is another example). As a portraiture device the male/female pair has a long history in European art reaching back to the Renaissance. Here the sitters face the viewer in boldly frontal placement, their presence emphasised by the strong Matissean reds of their clothing and the brusque, Picassoesque linear effects. The two figures are connected through the merging red tones of their clothing, yet the placement of the male figure's shoulder in front and his somewhat oblique glance separate the two personalities in a psychic sense.

As portraits of creative personalities — Katharine Church was and is a painter, Anthony West was first a painter then a writer — the painting relates to similar works of the period like Cedric Morris's *Portrait of Frances Hodgkins* herself (Auckland City Art Gallery, 1928). In Frances Hodgkins's own *oeuvre* there are other portraits of her artist peers, including *Man with Macaw,* 1930 (Cedric Morris) (Towner Art Gallery, Eastbourne) and *Portrait of Lett Haines,* 1927 (Minories Art Gallery, Colchester).

Frances Hodgkins was a close friend of the Wests, with whom she stayed on a number of occasions, and she frequently received gifts from Kitty West: 'They are 2 delightful Dears Anthony & Kitty —'. The settee in the portrait was a present from Anthony West's mother, the suffragette and writer Rebecca West, re-covered by her daughter-in-law in the yellow hessian edged with brown piping apparent in the painting.

While the date of the painting is usually given as 1937 from its inscription, this may be have been added subsequently (a common practice in Hodgkins's late work), for Katharine Church clearly remembers that 'This picture was painted from a watercolor of me and a pencil drawing of Anthony made at Chisbury Manor, near Hungerford in the first week of the War — 1939.' The drawing and watercolour are reproduced here.

August Month (Walls, Roofs and Flowers)

c.1939
GOUACHE, 633 x 487mm
SIGNED LOWER RIGHT: FRANCES HODGKINS
PRIVATE COLLECTION, NEW ZEALAND

Although titled *Walls, Roofs and Flowers* in the Penguin Modern Painters *Frances Hodgkins*, this exuberant painting was originally titled *August Month* and appeared in the Arts Council of Great Britain's Frances Hodgkins Memorial Exhibition (1952) as *August Month*. It was first shown (as *August Month*) in Hodgkins's April 1940 Lefevre Gallery exhibition, and so was quite probably produced in August 1939.

Unlike some other works from immediately before the outbreak of war, like the 'Barns' series, *August Month*'s warm, joyful, Mediterranean colouring relates to works by Hodgkins painted in, or inspired by, her experiences in the south of France or Spain in the 1930s. It displays her brilliant use of the gouache medium, as areas of colour and form are overlaid with a lively array of spritely gestural marks. This inspired 'handwriting', which had been developing earlier in paintings like *Private Bathing* (Fig. 49), gives the painting its special sense of vivid life, with the accents, swirls and squiggles operating as almost abstract signs of the objects that suggested them.

Perhaps *August Month* was painted during that August calm just before the war, when Frances Hodgkins wrote to her friend Dorothy Selby: 'I wish you were here — It is so divinely simple & smooth going — Jane's old Housekeeper cooking delicious vegetable meals — all fresh from the garden — great dishes of raspberries & cream — birds in the wood & a hedgehog on the Lawn — giving an exhibition of its tricks . . . I make the most of it — feeling it is a lull bfore a crash — & to be cherished —'.

Smithy

c.1940
GOUACHE ON PAPER, 495 x 650mm
SIGNED BRUSHPOINT LOWER RIGHT: FRANCES HODGKINS
PRIVATE COLLECTION, NEW ZEALAND

Farmyard, c.1940
Gouache, 485 x 640mm
Robert McDougall Art Gallery, Christchurch

Smithy's prominent wheels are a favourite motif in Frances Hodgkins's late paintings, as in *The Mill Wheel* (Fig. 60) and *Green Valley, Carmarthenshire* (Dunedin Public Art Gallery). Here, however, they dominate the image and are almost totally disengaged from a functional relationship with their setting, so that their pink, freely spinning spokes have a distinctly abstract appearance. As a motif, the wheel has a long history in Hodgkins's work and it was also common in neo-romantic, surrealist and surrealist-inflected imagery of the time: Burra, Agar, Trevelyan and Nash used it, the latter most notably as a central feature of his *Totes Meer (Dead Sea)*, 1940–41 (Tate Gallery). Its significations were various, ranging through suggestions of the self, of modernity, of transformation or, here, where a rustic setting is specified in the title, of English rural life. Yet the image also has an anthropomorphic look to it (in common with works like *Pleasure Boat* [see Pl. 27] and *Broken Tractor* [Fig. 56]), as the wheel hubs can be read as eyes, the white ovoid shape linking the two wheels as a kind of mouth, giving the image a bizarre, spectral presence, a surrealist dimension.

Formally, Hodgkins obviously found the possibilities of this motif intriguing, and here the double image with its two sets of rimless spokes is placed symmetrically in the centre, with the merest suggestion of setting in the child-art-like rendering of houses and windows. Above and below the twirling spokes a flurry of stabbing green brush marks lightly frame and accent the image.

Smithy was first exhibited in a group exhibition at the Leicester Galleries in the summer of 1940. It is closely related to *Farmyard*.

Walled Garden with Convolvulus

1942/3
WATERCOLOUR AND GOUACHE, 440 x 510mm
NOT SIGNED OR DATED
PRIVATE COLLECTION, NEW ZEALAND

Walled Garden with Convolvulus was first exhibited in Frances Hodgkins's 1943 show, *Gouaches by Frances Hodgkins — A New Series of Gouaches Painted during 1942–3*, at the Lefevre Galleries. Unlike many of her other solo exhibitions, which often included earlier as well as recent work, the fifteen works were recent and in the same medium, giving the selection a strong sense of cohesion.

This unusual painting explores further possibilities with the *plein air* still-life theme, the still-life arrangement reduced to a skeletal, spectral presence in the foreground, while the ambiguous architectural setting is transformed into a dream-like insubstantiality. But still life and setting are even more clearly here the basis only for an almost abstract play on colour, shape and mark, with the marvellously animated separate brush marks (the white dabs like daisy petals) creating an image whose expressive effects seem particularly innovatory in British painting of the time. Indeed, the freely dabbed brush marks foreshadow the painterly effects of a contemporary British colourist, Howard Hodgkin.

This vocabulary of lively gestural effects — especially the rhythmic dabs — is shared by other works of around this period, such as *The Mill Wheel* (Fig. 60) and *Root Crop* (Auckland City Art Gallery), which were also first exhibited in the same 1943 exhibition. In these two gouaches too, the appearance of objects is submerged beneath a complex and highly idiosyncratic language of form, line and colour, which teasingly baffles and delights the eye.

159

The China Shoe

1942

GOUACHE, 520 x 405mm

INSCRIBED LOWER LEFT: TO EARDLY [*SIC*] KNOLLYS FROM FRANCES HODGKINS 1942

PRIVATE COLLECTION

Ornaments with Flowers, 1942
Gouache, 460 x 514mm
Victoria & Albert Museum, London

Ornaments, 1942
Gouache, 559 x 381mm
Auckland City Art Gallery

As in *Walled Garden with Convolvulus* (Pl. 36), the still-life objects in this painting take on a ghostly quality, with the picture surface animated by an intriguing array of calligraphic flourishes. The subtly dark colouring and somewhat mysterious mood connect it closely with Neo-Romanticism, with work by artists like John Piper, John Craxton and John Minton, the painting's graphic effects being particularly close to those of Piper, an artist friend of Hodgkins's who was an admirer of and writer on her paintings.

The China Shoe was painted on an excursion to Wales in the autumn of 1942: at Dolaucothy she wrote to Eardley Knollys (whom she had met earlier on this visit) that she had 'made pictures of the funny chimney ornaments, which do lend themselves to decoration — I love them — tender silly unarranged things'. Eardley Knollys was to become a close friend for the rest of Hodgkins's life and also bought a number of her paintings. He introduced her to the china-ornament collector and the other two paintings based on these objects — *Ornaments with Flowers* and *Ornaments* — were exhibited in her March–April 1943 solo show at the Lefevre Galleries. This group of three provides another tightly knit small series like others in Hodgkins's late work.

Prominent in the foreground of each of these related paintings of ornaments is a shoe, a motif used by Hodgkins in *Self-Portrait: Still Life* (Pl. 30) and in *Still Life: Self-Portrait* (see Pl. 30) but here in ornament form. And amusingly and touchingly prominent on the shoe is a heart shape, given further focus by its placement in the centre foreground. What could be more emblematic of the affection felt by Frances Hodgkins towards the supportive friend to whom she gave this painting?

The New Rick, 1942
Gouache, 565 x 435mm
Dunedin Public Art Gallery

Corfe Castle, 1942
Watercolour & gouache, 415 x 560mm
Private collection, New Zealand

Peter Lanyon, *Porthleven*, 1951
Oil on board, 244.5 x 121.9mm
Tate Gallery, London

Church and Castle, Corfe

1942
GOUACHE ON PAPER GLUED TO CARD, 460 x 597mm
SIGNED LOWER LEFT: FRANCES HODGKINS 1942
(INSCRIBED ON REVERSE: CHURCH & CASTLE — CORFE 1942)
FERENS ART GALLERY, HULL CITY MUSEUMS AND ART GALLERIES

Church and Castle, Corfe is one of a number of paintings from 1942 which feature the impressive hilltop ruins and parish church of the Dorset village Corfe Castle. Rather than focusing on these buildings, however, the artist less predictably incorporates them as loosely sketched-in background motifs whose small-scale but insistent presence provides a subtle yet vital key to the neo-romantic mood of these works.

Church and Castle, Corfe, once in the collection of Sir Kenneth Clark, was shown with other works by Hodgkins in Paris in a 1945 British-Council-sponsored exhibition, *Quelques Contemporains Anglais,* with neo-romantic artists like John Piper, Henry Moore, Paul Nash, Graham Sutherland and Robert Colquhoun.

The image holds in perfect tension, verging on abstraction, identifiable and indistinct objects, a wonderful variety of graphic effects in line and brush mark, its colouring in eerie lightish yellows, greys and greens plus a touch of slate-blue and pale pink. The moonlit ambience gives the painting the somewhat 'gothic' character and atmosphere explored in other contemporary works, like John Piper's *Ruined Cottage* (1940, present location not known). But there is also an amorphous, free-floating abstract/surrealist aspect to this painting which has something in common with the work of the late Surrealists, while its expressive play within the gap between representation and abstraction – and its hilltop landmark — can be seen to foreshadow paintings like *Porthleven* (1951) by the St Ives artist Peter Lanyon.

Other paintings employing the motifs of church and castle include the oil *Corfe Castle* (Dunedin Public Art Gallery) and the gouaches *The New Rick*, which similarly features farm implements in the foreground, and *Corfe Castle*, which, despite its title, has the frontal, iconic image of an old farm barn dominating the foreground, its roof apparently sprouting on either side of the gable the twin structures of church and castle.

Purbeck Courtyard, Morning, 1944
Oil on board, 712 x 610mm
Southampton Art Gallery

Purbeck Courtyard, Early Afternoon, 1944
Oil on board, 620 x 720mm
Museum of New Zealand, Te Papa
Tongarewa

Graham Sutherland, *Devastation 1941 — East
End Street*, 1941
Ink, chalk & wash, 640 x 1102mm
Tate Gallery, London

The Courtyard in Wartime

1944

OIL ON BOARD, 610 x 762mm

INSCRIBED LOWER RIGHT IN BRUSHPOINT: FRANCES HODGKINS 1944

THE UNIVERSITY OF AUCKLAND ART COLLECTION

In a letter of 23 December 1944 to her friend Eardley Knollys Frances Hodgkins wrote: 'I propose to give and hand over to you . . . the problem picture you like fate-like as you say — Courtyard by Night I call it —'. The expressive and powerful *Courtyard by Night*, or as it is now known, *The Courtyard in Wartime*, is one of a group of three surviving oils inspired by the courtyard next to Hodgkins's cottage and ex-nonconformist-chapel studio in the village of Corfe Castle, where she was based from 1939 until her death in 1947.

These paintings are evidence yet again of Hodgkins's effective syntheses between adaptation and manipulation of the idiosyncrasies of place and a freely inventive formal approach. Each is of a similar size, is painted on board, relates to a specific time and is colouristically distinct: *Purbeck Courtyard, Morning*, mainly in peach, golden and sepia skeins of colour and line, looks up to the courtyard from the studio, while *Purbeck Courtyard, Early Afternoon* is painted in close tones of greens and tans from a viewpoint which appears to be looking downwards towards the opening through to the garden and studio.

Courtyard in Wartime is the most dramatic of the group with various elements of the setting — studio, cottage, porch, steps — disengaged from their context and transformed into cryptic signs of place which merge into areas of highly expressive colour and paintwork evoking the gruesome theatricality of the night raids: bright blue accents, foreground triangle of blue-black dabs on sienna, intense greens, pungent scarlets, dense blacks. The choice of an emotive night scene places this work in the context of the wartime nocturne, a theme treated by neo-romantic artists as a general signifier of doom, or, as in Hodgkins's painting, Piper's *All Saints Chapel, Bath* (1942) (Fig. 57), or Sutherland's *Devastation 1941 — East End Street*, as suggesting specifically apocalyptic overtones.

The Spanish Well, Purbeck

1945
OIL ON CANVAS, 670 x 646mm
SIGNED LOWER RIGHT: FRANCES HODGKINS 1945
AUCKLAND CITY ART GALLERY

Spanish Well, Purbeck's accents of more highly keyed colour show a move away from the generally sombre tones of the war years; and the lighter mood they generate in conjunction with the associations of the title recaptures something of the more expansive atmosphere of the paintings connected with her 1930s visits to the south of France and Spain. The painting's central, twisted tree and dabs of dark paint on a lighter ground may appear to relate to *Courtyard in Wartime* (Pl. 39), but the inclusion of the figure and the softly gleaming shafts of colour — a whole gamut of greens, dark greys, with pinks and oranges — give this painting a very different character.

The positioning of a male figure in *Spanish Well, Purbeck* within a landscape-related setting might suggest the relationship between figure (often male) and setting used by neo-romantic artists like John Craxton and John Minton. An aspect of neo-romantic practice was a focus on 'pastoral' man as an antidote to the dehumanisation and mechanisation of war. But Hodgkins's male figure, although integrated into the landscape in painterly terms, is not part of it in a primordial, rustic sense: instead he wears an urbane jacket and rather than being psychically absorbed in the setting, looks out at the viewer. This may well be a portrait of a kind. Thus, while an alertness to current ideas may be in evidence, these ideas are, typically for her late work, transformed by the artist's highly individual approach to colour and sophisticated and subtle display of painterly effects bordering on abstraction.

CHRONOLOGY

Frances Hodgkins, c. 1905
Alexander Turnbull Library, Wellington

1 8 6 9

28 April, born at Dunedin, third child and second daughter of William Mathew Hodgkins, solicitor, and Rachel Owen (née Parker).

1 8 9 0

Exhibits for the first time with the Canterbury Society of Arts, Christchurch, and Otago Art Society, Dunedin.

1 8 9 3

Takes classes given by the visiting Italian painter G. P. Nerli.

1 8 9 5

February, attends the Dunedin School of Art. Begins preparations for South Kensington examinations. In July, wins competition for the best study from life.

1 8 9 6

Obtains first-class passes in the South Kensington examinations. In August, opens a studio in Dunedin and places advertisements for pupils.

1 8 9 7

April–May, takes holiday at Timaru. In December visits Lake Wakatipu, Otago.

1 8 9 8

9 February, death of her father William Mathew Hodgkins. Illustrates *Otago Daily Times and Witness Christmas Annual*, 1898.

1 8 9 9

April, elected member of the Council, Otago Art Society. In September sketches at Moeraki and paints local Maori subjects. Does illustrations for the *New Zealand Illustrated Magazine*, November, and for the *Otago Daily Times and Witness Christmas Annual*, 1899. Visits Wellington in December and goes to the artists' colony at Silverstream.

1 9 0 0

Illustrates *New Zealand Illustrated Magazine* in January, February, May and June. Is appointed a member of the Otago Art Society's selection and hanging committee.

1 9 0 1

February, sails for Europe via Sydney, Colombo, Marseilles to London. April, arrives at London. June, attends Norman Garstin's sketching class at Caudebec, France. In September she travels from Caudebec to Paris. Stays in France until November when she travels to Italy visiting Rapallo and San Remo.

1 9 0 2

Spends part of January and February at San Remo. Late February, returns to London. March to June, she is at Penzance. In July joins Norman Garstin's sketching class at Dinan, France. August, shows new works at McGregor Wright's Gallery, Wellington. In October shows at John Baillie's Gallery, London. November, shows ten paintings at Doré Gallery, Bond Street, London. In November she travels to Tangier.

1 9 0 3

At Tangier January–March. Travels to Tetuan. In April returns to England. In May shows at the Royal Academy. July, shows ten works, with Fine Art Society, Bond Street, London. Mid-July to October in Belgium and Holland. November, sails for Sydney and Wellington. Arrives at Wellington December.

1 9 0 4

Based all year in Wellington. In February opens a studio in Bowen Street and starts teaching. Exhibits with Miss D. K. Richmond at McGregor Wright's Gallery, Wellington, in late February. In April shows at the Royal Academy, London.

1 9 0 5

Spends year in Wellington except for a visit to Rotorua in June–July. In April exhibits at Royal Academy, London.

1 9 0 6

January, leaves Wellington for England. Late February, reaches London. Spends April, June and part of July at Venice and Chioggia. In mid-July she travels to France and in August joins Norman Garstin's class at St Valery-sur-Somme. In November shows at *Société Internationale d'Aquarellistes*, Paris. In September visits Avignon and in November travels to Antibes, Alpes Maritimes.

1 9 0 7

In February she leaves Antibes for London. In March has a

solo exhibition at Paterson's Gallery, Old Bond Street, London. May, travels to Dordrecht, Holland. Stays in Holland for remainder of the year, except for a short trip to London in November. Exhibits two works at Amsterdam.

1 9 0 8

Stays in Holland, mainly at Dordrecht, until August. Wins prize shared with Thea Proctor, in the Australian section of Women's Art at the Franco-British Exhibition. August–November, based in England. Mid-November, travels to Paris. Takes lessons from Pierre Marcel-Beronneau in December, painting from the nude model in oils. Wins Whitney-Hoff Prize for best watercolour at the American (Women's) Student Hostel in the Boulevard Saint Michel, Paris.

1 9 0 9

Spends most of the year in Paris apart from a period at Montreuil-sur-Mer in May–July with a sketching class. Exhibits at Paris Salon. In July shows with Allied Artists, Albert Hall, London. In November shows twenty-seven works at Ryder Gallery, London.

1 9 1 0

In Paris until August, when she goes to Concarneau. Takes class in watercolours at the Académie Colarossi, Paris. In March shows at the Royal Institute of Painters in Watercolour. Shows at the *Société Internationale d'Aquarellistes* and *Société Internationale de la Peinture à l'Eau*, Paris.

1 9 1 1

January, at Concarneau. In February shows with *Société Internationale de la Peinture à l'Eau*, Paris. Canadian artist Emily Carr studies with her at Concarneau. October, travels to Paris and opens her own school for watercolour painting.

1 9 1 2

January, in Paris. In June leaves for sketching classes at St Valery-sur-Somme. October, sails for Melbourne from Toulon and arrives in November. Shows works in Melbourne. December, arrives at Wellington.

1 9 1 3

January, at Wellington. February–March, travels to Masterton and Rotorua. March, travels to Sydney. April, holds solo exhibition at Anthony Hordern's Gallery. June, has solo show at Society of Arts Gallery, Adelaide. July, arrives at Dunedin and opens solo exhibition at Dunedin Public Art Gallery. August, returns to Wellington and holds solo show at Walter Turnbull's Gallery. October, sails for Europe. November arrives at Naples and travels to Rome. December, at Naples and Capri.

1 9 1 4

Spends January at Capri and by May in Paris. Summer sketching class at Equihen and Concarneau ended by outbreak of war in August. September, returns to England

Frances Hodgkins, c.1913
Robert McDougall Art Gallery, Christchurch

and in November takes up residence at St Ives, Cornwall. Remains at St Ives except for brief visits to London and summer sketching classes.

1 9 1 5

January, begins teaching at St Ives. May, exhibits at the Royal Academy. October–November, exhibits six works with the International Society of Sculptors, Painters and Gravers, Grosvenor Gallery, London.

1 9 1 6

February–March, shows three works at the National Portrait Society, Grosvenor Gallery, London. May, exhibits at the Royal Academy and May–July, has four works at the International Society. Summer class June–September at Chipping Campden, Gloucester. October, shows six works at the International Society.

1 9 1 7

At St Ives. April, exhibits with the National Portrait Society. Summer class at Burford in June and that month exhibits six works at the International Society.

1 9 1 8

At St Ives. February–March, exhibits three works with the National Portrait Society. May, shows six works at the International Society. June–September, summer class at Porlock, Somerset. October, exhibits twenty-one works in the Private Gallery at the International Society. October, exhibition of thirty-five works at Anthony Hordern's Gallery, Sydney. December, rents a studio in Kensington, London. Comes into contact with Cedric Morris and Arthur Lett Haines, who sublets her Kensington studio.

1 9 1 9

January, in London. February, exhibits three works with the National Portrait Society and Australian exhibition opens at the Fine Art Society, Melbourne. March, shows eight works with the Women's International Art Club, Grafton Galleries. May, exhibits at the International Society. May–August, summer class at Ludlow and Great Barrington. October, shows six works at the International Society, lets London studio and by November in St Ives.

1 9 2 0

January, in St Ives. February, one-woman exhibition at Hampstead Art Gallery. March, exhibits two works with the Women's International Art Club. April, sketching class Topsham, Exeter. May, returns to St Ives. November, leaves St Ives for London and south of France. December, at St Tropez and Cassis.

1 9 2 1

January, at Cassis. Moves to Martigues. May, summer class at Douarnenez, Brittany. July, moves to Tréboul. November, returns to England and stays with friends in London.

1 9 2 2

January, settles in Burford. Gives classes and submits designs for poster competitions. June, drawing, *The Cinema*, reproduced in the magazine *Colour*. October–November, in Manchester to give class at Girls' High School. Stays with Hannah Ritchie and Jane Saunders.

1 9 2 3

January, at Burford. February–March, visits Manchester. Teaches over the summer at Burford. October, leaves for London and the south of France. Early November, one-woman exhibition, Little Art Rooms, Adelphi, London. By end of November at St Paul du Var, near Nice.

1 9 2 4

January, at St Paul du Var. February, sketching class at Nice. June–October, summer class at Montreuil-sur-Mer, Normandy. October, at St Valery-sur-Somme. Shows seven works at *Salon d'Automne*, Paris. December, leaves St Valery for Martigues in the south of France.

1 9 2 5

January, at Martigues. February, returns to London via Paris. Stays with friends in London and books passage to Melbourne. May, visits Manchester and accepts post of textile designer for Calico Printers' Association on a six-month contract. August, sent by the CPA to Paris to see *Exposition Internationale des Arts Décoratifs et Industriels Modernes*. December, contract with CPA expires and is not renewed. Continues to paint in Manchester.

1 9 2 6

January, at Manchester. About March–April meets Lucy Wertheim. April, death of her mother in Wellington. June, summer class at Ludlow and Bridgnorth. October, returns to Manchester and has one-woman exhibition at All Saints, Manchester.

1 9 2 7

January, at Manchester. June, exhibits with the London Group, RWS Gallery and leaves for Tréboul. September, at Concarneau. November, returns to London and in December exhibits with the New English Art Club. December, leaves London for Martigues.

1 9 2 8

January–March, at Martigues. Returns to London and in April holds one-woman show, Claridge Gallery. Exhibits in June and December at the New English Art Club. October–November, seriously ill.

1 9 2 9

January, in London. Elected to the Seven and Five Society and shows six works at the Society's March exhibition at Arthur Tooth & Sons. May, at Haywards Heath and shows seven works at the Mansard Gallery. October, returns to London and in November leaves for Pastorale, south of France. November, exhibits with Vera Cuningham at the Bloomsbury Gallery.

1 9 3 0

January, at Pastorale. February, moves to St Jeannet and signs contract with Arthur Howell of the St George's Gallery to supply watercolours. April, leaves St Jeannet for London via Paris. June, at Flatford Mill, East Bergholt. October, shows four works at the opening exhibition, Wertheim Gallery, and later that month has one-woman exhibition at St George's Gallery. October–November, at St Osyth. November, at Wilmington. December, at Bradford-on-Tone.

1 9 3 1

January, in London. Exhibits in the tenth Seven and Five Society exhibition in February. Group exhibition at the Wertheim Gallery. February–August, in the south of France, in contact first with Maurice Garnier and then staying with the expatriate New Zealand artist Maud Burge and husband at St Tropez. Autumn in London. December, in Cornwall. The St George's Gallery closes.

1 9 3 2

January, in Cornwall. February, exhibits in eleventh Seven and Five Society exhibition and visits London, returning to Cornwall in March, staying until c.June. Contract with the Lefevre Galleries from February. Exhibits in group shows: in *Room and Book* at Zwemmers in April and at the Wertheim Gallery. In August works in Bridgnorth,

Shropshire with Dorothy Selby, Jane Saunders and Hannah Ritchie. Travels to Ibiza in October.

1 9 3 3

In Ibiza until July, with Maud Burge and two other expatriate New Zealand artists, Gwen Knight and May Smith. Exhibited in the twelfth Seven and Five Society exhibition in February and in other group exhibitions at the Zwemmer and Wertheim Galleries. Invited to join Unit One by Paul Nash in May. In London from July until the end of the year. Resigns from Unit One in October.

1 9 3 4

January–March, in London, April in Cornwall, July in Bradford-on-Tone, Somerset, September in London. In December moves to Corfe Castle, Dorset, using ex-nonconformist chapel as studio. Exhibits in group exhibition at the Wertheim Gallery and in the thirteenth Seven and Five Society exhibition in October–November.

1 9 3 5

January, at Corfe Castle. February, visits London and exhibits at the Leicester Galleries with Orovida and Mariette Lydis, returning to Corfe Castle in March. In London in June, visits Wales in August, where she meets Cedric Morris again. Leaves for Tossa de Mar, Spain in October. Exhibits in the Brussels Universal International Exhibition.

1 9 3 6

January–April, at Tossa de Mar. Exhibits at the Wertheim Gallery in February. May, at Corfe Castle; August, at Llangenith and Solva in Wales, returning to Corfe Castle by November. In group exhibition at the Wertheim Gallery.

1 9 3 7

January–February, at Corfe Castle, moving to Bradford-on-Tone for March and April. Establishes herself at Worth Matravers, Dorset, using ex-cowshed as studio, from May. Visits Tréboul, Brittany, in August. Visits London and has solo exhibition at the Lefevre Galleries in October, returning to Worth Matravers in November. Group exhibition at the Leicester Galleries.

1 9 3 8

Based in Worth Matravers until the end of the year. February holiday in France with Rée Gorer. With Kitty and Anthony West c.May. Contract with Lefevre Galleries renegotiated in July. Visits London in June and Kimmeridge, Dorset, in July. In Wales in September and again in November. Group exhibitions at the Lefevre Galleries, the Redfern Gallery and the Wertheim Gallery. Exhibited at the *Salon d'Automne*, Paris, October–November.

1 9 3 9

January, at Worth Matravers. Visits London in February and exhibits in the London Gallery surrealist exhibition, *Living Art in England*, in January–February. Short visit to St Tropez in March. January, invitation to exhibit in

Contemporary British Art, selected by Kenneth Clark, at the World's Fair Exhibition in New York. Stays in Bradford-on-Tone from May until July, when she moves back to Corfe Castle. August in Northumberland with Jane Saunders and also with the Wests in Wiltshire, returning to Corfe Castle by the beginning of September and the outbreak of war. Contract with the Lefevre Galleries cancelled in November. In December invited to exhibit in the *Biennale di Venezia* in May 1940. Group exhibitions at the Leicester, Lefevre and Redfern galleries.

1 9 4 0

January–April, at Corfe Castle. Visits London in April for solo exhibition at the Lefevre Galleries, returning to Corfe Castle by May. *Biennale* work shown at Hertford House in May. Late May–October at Bradford-on-Tone, with holiday in Hertfordshire late October. Group exhibitions at the Leicester Galleries. Work also shown in the New Zealand Centennial Exhibition.

Frances Hodgkins at Corfe Castle, 1945
Felix H. Man Collection,
Alexander Turnbull Library, Wellington

1941

January–May, at Bradford-on-Tone, with visits to Corfe Castle in April, to Clun, Wales in May and later that month to John and Myfanwy Piper at Henley-on-Thames, where she becomes ill and is hospitalised. Leaves hospital in August and convalesces at the Wests' in Berkshire. Returns to Corfe Castle, where she stays for the rest of the year. Solo exhibition at the Leicester Galleries in October and group exhibitions at the Redfern, Leger and Leicester galleries.

1942

At Corfe Castle from January, with short visits to Studland, Dorset, in May, to Brixham, Devon, in August. In September–November stays at Dolaucothy, Wales, where she meets Eardley Knollys. Group exhibitions at the Lefevre, Leicester and Redfern galleries. John Piper negotiates a Civil List pension for her.

1943

At Corfe Castle all year, except for a few weeks in Cerne Abbas, Dorset with Dorothy Selby in September. Solo exhibition at the Lefevre Galleries in March–April. Group exhibition at the Redfern Gallery. Studio roof collapses in June, repaired later in year.

1944

At Corfe Castle all year, except for brief visit to Bridport, Dorset in July. Moves to the Greyhound Inn in June. Group exhibitions at the Redfern and Leicester galleries.

1945

At Corfe Castle all year, except for two-week stay in Wales in April. Work included in group exhibitions at the Leicester and Redfern galleries, at the Lefevre Galleries (with Bacon, Smith, Moore and Sutherland) and in *Quelques Contemporains Anglais*, Paris.

1946

At Corfe Castle most of the year, with visits to London in February, to Bradford-on-Tone in March and October and to London again in November for her Retrospective Exhibition at the Lefevre Galleries.

1947

January–March, at Corfe Castle. Late March, admitted to Herrison House, a psychiatric hospital near Dorchester, where she dies on 13 May.

EXHIBITIONS

INDIVIDUAL EXHIBITIONS

1904 FEBRUARY Wellington, McGregor Wright's Gallery (with D. K. Richmond) (37 works).

1907 MARCH London, Paterson's Gallery (22 works).

1909 NOVEMBER London, Ryder Gallery (27 works).

1912 NOVEMBER Melbourne, Theosophical Society's Room. *An Exhibition of Water Colours by Miss Frances Hodgkins* (74 works). Travelling to Sydney (Anthony Hordern's Fine Art Gallery: with the addition of two works, April 1913), Adelaide (Society of Arts Gallery, June 1913), Dunedin (Art Gallery: a reduced group of 44 works, July 1913), Wellington (Walter Turnbull's Gallery, August 1913).

1918 OCTOBER Sydney, Anthony Hordern's Fine Art Gallery (35 works). Travelling to Melbourne (Fine Art Society, February 1919).

1920 FEBRUARY London, Hampstead Art Gallery. Introduction Frank Rutter. (No catalogue traced.)

1923 NOVEMBER London, Little Art Rooms, Adelphi. (No catalogue traced.)

1926 NOVEMBER Manchester, All Saints. *Exhibition of Paintings by Frances Hodgkins* (80 works). Introduction O. Raymond Drey.

1928 APRIL London, Claridge Gallery. *Exhibition of Paintings and Water-colours by Frances Hodgkins* (48 works).

1929 NOVEMBER London, Bloomsbury Gallery (with Vera Cunningham). (No catalogue traced.)

1930 OCTOBER London, St George's Gallery. *Paintings and Watercolours by Frances Hodgkins* (21 works).

1933 OCTOBER London, Lefevre Gallery. *New Watercolour Drawings by Frances Hodgkins* (32 works).

1935 FEBRUARY London, Leicester Galleries. *Paintings and Watercolours by Frances Hodgkins* (32 works).

1936 FEBRUARY London, Wertheim Gallery (32 works). (No catalogue traced.)

1937 OCTOBER London, Lefevre Gallery. *New Paintings and Watercolours by Frances Hodgkins* (63 works).

1940 APRIL London, Lefevre Gallery. *Gouaches and Pencil Drawings by Frances Hodgkins* (38 works).

1941 OCTOBER London, Leicester Galleries. *Paintings and Watercolours by Frances Hodgkins* (32 works).

1943 MARCH London, Lefevre Gallery. *Gouaches by Frances Hodgkins — A New Series of Gouaches Painted during 1942–43* (15 works).

1946 NOVEMBER London, Lefevre Gallery. *Retrospective Exhibition, Frances Hodgkins* (79 works). Foreword Eric Newton.

1947 AUGUST Manchester, City Art Gallery. *Pictures by Frances Hodgkins* (44 works). Foreword David Baxandall.

1948 MARCH Swanage, Isle of Purbeck Arts Club. *An Exhibition of Pictures by Frances Hodgkins* (44 works). Foreword Eardley Knollys. Travelling to Bournemouth (Bournemouth Arts Club, March–April), Totnes (Dartington Hall, April–May), St Ives (New Gallery, May).

1949 MARCH London, St George's Gallery. *Homage to Frances Hodgkins* (38 works). Foreword Arthur R. Howell.

1952 MAY London, Tate Gallery. *Ethel Walker, Frances Hodgkins, Gwen John. A Memorial Exhibition* (43 works with an addenda of a further 14). Foreword John Rothenstein & Philip James. Essay Myfanwy Piper.
London, Arts Council. *Memorial Exhibition of the Works of Frances Hodgkins 1869–1947* (the Hodgkins section of the 1952 Tate exhibition, including the essay by Myfanwy Piper and an additional two works, but not the 14-work Tate addenda).

1954 JUNE Auckland, City Art Gallery. *Frances Hodgkins and her Circle* (65 works). Catalogue introduction & notes E. H. McCormick.

1956 JUNE London, Leicester Galleries. *Paintings, Watercolours and Gouaches by Frances Hodgkins* (35 works).

1959 APRIL Auckland, City Art Gallery. *Frances Hodgkins, Paintings and Drawings* (35 works). Catalogue introduction & notes Colin McCahon.

1966 OCTOBER Blandford, Hambledon Gallery. *Frances Hodgkins* (24 works).

1969 APRIL London, New Zealand High Commission. *Frances Hodgkins 1869–1947* (24 works).
APRIL Dunedin Public Art Gallery. *Frances Hodgkins 1869–1947, A Centenary Exhibition* (101 works). Catalogue introduction & notes Ian Roberts & David Armitage. Organised by the Queen Elizabeth II Arts Council of New Zealand and travelling to Christchurch (Robert McDougall Art Gallery, June 1969), Wellington (National Art Gallery, July 1969), Auckland (City Art Gallery,

August 1969), Melbourne (National Gallery of Victoria, October 1969), London (Commonwealth Institute Gallery, February 1970).
Dunedin, Hocken Library, University of Otago. *The Origins of Frances Hodgkins* (100 works). Introduction & catalogue Una Platts.

1979 NOVEMBER Auckland, City Art Gallery. *Frances Hodgkins* (52 works).

1987 NOVEMBER London, Gillian Jason Gallery. *A Tribute to Frances Hodgkins* (29 works).

1988 APRIL Hawke's Bay Art Gallery and Museum. *Frances Hodgkins and Maud Burge — Two Expatriates* (20 works). Introduction Margaret Cranwell.

1989 AUGUST Wellington, The Gallery, Kirkcaldie & Stains Ltd. *Frances Hodgkins, Works from Private Collections* (43 works).

1990 JULY London, Whitford & Hughes. *Frances Hodgkins 1869–1947* (32 works). Introduction & catalogue Avenal McKinnon.
NOVEMBER Colchester, Minories Art Gallery. *Frances Hodgkins — The Late Work* (43 works). Introduction Liz Reintjes, essays Rosemary Pawsey & Lindsey Bridget Shaw. Minories Art Gallery touring exhibition, travelling to Eastbourne (Towner Art Gallery, January–March 1991), Newton (Oriel 31, Davies Memorial Gallery, March–April 1991), Sheffield (Graves Art Gallery, April–June 1991).

1991 OCTOBER Auckland, City Art Gallery. *Works from the Studio* (60 works).

1992 JULY Auckland, John Leech Gallery. *Frances Hodgkins and her Contemporaries* (17 works).

1993 SEPTEMBER Wellington, Museum of New Zealand Te Papa Tongarewa. *Frances Hodgkins* (51 works). Catalogue Jill Trevelyan.

1994 FEBRUARY Auckland, City Art Gallery. *Late Summer by Frances Hodgkins* (49 works).

SELECTED GROUP EXHIBITIONS

1890 NOVEMBER Christchurch, Canterbury Society of Arts (1 work).
NOVEMBER Dunedin, Otago Art Society (1 work).

1892 SEPTEMBER Wellington, New Zealand Academy of Fine Arts (4 works).

1895 NOVEMBER Dunedin, Otago Art Society (7 works).

1896 NOVEMBER Dunedin, Otago Art Society (8 works).

1898 JULY Wellington, New Zealand Academy of Fine Arts (6 works).
NOVEMBER Dunedin, Otago Art Society (7 works).

1900 SEPTEMBER Wellington, New Zealand Academy of Fine Arts (5 works).
NOVEMBER Dunedin, Otago Art Society (7 works).

1901 NOVEMBER Dunedin, Otago Art Society (12 works).

1902 NOVEMBER Dunedin, Otago Art Society (16 works).
NOVEMBER London, Doré Gallery (10 works).

1903 MAY London, Royal Academy (1 work).
JULY London, Fine Art Society (10 works).

1904 APRIL London, Royal Academy (1 work).

1905 APRIL London, Royal Academy (2 works).

1906 NOVEMBER Paris, *Société Internationale des Aquarellistes* (5 works).

1909 MAY Paris, *Salon des Artistes Françaises*, 85 rue Vaneau (2 works).

1910 OCTOBER Paris, *Société Internationale des Aquarellistes*, Galerie Georges Petit (6 works).

1911 FEBRUARY Paris, *Société Internationale de la Peinture à l' Eau*, Galerie des Artistes Modernes (5 works).
NOVEMBER Paris, *Société Internationale des Aquarellistes*, Galerie Georges Petit (no catalogue located).
Paris, *Salon de la Société Nationale des Beaux-Arts* (1 work).

1912 Paris, *Salon de la Société Nationale des Beaux-Arts* (1 work).

1915 MAY London, Royal Academy (1 work).
OCTOBER London, 19th Exhibition International Society, Grosvenor Gallery (6 works).

1916 FEBRUARY London, 5th Exhibition National Portrait Society (3 works).
MAY London, Royal Academy (1 work).
OCTOBER London, 21st Exhibition International Society, Grosvenor Gallery (6 works).

1917 JUNE London, 22nd Exhibition International Society, Grosvenor Gallery (7 works).

1918 FEBRUARY London, 7th Exhibition National Portrait Society, Grosvenor Gallery (3 works).
MAY London, 23rd Exhibition International Society, Grosvenor Gallery (6 works).
OCTOBER London, 24th Exhibition International Society, Grosvenor Gallery (22 works).

1919 FEBRUARY London, 8th Exhibition National Portrait Society, Grosvenor Gallery (3 works).
MARCH London, 18th Exhibition Women's International Art Club, Grafton Gallery (8 works).
OCTOBER London, 26th Exhibition International Society, Grosvenor Gallery (6 works).

1920 JULY London, 12th Salon Allied Artists' Association, Grafton Galleries (3 works).

1921 JUNE London, 13th Salon Allied Artists' Association, Mansard Gallery (3 works).

1924 OCTOBER London, Women's International Art Club, Suffolk Street Galleries (2 works).
NOVEMBER Paris, *Salon d'Automne* (7 works).

1927 JUNE London, 25th Exhibition London Group, R.W.S. Gallery (1 work).
DECEMBER London, 76th Exhibition New English Art Club, New Burlington Galleries (2 works).

1928 NOVEMBER London, 78th Exhibition New English Art Club, New Burlington Galleries (1 work).

1929 MARCH London, 9th Exhibition Seven and Five Society, Arthur Tooth & Sons (6 works).
OCTOBER London, 27th Exhibition London Group, New Burlington Galleries (2 works).

1930 OCTOBER London, Wertheim Gallery. *Modern Paintings* (4 works).

1931 JANUARY London, 10th Exhibition Seven and Five Society, Leicester Galleries (2 works).

1932 FEBRUARY London, 11th Exhibition Seven and Five Society, Leicester Galleries (6 works).
APRIL London, Zwemmer Gallery. *Room and Book* (1 work).

1933 FEBRUARY London, 12th Exhibition Seven and Five Society, Leicester Galleries (6 works).

1934 MARCH London, 13th Exhibition Seven and Five Society, Leicester Galleries (7 works).

1935 AUGUST Salford, Royal Museum & Art Galleries. *One Hundred Watercolour Drawings* (6 works). Exhibition selected by Lucy Wertheim.

1938 JANUARY London, Lefevre Gallery. *New Paintings* (9 works).
SEPTEMBER London, Leicester Galleries. *Lithographs in Colour* (1 work).
NOVEMBER Paris, *Salon d'Automne* (2 works, as part of an invited group of British artists).

1939 JANUARY London, London Gallery. *Living Art in England* (2 works).
JULY London, Lefevre Gallery. *L'Entente Cordiale, Painting by Contemporary British and French Artists* (2 works).
NOVEMBER Wellington, National Gallery. *Centennial Exhibition of International and New Zealand Art* (2 works).

1940 MAY London, Hertford House. *Paintings Selected for Inclusion in the 22nd Biennale di Venezia* (26 works). The other participating artists were Duncan Grant, Glyn Philpot, Alfred Munnings, Edward Wadsworth & Frank Dobson.

1944 JANUARY London, Leicester Galleries. *Selected Paintings, Drawings and Sculpture from the Collection of the Late Sir Michael Sadler* (3 works). Preface by John Piper.

1945 APRIL London, Lefevre Gallery. *Recent Paintings by Francis Bacon, Frances Hodgkins, Henry Moore, Matthew Smith, Graham Sutherland* (8 works).
Paris, British Council, 28 avenue des Champs Elysées. *Quelques Contemporains Anglais* (6 works). Preface Philip Hendy.

1946 Paris, Musée du Jeu de Paume. *Tableaux Britanniques Modernes Appartenant à la Tate Gallery* (3 works). Organised by the British Council. Selection & essay John Rothenstein.
Buffalo, Albright Art Gallery, Buffalo Fine Arts Academy. *British Contemporary Painters* (4 works). Introduction Andrew C. Ritchie.
JULY London, Lefevre Gallery. *British Painters Past and Present* (9 works).

1947 SEPTEMBER London, Lefevre Gallery. *Ascher Squares designed by Matisse, Moore, Derain, Sutherland, Hitchens, Hodgkins, Laurens, Cocteau and others* (1 work).

1947–48 British Council, Sweden. *Engelsk Nutidskonst, Contemporary British Painting* (5 works). Introduction Patrick Heron.

1949 British Council, Australia. *Eleven British Artists* (5 works). Introduction A. J. L. McDonnel. Travelling to the State Galleries of Perth, Adelaide, Melbourne, Sydney, Brisbane, Hobart & Launceston.

1950 OCTOBER Birmingham, Museum & Art Gallery. *Six Contemporary British Painters* (10 works). Introduction Richard James.

1951 Vancouver, Art Gallery. *21 Modern British Painters* (3 works). Introduction Doris Shadbolt. Organised by the British Council in conjunction with the Vancouver Art Gallery. Travelling to Seattle Art Museum, San Jose, San Francisco, De Young Memorial Museum, Salt Lake City, Portland Art Museum.

1958 AUGUST Auckland, City Art Gallery. *Thirty-seven New Zealand Paintings from the Collection of Charles Brasch and Rodney Kennedy* (2 works). Introduction Charles Brasch.

1962 OCTOBER Cardiff, National Museum of Wales. *British Art and the Modern Movement* (2 works). Introduction Alan Bowness. Organised by the Welsh Committee of the Arts Council.

1964 APRIL Edinburgh, Scottish National Gallery of Modern Art. *Modern Paintings and Drawings from the Collection of Dr Peter Davis* (8 works). Introduction Peter Davis.

1975 Auckland, City Art Gallery. *New Zealand's Women Painters*. Introduction Anne Kirker & Eric Young.

1980 London, Hayward Gallery. *The Thirties* (1 work).

1982 Nottingham, Castle Museum. *The Women's Art Show 1550–1970* (1 work). Essays by Jennifer Fletcher, Pamela Gerrish Nunn, J. Hunt.

1983 APRIL London, Hayward Gallery. *Landscape in Britain 1850–1950* (1 work). Essay Frances Spalding. Travelling to Bristol (City Museum and Art Gallery), Stoke-on-Trent (City Museum & Art Gallery), Sheffield (Mappin Art Gallery).

1987 JULY Dunedin, Hocken Library, University of Otago. *Under the Spell, Frances Hodgkins, Nellie Hutton and Grace Joel* (14 works). Introduction R. J. Entwisle.

1988 Liverpool, Walker Art Gallery, Sudley Art Gallery; Port Sunlight, Lady Lever Art Gallery. *Women's Works* (1 work). Catalogue June Sellars.
OCTOBER Leeds, City Art Gallery. *100 Years of Art in Britain* (1 work). Introduction Frances Spalding.

1989 Liverpool, Tate Gallery. *World War Two* (1 work). Essay Penelope Curtis.

1991 AUGUST Liverpool, Tate Gallery. *Echo, Works by Women Artists 1850–1940* (1 work). Essay Maud Sulter.
DECEMBER Salford, Museum & Art Gallery. *Adventure in Art, Modern British Art under the Patronage of Lucy Wertheim* (6 works). Introduction Jimmy Hume. Essays Penny Johnston & Judith Collins. Travelling to Eastbourne (Towner Art Gallery), Wakefield (Art Gallery), Dudley (Museum & Art Gallery). Exhibition organised by Salford Museum & Art Gallery and the Towner Art Gallery.

1993 OCTOBER London, Tate Gallery. *Writing on the Wall* (1 work). Compiled by Judith Collins.

1994 JANUARY London, Victoria & Albert Museum. *Prospects, Thresholds, Interiors: Watercolours from the National Collection* (1 work).

BIBLIOGRAPHY

BOOKS

Evans, Myfanwy. *Frances Hodgkins*, Penguin Modern Painters, Harmondsworth, 1948.

Gill, Linda, ed. *Letters of Frances Hodgkins*, Auckland, 1993.

Howell, Arthur R. *Frances Hodgkins, Four Vital Years*, London, 1951.

McCormick, E. H. *The Expatriate, A Study of Frances Hodgkins*, Wellington, 1954.

McCormick, E. H. *Works of Frances Hodgkins in New Zealand*, Auckland, 1954.

McCormick, E. H. *Portrait of Frances Hodgkins*, Auckland, 1981.

MAJOR EXHIBITION CATALOGUES

Frances Hodgkins 1869–1947, A Centenary Exhibition. Foreword G. C. Docking, essay David Armitage and Ian Roberts. Queen Elizabeth II Arts Council of New Zealand, Auckland City Art Gallery, 1969.

Frances Hodgkins 1869–1947. Introduction Avenal McKinnon. Whitford & Hughes, London, 1990.

Frances Hodgkins — The Late Work. Foreword Richard Stokes, introduction Liz Reintjes, essays Rosemary Pawsey & Lindsey Bridget Shaw. Minories Art Gallery, Colchester, 1990.

Frances Hodgkins, Women's Suffrage Exhibition. Introduction Jill Trevelyan. Museum of New Zealand Te Papa Tongarewa, Wellington, 1993.

SELECTED ARTICLES
(including radio and tape-recorded material)

Anon. 'Miss F. Hodgkins', *Otago Daily Times & Witness* (Dunedin), Christmas Annual, December 1902, p.10.

Art New Zealand, 16, 1980. Articles by Gordon H. Brown, Anne Kirker, E. H. McCormick, E. A. Sheppard.

Ascent, Frances Hodgkins commemorative issue, 1969. Articles by Melvin Day, Shay Docking, Anthony S. G. Green, June Opie, E. H. McCormick.

Brasch, Charles. 'Frances Hodgkins at One Hundred', *Landfall*, 92, 1969, pp.265-76.

Buchanan, Iain. 'Frances Hodgkins and Neo-Romanticism', in *Writing a New Country, A Collection of Essays Presented to E. H. McCormick in his 88th year*, eds James Ross, Linda Gill & Stuart McRae, Auckland, 1993, pp.155-64.

Collins, R. D. J. 'A Long Attachment: Frances Hodgkins in France', in *Writing a New Country*, pp.84-95.

Cornstalk, Ann. 'Frances Hodgkins', *Lone Hand* (Sydney), 2 June 1913, pp.xxxviii-xl.

Davison, Anne-Marie. 'G. P. Nerli and Frances Hodgkins: The Dunedin Years', *Art New Zealand*, 58, Autumn 1991, pp.78-82.

Entwisle, Peter. 'Frances Hodgkins at the Dunedin Public Art Gallery: A History of the Collection and a Checklist', *Bulletin of New Zealand Art History*, 14, 1993, pp.41-70.

Evans, Myfanwy. 'Frances Hodgkins', *Vogue*, August 1947, pp.53, 91.

Frances Hodgkins: Recollections by Various People, audio tape, 19 April 1961, Radio New Zealand. Includes memories of FH by May Smith and Gwen Knight.

Frances Hodgkins: The European Years. Reminiscences of friends and fellow artists including Henry Moore, Barbara Hepworth, Douglas Glass, Ben Nicholson, Katharine West: tape-recorded interviews by June Opie, 1969.

Frances Hodgkins, 1984 calendar, Government Printing Office, Wellington. Plate commentaries Anne Kirker.

Frankel, Margaret. 'The "Pleasure Garden" Incident at Christchurch', *Year Book of the Arts in New Zealand*, 5, Wellington, 1949, pp.10-21.

Fairburn, A. R. D. 'About Frances Hodgkins', *New Zealand Listener*, 16 May 1947, pp.24-25.

Fairburn, A. R. D. 'The Wertheim Collection', *Year Book of the Arts in New Zealand*, 5, Wellington, 1949, pp.11-17.

Gill, Linda. 'The Letters of Frances Hodgkins', *Art New Zealand*, 68, Spring 1993, pp.106-9, 117.

Gorer, Geoffrey. 'The Art of Frances Hodgkins', *Listener*, 17 November 1937, pp.1082-3. Repr. in *Art in New Zealand*, March 1938, pp.160-3.

Gorer, Geoffrey. 'Remembering Frances Hodgkins', *Listener*, 19 June 1947, p.968.

Grigson, Geoffrey. '"Childishness" in Contemporary Art', *Bookman*, December 1933, pp.170-1.

Hay, Thomson C. 'An Artist of the Moderns', *Everylady's Journal* (Melbourne), 6 January 1913, p.12.

Kirker, Anne. '*Adoration*: a pencil and watercolour drawing by Frances Hodgkins', *Auckland City Art Gallery Quarterly*, no. 58, 1975, n.p.

McCormick, E. H. 'Some recently acquired drawings by Frances Hodgkins', *Auckland City Art Gallery Quarterly*, no. 58, 1975, pp.1-8.

McCormick, E. H. 'Illustrated by Miss F. Hodgkins', *Landfall*, 18, 1951, pp.117-21.

McCormick, E. H. *Late Attachment, Frances Hodgkins & Maurice Garnier*, Auckland City Art Gallery, 1988.

McLean, Fred. Five-part series on Frances Hodgkins in *Dominion*, 13–17 January 1992.

Newton, Eric. 'Frances Hodgkins — A Painter of Genius',

Art in New Zealand, September 1940, p.36, repr. from *Sunday Times*, 14 September 1940.

Nunn, Pamela Gerrish. 'Frances Hodgkins, The "Arrival" in Context', *Art New Zealand*, 56, 1990, pp.86-89.

Piper, John. 'Frances Hodgkins', *Horizon*, vol. 4, no. 24, London, 1941, pp.413-6.

Piper, Myfanwy. 'The Life and Art of Frances Hodgkins', *Listener*, 21 November 1946, pp.705-6.

Read, Herbert. 'Unit One', *Architectural Review*, 74, October 1933, pp.125-8.

Read, Herbert. 'L'Art Contemporain en Angleterre', *Cahiers d'Art*, no. 1, 1938, pp.29-42.

Rothenstein, John. 'Frances Hodgkins', *Modern English Painters*, vol. 1: *Sickert to Smith*, London, repr. 1976.

Scott, T. H. 'The Frances Hodgkins Controversy', *Landfall*, 12, 1949, pp.360-74.

Scott, T. H. 'The "Pleasure Garden", A Postscript', *Landfall*, 20, 1951, pp.311-13.

Stephens, A. G. 'Frances Hodgkins', *Bookfellow* (Sydney), 1 May 1913, pp.ix-x.

Stephens, A. G. 'Frances Hodgkins, a Dunedin girl who conquered Paris', *Otago Witness*, 28 May 1913.

Warner, Tony. 'Frances Hodgkins', *Arts Review*, 25 January 1991, p.49.

Westbrook, Eric. 'Pupil and Teacher: Some Works by Frances Hodgkins and G. P. Nerli in Melbourne', *Quarterly Bulletin of the National Gallery of Victoria*, 11, no. 1, 1957, pp.3-5.

GENERAL: BOOKS & ARTICLES

Agar, Eileen, with Lambirth, Andrew. *Eileen Agar, A Look at My Life*, London, 1988.

Ayrton, Michael. Introduction to Turner, W. J., ed., *Aspects of British Art*, London, 1947.

Ayrton, Michael. 'British Art', *Studio*, 132, 1946, p.144.

Bell, Graham. 'Art in the "Island Fortress", A Review of Contemporary British Painting', *Studio*, 120, 571, Oct. 1940, pp.98-109.

Bell, Leonard. *The Maori in European Art, A Survey of the Representation of the Maori by European Artists from the Time of Captain Cook to the Present Day*, Wellington, 1980.

Bell, Leonard. *Colonial Constructs, European Images of Maori 1840-1914*, Auckland, 1992.

Berlin, Sven. *Alfred Wallis Primitive*, London, 1949.

Bowness, Alan. Introduction to *British Art and the Modern Movement*, London, 1962.

Brill, Reginald. *Modern Painting and its Roots in European Tradition*, London, 1946.

Brown, G. & Keith, H. *An Introduction to New Zealand Painting 1839-1980*, 2nd ed., Auckland, 1982.

Brusatin, Manlio. *A History of Colors*, Boston & London, 1991.

Bryson, Norman. *Looking at the Overlooked, Four Essays on Still Life Painting*, London, 1990.

Causey, Andrew. *Paul Nash*, Oxford, 1980.

Christopher Wood, exhibition catalogue, Minories Gallery, Colchester, 1979.

Collins, Judith. *Winifred Nicholson*, Tate Gallery, London, 1987.

Collins, R. D. J. 'Grace Joel and Australia', *Bulletin of New Zealand Art History*, 14, 1993, pp.29-40.

Compton, Susan, ed. *British Art in the 20th Century*, exhibition catalogue, Royal Academy of Arts, London, 1987.

Cooper, Douglas. *The Work of Graham Sutherland*, London, 1961.

Cooper, Douglas. *The Cubist Epoch*, London, 1970.

Cooper, Emmanuel. *The Sexual Perspective: Homosexuality and Art in the Last 100 Years in the West*, London, 1986.

Cork, Richard. *Vorticism and Abstract Art in the First Machine Age*, vol. 1: *Origins and Development*; vol. 2: *Synthesis and Decline*, London, 1976.

Cross, Tom. *Painting in the Warmth of the Sun, St Ives Artists 1939-1975*, exhibition catalogue, Guildford, 1984.

Cowling, Elizabeth & Mundy, Jennifer. *On Classic Ground, Picasso, Léger, de Chirico and the New Classicism 1910-1930*, exhibition catalogue, Tate Gallery, London, 1990.

Deepwell, Katy. 'The Memorial Exhibition of Ethel Walker, Gwen John and Frances Hodgkins', synopsis of MA thesis, Leeds University, 1986, *Women Artists Slide Library Journal*, no. 16, April/May 1987, pp.5-6.

Docking, Gill. *Two Hundred Years of New Zealand Painting*, Wellington, 1971.

Dunn, Michael. 'Girolamo Nerli: An Italian Painter in New Zealand', *Art New Zealand*, 49, 1988, pp.60-65.

Dunn, Michael. *A Concise History of New Zealand Painting*, Sydney, 1991.

Eastmond, Elizabeth & Penfold, Merimeri. *Women and the Arts in New Zealand 1936-1986: Forty Works*, Auckland, 1986.

Entwisle, Peter. *William Matthew Hodgkins and his Circle*, exhibition catalogue, Dunedin Public Art Gallery, 1984.

Entwisle, Peter. *Treasures of the Dunedin Public Art Gallery*, exhibition catalogue, Dunedin Public Art Gallery, 1990.

Entwisle, Peter, Dunn, Michael & Collins, Roger. *Nerli, Paintings and Drawings*, Dunedin Public Art Gallery, 1988.

Evans, Myfanwy, ed. *The Painter's Object*, London, 1937.

Fox, Caroline. *Painting in Newlyn 1900-1930*, exhibition catalogue, Penzance, Cornwall, 1985.

Fox, Caroline. *Dame Laura Knight*, Oxford, 1988.

Glazebrook, Mark. *Art in Britain 1930-40 centred around Axis, Circle, Unit One*, exhibition catalogue, Marlborough Fine Art, London, 1965.

Glazebrook, Mark. *The Seven and Five Society 1920-35*, exhibition catalogue, Michael Parkin Fine Art, London, 1979-80.

Golding, John. *Cubism: A History and an Analysis, 1907-1914*, London, 1968.

Gorer, Geoffrey. *Bali and Angkor, or Looking at Life and Death*, London, 1936.

Green, Christopher. *Cubism and its Enemies*, New Haven & London, 1987.

Griffiths, Antony. 'Contemporary Lithographs Ltd', *Print Quarterly*, December 1991, pp.388-402.

Grimes, Teresa, Collins, Judith & Baddeley, Oriana. *Five Women Painters*, Oxford, 1989.

Harrison, Charles. *English Art and Modernism 1900-1939*, London, 1981.

Heron, Patrick. *The Changing Forms of Art*, London, 1955.

Hills, Paul. *David Jones*, exhibition catalogue, Tate Gallery, 1981.

Hubbard, Eric Hesketh. *A Hundred Years of British Painting 1851-1951*, London, 1951.

Hutchings, P. A. E. & Lewis, Julie. *Kathleen O'Connor: Artist in Exile*, Fremantle, 1987.

Ironside, Robin. *Painting Since 1939*, London, 1947.

Jacobs, Michael. *The Good and Simple Life, Artist Colonies in Europe and America*, Oxford, 1985.

Jeffrey, Ian. *The British Landscape 1920-1950*, London, 1984.

Kay, Robin & Eden, Tony. *Portrait of a Century: The History of the New Zealand Academy of Fine Arts, 1882-1982*, Wellington, 1983.

King, Julie. *Sydney Lough Thompson at Home and Abroad*, exhibition catalogue, Robert McDougall Art Gallery, Christchurch, 1990.

Kirker, Anne. 'The Last Years of the Seven and Five Society', MA Report, Courtauld Institute of Art, London, 1979.

Kirker, Anne. *New Zealand Women Artists*, Auckland, 1986; revised edition, Sydney, 1993.

Kirker, Anne. *The First Fifty Years, British Art of the 20th Century*, exhibition catalogue, National Art Gallery, Wellington, 1981.

Krauss, Rosalind E. *The Originality of the Avant-Garde and other Modernist Myths*, Cambridge, Mass. & London, 1985.

Lewison, Jeremy. *Ben Nicholson*, Oxford, 1991.

McCormick, E. H. 'From Charles Heaphy to Frances Hodgkins, a Biographical View of New Zealand Painting', *Arts Year Book*, 7, 1951, pp.145-52.

McCormick, E. H. *Letters and Art in New Zealand*, Wellington, 1940.

McKay, Agnes. *Arthur Melville, Scottish Impressionist*, Leigh-on-Sea, 1951.

Mellor, David, ed. *A Paradise Lost, The Neo-Romantic Imagination in Britain 1935-55*, exhibition catalogue, Barbican Art Gallery, 1987.

Mendes, V. D. & Hinchcliffe, M. *Ascher — Fabric — Art*, exhibition catalogue, Victoria & Albert Museum, 1987.

Mendes, E. L. T., ed. 'Living Art in England', *London Bulletin*, no.8-9, January-February 1939, pp.8ff, pp.57-58.

Morphet, Richard. *Cedric Morris*, exhibition catalogue, Tate Gallery, 1984.

Mourey, G. 'The Art of Lucien Simon', *Studio*, 25, 109, 1902, pp.157-70.

Mullins, Edwin. *Alfred Wallis, Cornish Primitive Painter*, London, 1967.

Nash, Paul. *Dorset, Shell Guide*, London, n.d. but 1936.

Nash, Paul. *Outline: An Autobiography and Other Writings*, London, 1949.

Newton, Eric. 'The Centre Party in Contemporary Painting', *Listener*, 23 May 1934, pp.862-3.

Newton Eric. *British Painting*, London, 1945.

Newton, Eric. *In My View*, London, 1950 (includes review first published *Listener*, 2 October 1941).

Nicholson, Winifred. *Unknown Colour: Paintings, Letters, Writings by Winifred Nicholson*, London, 1987.

Painting in Newlyn, exhibition catalogue, Barbican Gallery, 1985.

Paris, H. J. *English Watercolour Painters*, London, 1945.

Perez-Tibi, Dora. *Dufy*, New York, 1989.

Piper, John. *British Romantic Artists*, London, 1947.

Piper, M. 'Back in the Thirties', *Art and Literature, An International Review*, 7, Winter 1965, p.136.

Post-Impressionism, exhibition catalogue, Royal Academy

of Arts, London, 1980.

Raoul Hausmann Architecte Ibiza, exhibition catalogue, Fondation pour l'Architecture, Bruxelles, 1990.

Read, Herbert, ed. *Unit One, The Modern Movement in English Architecture, Painting and Sculpture*, London, 1934.

Read, Herbert. 'Art in Britain 1930–40', in *Art in Britain centred around Axis, Circle, Unit One*, Marlborough Fine Art, London, 1965.

Reynolds, Graham. *British Water-Colours*, Victoria & Albert Museum; revised 1969.

Robertson, Bryan. '1893–1963 British Painting', *Studio*, 165, 840, 1963, pp.136-47.

Rothenstein, Michael. *Looking at Paintings*, London, 1947.

Sackville-West, Edward. *Graham Sutherland*, The Penguin Modern Painters, Harmondsworth, 1943.

Schapiro, Meyer. 'The Apples of Cézanne, An Essay on the Meaning of Still-Life' in *Modern Art, 19th and 20th Centuries*, London, 1978, pp.1-38.

Sheldon, Michael. *Friends of Promise: Cyril Connolly and the World of* Horizon, London, 1989.

Shone, Richard. *The Century of Change: British Painting Since 1900*, London, 1977.

Silver, Kenneth E. *Esprit de Corps: the Art of the Parisian Avant Garde and the First World War, 1914–1925*, Princeton N.J., 1989.

Smith, Gary, ed. *On Walter Benjamin, Critical Essays and Recollections*, Cambridge Mass., 1991.

Spalding, Frances. *Roger Fry: Art and Life*, London, 1980.

Spalding, Frances. *British Art Since 1900*, 2nd ed., London, 1989.

Spalding, Frances. *Dance till the Stars Come Down, A Biography of John Minton*, London, 1991.

The Fauve Landscape, exhibition catalogue, Los Angeles County Museum, 1990.

Thom, Ian M. *Emily Carr in France*, exhibition catalogue, Vancouver Art Gallery, 1991.

Tippett, Maria. *Emily Carr, a Biography*, Oxford, 1979.

Tombs, H. H., ed. *A Century of Art in Otago*, Wellington, 1948.

Turner, W. J., ed. *Aspects of British Art*, London, 1947.

Weinberg, Barbara H. *The Lure of Paris: 19th Century American Painters and their French Teachers*, New York, 1991.

Wertheim, Lucy Carrington. *Adventure in Art*, London, 1947.

West, Anthony. *John Piper*, London, 1979.

Wilson, Simon. *British Art from Holbein to the Present Day*, London, 1979.

Yorke, Malcolm. *The Spirit of Place, Nine Neo-Romantic Artists and their Times*, London, 1988.

MANUSCRIPT PAPERS

Hodgkins, Frances. Correspondence 1875–1946, MS 85, Alexander Turnbull Library, Wellington.

Hodgkins, Frances. Manuscript papers, Alexander Turnbull Library, Wellington.

Hodgkins, Frances. Manuscript papers, Research Library, Auckland City Art Gallery.

Hodgkins, Frances. Transcription (by E. H. McCormick) of FH letters, Research Library, Auckland City Art Gallery.

Hodgkins, Frances. Manuscript papers, Tate Gallery Archive.

Howell, Arthur R. Manuscript papers, Tate Gallery Archive.

Morris, Cedric. Manuscript papers, Tate Gallery Archive.

Nash, Paul. Paul Nash archive, Tate Gallery Archive.

Saunders, Jane. Manuscript papers, Tate Gallery Archive.

Seven and Five Society Records, Tate Gallery Archive.

Unit One Archive, Press Cuttings Book 6, Tate Gallery Archive.

LIST OF COLOUR PLATES

PLATE 1
The Girl with the Flaxen Hair, 1893
Watercolour, 485 x 381mm
Museum of New Zealand, Te Papa Tongarewa

PLATE 2
Mountain Scene, 1897
Watercolour, 191 x 315mm
Hocken Library, Dunedin

PLATE 3
Orange Sellers, Tangier, 1903
Watercolour, 510 x 395mm
Theomin Gallery, Olveston, Dunedin

PLATE 4
Ayesha, 1904
Watercolour, 750 x 495mm
Dunedin Public Art Gallery

PLATE 5
Red Sails, 1906
Watercolour, 686 x 448mm
Dunedin Public Art Gallery

PLATE 6
The Window Seat, 1907
Watercolour, 645 x 515mm
Art Gallery of New South Wales, Sydney

PLATE 7
The Bridge, c.1907
Watercolour, 410 x 475mm
Private collection

PLATE 8
Dordrecht, c.1908
Watercolour, 680 x 455mm
Dunedin Public Art Gallery

PLATE 9
Summer, c.1912
Watercolour & charcoal, 586 x 498mm
Dunedin Public Art Gallery

PLATE 10
At the Window, c.1912
Watercolour, 653 x 628mm
Art Gallery of South Australia, Adelaide

PLATE 11
Loveday and Anne, 1916
Oil on canvas, 670 x 670mm
Tate Gallery, London

PLATE 12
Mr and Mrs Moffat Lindner and Hope, 1916
Tempera on linen, 2000 x 1022mm
Dunedin Public Art Gallery

PLATE 13
Belgian Refugees, c.1916
Oil & tempera on canvas, 710 x 800mm
Robert McDougall Art Gallery, Christchurch

PLATE 14
Threshing Scene, c.1919
Watercolour, 535 x 688mm
Private collection, Auckland

PLATE 15
Three Children, c.1923–24
Oil on canvas, 560 x 660mm
Private collection, Auckland

PLATE 16
The Red Cockerel, 1924
Oil on canvas, 707 x 914mm
Dunedin Public Art Gallery

PLATE 17
Double Portrait, c.1922–25
Oil on canvas, 610 x 770mm
Hocken Library, Dunedin

PLATE 18
Lancashire Family, c.1927
Oil on canvas, 685 x 705mm
Auckland City Art Gallery

PLATE 19
Lancashire Children, c.1927
Oil on canvas, 740 x 610mm
Private collection

PLATE 20
The Bridesmaids, 1930
Oil on canvas, 737 x 597mm
Auckland City Art Gallery

PLATE 21
The White House, c.1930

Oil on canvas, 635 x 610mm
Art Gallery of New South Wales, Sydney

PLATE 22
Berries and Laurel, c.1930
Oil on canvas, 640 x 763mm
Auckland City Art Gallery

PLATE 23
Still-Life Landscape, c.1931
Watercolour, 359 x 471mm
Private collection, Auckland

PLATE 24
Pastorale, 1929–30
Oil on canvas, 630 x 730mm
Private collection, Auckland

PLATE 25
Wings Over Water, 1931–32
Oil on canvas, 710 x 910mm
Tate Gallery, London

PLATE 26
Arum Lilies, c.1931
Oil on board, 640 x 540mm
Private collection, United Kingdom

PLATE 27
Enchanted Garden (A Cornish Garden), 1932
Watercolour & pencil on paper, 546 x 451mm
Sheffield City Art Galleries

PLATE 28
Evening, 1932-33
Oil on canvas, 535 x 640mm
Private collection, New Zealand

PLATE 29
Spanish Shrine, 1933–34
Oil on canvas, 654 x 927mm
Auckland City Art Gallery

PLATE 30
Self-Portrait: Still Life, c.1935
Oil on cardboard, 762 x 635mm
Auckland City Art Gallery

PLATE 31
Pumpkins and Pimenti, c.1935–36
Gouache, pencil, chalk, 510 x 710mm
Fletcher Challenge Art Collection

PLATE 32
Arrangement of Jugs, 1938
Lithograph, 610 x 457mm
Published by Contemporary Lithographs Ltd, London

PLATE 33
Double Portrait No. 2 (Katharine and Anthony West), 1937/39
Oil, 690 x 825mm
Museum of New Zealand, Te Papa Tongarewa

PLATE 34
August Month (Walls, Roofs and Flowers), c.1939
Gouache, 633 x 487mm
Private collection, New Zealand

PLATE 35
Smithy, c.1940
Gouache on paper, 495 x 650mm
Private collection, New Zealand

PLATE 36
Walled Garden with Convolvulus, 1942/43
Watercolour & gouache, 440 x 510mm
Private collection, New Zealand

PLATE 37
The China Shoe, 1942
Gouache, 520 x 405mm
Private collection

PLATE 38
Church and Castle, Corfe, 1942
Gouache on paper glued to card, 460 x 597mm
Ferens Art Gallery, Hull City Museums & Art Galleries

PLATE 39
The Courtyard in Wartime, 1944
Oil on board, 610 x 762mm
The University of Auckland Art Collection

PLATE 40
The Spanish Well, Purbeck, 1945
Oil on canvas, 670 x 646mm
Auckland City Art Gallery

LIST OF FIGURES

Whereabouts unknown, photograph Auckland City Art
Gallery

FIGURE 22
Mediterranean Landscape, c.1921
Black chalk
Private collection

FIGURE 23
Olives, St Tropez, c.1921
Black chalk, 252 x 318mm
Hocken Library, Dunedin

FIGURE 24
Les Martigues, c.1921
Pencil, 375 x 419mm
Tate Gallery Archive, London

FIGURE 25
Chez M. le Chef, c.1921
Black chalk, 275 x 425mm
Auckland City Art Gallery

FIGURE 26
The Cinema, c.1922
Charcoal
Tinakori Gallery, Wellington

FIGURE 27
Mother and Child, c.1921
Watercolour, 406 x 361mm
Auckland City Art Gallery

FIGURE 28
Fabric design, c.1925
Gouache, 141 x 305mm
Tate Gallery Archive, London

FIGURE 29
Handkerchief designed by Frances Hodgkins, c.1940?
242 x 257mm
Dunedin Public Art Gallery

FIGURE 30
Seated Woman, c.1926
Pencil & black chalk, 940 x 600mm
Tate Gallery, London

FIGURE 31
Adoration, c.1925
Pencil & watercolour, 529 x 378mm
Whitworth Art Gallery, University of Manchester

FIGURE 32
Cedric Morris, *Herstmonceaux Church*, c.1928
Oil, 594 x 730mm
Towner Art Gallery, Eastbourne

FIGURE 33
The Sisters, 1927–28
Oil, 727 x 597mm
Auckland City Art Gallery

FIGURE 34
Alfred Wallis, *Houses at St Ives, Cornwall*, c.1935

Oil, 270 x 315mm
Tate Gallery, London

FIGURE 35
Still Life in a Landscape, c.1928
Oil, 813 x 721mm
Ministry of Foreign Affairs & Trade, New Zealand

FIGURE 36
Vase with Handles, c.1928
Pencil, 305 x 228mm
Auckland City Art Gallery

FIGURE 37
A Country Window, c.1929
Oil, 555 x 675mm
Dunbar Sloane, Wellington

FIGURE 38
Cut Melons, c.1931
Oil on canvas, 535 x 643mm
Museum of New Zealand, Te Papa Tongarewa

FIGURE 39
Two Plates, c.1931
Pencil, pastel & watercolour, 395 x 575mm
Museum of New Zealand, Te Papa Tongarewa

FIGURE 40
Sabrina's Garden, 1932/33
Oil on canvas, 645 x 920mm
Bristol Art Gallery

FIGURE 41
Phoenician Pottery and Gourds, c.1933
Watercolour, 406 x 542mm
Auckland City Art Gallery

FIGURE 42
Flute Players, c.1933
Pencil, 533 x 393mm
Auckland City Art Gallery

FIGURE 43
Ibiza, Study for Oil, c.1933
Watercolour, 428 x 558mm
Auckland City Art Gallery

FIGURE 44
Raoul Hausmann, *Maison Paysanne — Cal Tio — Ile d'Ibiza*,
1933
Photograph, 127 x 180mm
Musée Départemental de Rochechouart, Limoges, France

FIGURE 45
Poet Resting under a Tree, Spain, c.1932/33
Oil on canvas, 560 x 685mm
Private collection, New Zealand

FIGURE 46
Paul Nash, *Event on the Downs*, 1934
Oil, 508 x 610mm
Government Art Collection, Department of National
Heritage, UK

FIGURE 47
Decorative Motif, c.1933/34
Oil on canvas, 492 x 590mm
Museum of New Zealand, Te Papa Tongarewa

FIGURE 48
Christmas Decorations, 1935
Watercolour, 412 x 570mm
Private collection, New Zealand

FIGURE 49
Private Bathing, 1935/36
Gouache, 546 x 750mm
Private collection, UK

FIGURE 50
In Perspective (En Perspective), 1936
Gouache & watercolour, 510 x 655mm
Victoria & Albert Museum, London

FIGURE 51
Paul Nash, *Landscape from a Dream*, 1936–38
Oil on canvas, 679 x 1016mm
Tate Gallery, London

FIGURE 52
Solva, 1936
Gouache, 545 x 753mm
Birmingham Museums & Art Gallery

FIGURE 53
Empty Drums and Barrel, 1939
Gouache, 420 x 560mm
Private collection, New Zealand

FIGURE 54
Kimmeridge Foreshore, c.1938
Oil on canvas, 760 x 1015mm
Victoria University of Wellington

FIGURE 55
Houses and Outhouses, Purbeck, c.1938
Oil on canvas, 1285 x 1025mm
British Council

FIGURE 56
Broken Tractor, 1942
Gouache, 381 x 571mm
Tate Gallery, London

FIGURE 57
John Piper, *All Saints Chapel, Bath*, 1942
Watercolour, 425 x 559mm
Tate Gallery, London

FIGURE 58
Landscape with Engine, 1941
Gouache, 437 x 568mm
Ministry of Foreign Affairs & Trade, New Zealand

FIGURE 59
Window Group (Window Piece), c.1940
Gouache, 485 x 684mm
Private collection, New Zealand

Sketch of a cat
45 x 83mm
E. H. McCormick Collection,
Alexander Turnbull Library, Wellington

INDEX